JUNKERS Ju 88
KAMPFGESCHWADER
ON THE RUSSIAN FRONT

SERIES EDITOR: TONY HOLMES

OSPREY COMBAT AIRCRAFT • 79

JUNKERS Ju 88

KAMPFGESCHWADER

ON THE RUSSIAN

FRONT

JOHN WEAL

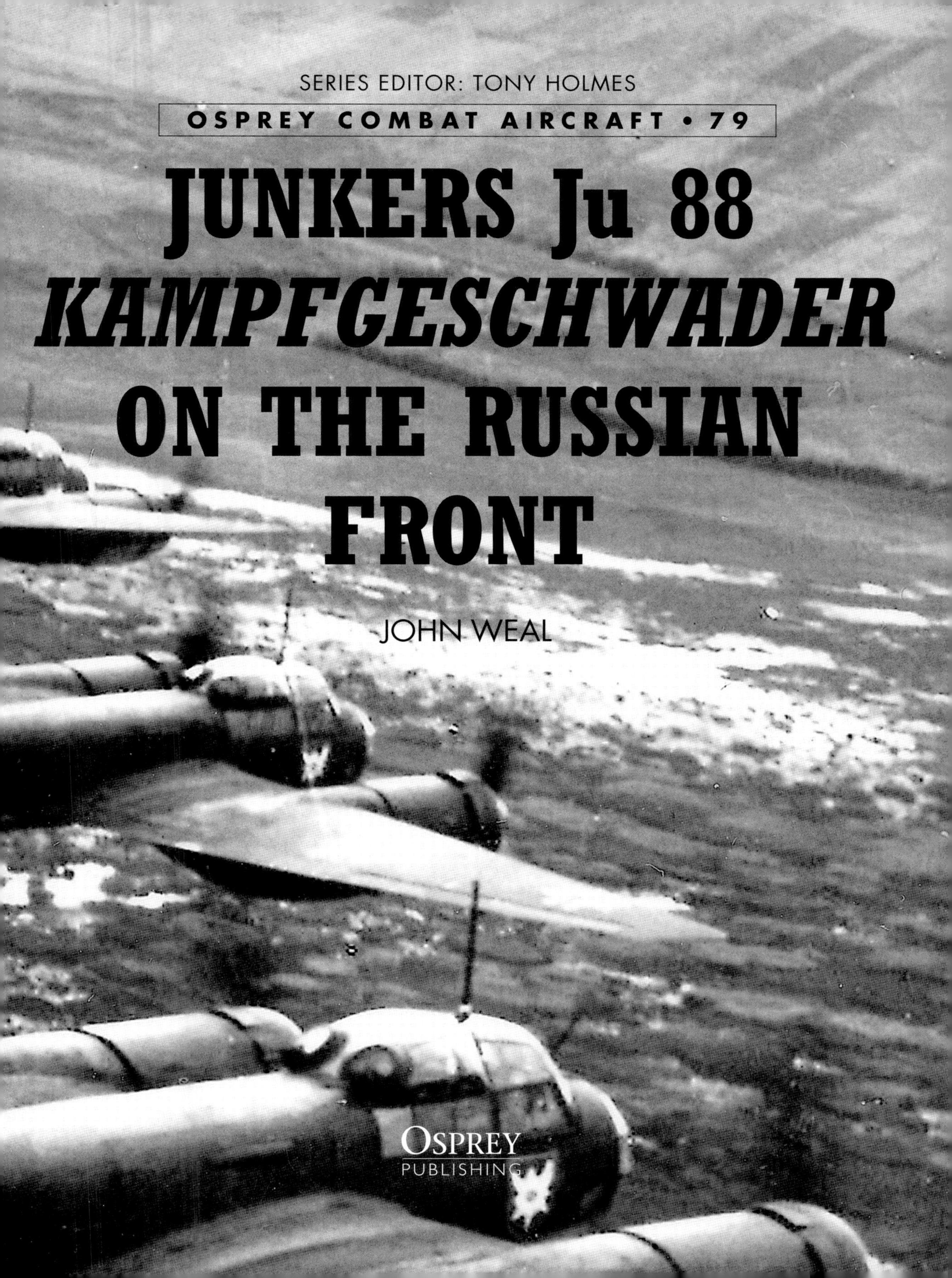

OSPREY
PUBLISHING

Front Cover
In the war against the Soviet Union the Ju 88 bomber was employed in two major roles. Its primary function was as a tactical strike weapon supporting Axis ground forces in the field, but it also saw a great deal of use against the enemy's rear area lines of supply and communication. These latter included road, rail and sea transport routes.

In order to increase their effectiveness against the Soviets' extensive rail network in particular, most Ju 88 *Kampfgeschwader* on the Russian front were ordered to re-equip one of their component *Staffeln* with cannon-armed Ju 88C-6 heavy fighters. And it is one such 'train-buster' – a machine of 4.(Eis)/KG 76, winter-camouflaged and with dummy transparencies painted on its solid nose to deceive enemy fighters – that provides the subject of Mark Postlethwaite's dramatic cover artwork as it attacks a Soviet armoured train on the southern sector of the front late in 1942 (*Cover artwork by Mark Postlethwaite*)

First published in Great Britain in 2010 by Osprey Publishing
Midland House, West Way, Botley, Oxford, OX2 0PH
44-02 23rd St, Suite 219, Long Island City, New York, 11101

E-mail; info@ospreypublishing.com

ISBN: 978 1 84603 419 0
E-book ISBN: 978 1 84908 305 8

Edited by Tony Holmes
Page design by Tony Truscott
Cover Artwork by Mark Postlethwaite
Aircraft Profiles by John Weal
Index by Michael Forder
Originated by PDQ Digital Media Solutions, Suffolk, UK
Printed in China through Bookbuilders

10 11 12 13 14   10 9 8 7 6 5 4 3 2 1

Osprey Publishing is supporting the Woodland Trust, the UK's leading woodland conservation charity by funding the dedication of trees.

www.ospreypublishing.com

ACKNOWLEDGEMENTS
The author wishes to thank the following individuals for their generous help in providing information and photographs – Helmut Ahrens, Desmond Allan, Gerhard Baeker (deceased), Manfred Griehl, Walter Matthiesen, Dr Alfred Price, Robert Simpson, Andrew Thomas, Nigel Tilley and Bruce Weaver.

CONTENTS

BARBAROSSA – OPENING ROUND

By mid May 1941 the Luftwaffe's nocturnal *Blitz* on Britain, which had begun in September 1940 and peaked with the devastating raid on London during the night of 10/11 May, was clearly starting to lose momentum. Even so, it still came as a surprise to many in the *Kampfgruppen* involved in the nightly forays over the British Isles when they were taken off operations for no discernible reason.

II./KG 1's experiences were typical. This was one of the five *Gruppen* that had been rushed to western France in late May in an abortive attempt to aid the stricken battleship *Bismarck*. But with the pride of the Kriegsmarine sent to the bottom of the Atlantic by the pursuing Royal Navy before they could intervene, the Luftwaffe's bombers were recalled to their bases in the north of France just two days later.

Back at Rosières-en-Santerre, 20 miles to the southeast of Amiens, the crews of II./KG 1 fully expected to resume their night *Blitz* on Britain. But instead they were taken off operations to undergo a thorough overhaul. III./KG 1, their sole sister *Gruppe* (I./KG 1 having been redesignated to become III./KG 40 back in March), received an even more unexpected order. They were to return to the homeland, where their Ju 88A-5s were to be converted back to Category 'A' configuration. This entailed the removal of the long-range fuel tanks in the fuselage and their replacement by weapons racks. At the same time the machines' undersides were to be stripped of their matt-black camouflage paint.

Speculation was rife. The unit's lengthy missions in the night skies over Britain were clearly a thing of the past. But what was to take their place? With their aircraft equipped solely with wing tanks, and now fitted with internal weapons racks accommodating bombs of 50 kg or less, all the signs were that the *Gruppe's* future role was to be tactical, presumably in support of the army in the field – but where, and against whom?

Theories abounded. Some of the younger crews were convinced that the cross-Channel invasion was at long last about to be launched, and that they would be employed in covering the Wehrmacht's advance through England's southern counties. But the *Gruppe's alte Hasen* (experienced veterans) were aghast at the very thought. They were only too well aware that the RAF's defences were now even stronger than they had been in the summer of 1940. The lack of any form of tropical equipment seemed to rule out the

9./KG 1's bomb-laden 'HT' taxies out at Amy in the late spring of 1941 for yet another night raid on the English Midlands. That all-concealing coat of black camouflage paint is soon to be removed, however, as the two *Gruppen* of KG 1 are about to head eastwards to take part in the invasion of the Soviet Union. There, the machine will survive for just 14 weeks, for this is believed to be the 'V4+HT' that was lost 'to unknown causes' near Leningrad on 28 September 1941

possibility of deployment to North Africa. And as far as the east was concerned, the German-Soviet pact of non-aggression – signed just before the outbreak of war – was still in place and working to the mutual benefit of both nations. In fact, one of the wilder flights of fancy even suggested that Germany and the Soviet Union were about to join forces in a combined drive southwards to the oilfields of Persia!

Then, after more than two weeks of rumour and uncertainty, II. and III./KG 1 were transferred up to airfields close to the Baltic coast. In order to disguise the move they did not fly in massed formation, but were sent off in widely spaced *Ketten*, or vics of three. The following day, 17 June, the two *Gruppenkommandeure*, Hauptmann Otto Stams and Major Walter Lehwess-Litzmann, opened the sealed green envelopes that were to reveal their units' final destinations. Both were to move forward into East Prussia, II./KG 1 to Powunden, close to the provincial capital Königsberg, and III./KG 1 some 25 miles further to the northeast to Eichwalde, near the shores of the Kurisches Haff lagoon.

The unpalatable truth began to dawn. The *Führer* was about to risk a two-front war by launching a surprise attack on the Soviet Union. All doubts were dispelled over the course of the next few days as lorry-load after lorry-load of bombs and ammunition was delivered to the two fields. Finally, on the evening of 21 June, the *Staffeln* were assembled and Hitler's call-to-arms was read aloud to them;

'Soldiers of the eastern front, after months of great anxiety and self-imposed silence the time has now come, my soldiers, when I can speak to you quite openly. There are about 160 Russian divisions massed along our border. For weeks past this border has been subject to constant violation. And not only our border, but also those of Finland to the far north and of Rumania. At this moment, soldiers of the eastern front, a concentration of fighting power is being assembled which, in size and scope, is the largest the world has ever seen. In alliance with Finnish divisions, your comrades are poised on the shores of the Arctic Ocean. You are standing on the eastern front.

'In Rumania, along the banks of the River Pruth and on the Danube down to the Black Sea coast, German and Rumanian troops are united under Head of State Antonescu. When this greatest fighting front in the history of the world now takes up arms, it does so not only to ensure the successful outcome of the present conflict – or to protect those nations currently under threat – but save Europe's entire civilisation and culture. German soldiers! You are thus embarking on a hard struggle fraught with responsibility. For the fate of Europe, the future of the German Reich, the very existence of our *Volk*, now lie in your hands, and your hands alone!'

The two *Gruppen* of KG 1 were just one small part of the vast array of military might that the Wehrmacht had gathered along Germany's eastern border provinces. More than two-thirds of all the Luftwaffe's operational *Kampfgruppen* had been redeployed in readiness for the attack. Numbering 32 in total, 18 of them were equipped with Ju 88s.

These 18 *Gruppen* were divided somewhat unequally between the four *Luftflotten* (Air Fleets) stretching from the Arctic Ocean to the Black Sea. By far the greatest concentration of Ju 88 bombers along what was to become the main eastern front was on the northern sector, where all nine of *Luftflotte* 1's *Kampfgruppen* were equipped with this type. In addition to

At the start of the hostilities against Russia the only Ju 88 bomber presence on the central sector of the front was provided by two *Gruppen* of KG 3. Although the full code of this II. *Gruppe* aircraft is not decipherable in this illustration from a wartime magazine, the white lightning bolt (on a red shield) below the cockpit that gave the *Geschwader* its name – 'Blitz' – is clearly visible

For much of the first half of the war against the Soviet Union, bomber operations above the Arctic Circle were almost the sole preserve of KG 30, the famous *'Adler'*, or 'Eagle', *Geschwader*

the two *Gruppen* of Oberst Karl Angerstein's KG 1 'Hindenburg', this Air Fleet also controlled two other *Kampfgeschwader* – Oberst *Dr.Ing.* Ernst Bormann's KG 76 and Oberst Johann Raithel's KG 77, each of which had a full establishment of three component *Gruppen*.

The above eight *Gruppen* together formed I. *Fliegerkorps*, the northern sector's primary bomber force. The ninth *Gruppe* was the semi-autonomous *Kampfgruppe* 806 commanded by Major Hans Emig. This was subordinated to the *Fliegerführer Ostsee* (Air Commander Baltic), which, as its name implies, would be engaged predominantly in maritime operations.

Luftflotte 2 on the central sector of the front had eight *Kampfgruppen* in all. But of this number only two, I. and II./KG 3 'Blitz', which formed part of II. *Fliegerkorps*, were flying Ju 88s. Although assigned to the same Air Fleet, the *Geschwader's* third *Gruppe* was still equipped with Do 17s and currently operating within neighbouring VIII. *Fliegerkorps*.

Along the southern sector the two *Fliegerkorps* of *Luftflotte* 4 included no fewer than 12 *Kampfgruppen*, the largest number of any of the Air Fleets. Five of the 12 were equipped with the Ju 88, and these were all attached to V. *Fliegerkorps*. They comprised the three *Gruppen* of Major Hans Bruno Schulz-Heyn's KG 51 'Edelweiss', together with I. and II./KG 54 'Totenkopf'. Like KG 1 to the north, Oberstleutnant Otto Höhne's KG 54 consisted at this time of only two *Gruppen*, III./KG 54 having been disbanded back in July 1940.

Finally, in the far north, two of the three *Kampfgruppen* available to *Luftflotte* 5 for operations above the Arctic Circle were also flying Ju 88s. In fact, I. and II./KG 30 'Adler' were the longest serving Ju 88 units in the Luftwaffe, having been activated on the then-new *Wunderbomber* in the opening weeks of the war. A third *Gruppe* had been established early in 1940 but this unit, III./KG 30, was presently serving alongside the Ju 88s of LG 1 in the Mediterranean (see *Osprey Combat Aircraft Nos 17* and *75* respectively).

Despite the magnitude of the undertaking, Operation *Barbarossa* – the invasion of the Soviet Union – was to begin in exactly the same manner as every other successful *Blitzkrieg* campaign launched by the Wehrmacht to date, with a series of surprise attacks on the enemy's airfields. Much has been written in the past on the part played by the Luftwaffe's fighter and Stuka units in these pre-emptive strikes, but the *Kampfgruppen* also had a vitally important role to perform.

Some 100+ specially selected crews – including, for example, almost a dozen from the two Ju 88 *Gruppen* of KG 3, based near Deblin in Poland – would form the spearhead of the assault on Russia. All highly experienced in night flying from their recent operations during the *Blitz* on Britain, these crews were to take off in the very early hours of 22 June 1941. Split up into small groups of no more than three to five aircraft, their job would be to locate and illuminate the 30+ major Soviet airfields strung along the frontier from the Baltic to the Black Sea.

By 0300 hrs on the opening morning of *Barbarossa,* these *ad hoc* pathfinders were nearing their assigned objectives. Soon, showers of incendiaries were raining down on the forward Russian fields, lighting the way for the first waves of the main attacking force, which were following hard on the heels of the small vanguard formations. Once the latter had completed their initial task, each returned to base to rearm and add its weight to the continuing attacks on the Red Air Force that would be kept up until last light. KG 3's most successful pilot on this first day of hostilities in the east was undoubtedly Leutnant Ernst-Wilhelm Ihrig, the *Kapitän* of 3. *Staffel,* who alone claimed the destruction of 60 enemy aircraft on the ground after making half a dozen low-level passes over the airfield at Pinsk, some 100 miles due east of Brest-Litovsk.

While I. and II./KG 3 constituted the sole Ju 88 bomber presence on the central sector, eight of the nine Ju 88 *Kampfgruppen* controlled by *Luftflotte* 1 to the north were also employed in strikes against airfields.

KG 1's objectives were the Red Air Force bases protecting the two main ports on the west coast of Latvia's Courland Peninsula, with II./KG 1 being despatched against Windau (Ventspils) close to the peninsula's northern tip, and III./KG 1 targeting the much larger Libau (Liepaja) to the south. Taking off from forward fields in East Prussia at 0215 hrs, the two units reached their respective targets 45 minutes later. In the half-light of the false dawn that was 'illuminating a thin strip of sky to the north', the crews of III. *Gruppe* could make out the long orderly rows of Russian fighters parked wingtip to wingtip around the edges of Libau airfield. They presented a target that was impossible to miss. After releasing its bombs 'almost as if on exercise', the *Gruppe* returned to base, all landing back before sunrise without loss. A second mission against Libau was flown later that morning, and although the Ju 88s encountered both fighters and flak on this occasion, again all crews returned safely.

The six *Gruppen* of KGs 76 and 77, which were similarly engaged against other Soviet airfields in the Baltic states and in that part of northeastern Poland that had been occupied by the Russians in September 1939, apparently fared less well. They reported several inexplicable losses that were at first attributed to the over-zealousness of their own troops – what today would be termed 'friendly fire incidents'.

Luftflotte 1's ninth Ju 88 bomber *Gruppe* was Major Emig's *Kampfgruppe* 806. As befitted its past history (it had originally been activated as a coastal unit back in November 1939) and its current subordination to the *Fliegerführer Ostsee,* KGr 806 did not participate in the raids on the Red Air Force's forward fields, but was employed instead in a maritime role. Undertaking possibly the longest mission flown by any unit on the opening day of *Barbarossa,* Emig's crews made the 1000-mile round trip from East Prussia to the Soviet Baltic Fleet's main naval base at

Kronstadt, off Leningrad, where they laid 27 aerial mines. The end result hardly justified the effort and the losses involved (at least one source refers to six aircraft failing to return), for the only known victim of the minefield was the 499-ton Estonian steamer *Ruhno*, which went down later that same day. During the course of the operation, however, KGr 806 machines reportedly sank the 2329-ton Soviet freighter *Luga*.

Further to the north still, high above the Arctic Circle, the Ju 88 bombers of *Luftflotte* 5 were also to make their first contribution to *Barbarossa* by attacking the Soviet airfields around Murmansk. Once this had been done, they would then be required to mine the port and its approaches. These two tasks were something of a tall order given the fact that fewer than a dozen of the Air Fleet's 40+ available Ju 88s were scheduled to carry them out. In fact, of the two *Gruppen* of KG 30 currently assigned to *Luftflotte* 5 in Norway, only a single *Staffel* had initially been instructed to transfer from Stavanger-Sola in the south of the country up to Banak, close to the Finnish border in the far north.

Reference sources are at odds as to the exact identity of this particular *Staffel*. Some state that it was 5./KG 30, while others (including the memoirs of an ex-member of the unit concerned) maintain that it was 6./KG 30. Whatever the truth of the matter, the question is now academic, for bad weather in the northern area on 22 June prevented most machines from taking off. Some did manage to get into the air the following day. Among the sorties flown was one sent out to mine the Kola Inlet. By this time, however, the remaining two *Staffeln* of II./KG 30 had also been ordered north from Stavanger to bolster the Luftwaffe's strength in its isolated campaign against Soviet forces in the Arctic.

No such problems beset the units of *Luftflotte* 4 on the southern sector of the main eastern front, where the five *Kampfgruppen* of KGs 51 and 54 were grouped together under V. *Fliegerkorps* around Krosno and Lublin, in German-occupied Poland. The main objective of the Wehrmacht's ground forces on the southern sector was the Ukrainian capital Kiev. It was in order to support *Panzergruppe* 1's drive due east out of Poland through the forward Kiev Military District towards this city that the Air Fleet's Ju 88 *Gruppen* were ordered to bomb specific Soviet airfields along the route of advance. For KG 51 it was to prove a costly venture.

After the obligatory reading of the *Führer's* stirring call-to-arms to all 'Soldiers of the Eastern Front', the heavily laden Junkers began to take off for the first of the day's four missions – the *Geschwaderstab*, together with I. and II. *Gruppen* from Krosno, and III./KG 51 from nearby Lezany – a total of some 80 bombers in all.

Major Walter Marienfeld's III. *Gruppe* fared worst. Although crews reportedly destroyed at least 34 Polikarpov biplanes on the ground at their assigned target, an airfield south of Lvov (Lemberg) that was just 40 miles beyond the border, they were set upon by other Soviet fighters as they turned for home. A running battle developed and seven of the 28 bombers despatched by III./KG 51 did not make it back to base, five of the losses being suffered by 9. *Staffel* alone.

Further casualties were sustained during the three subsequent missions in and around the Kiev District later in the day. After the last machine had landed at 2023 hrs the mood in Major Schulz-Heyn's *Geschwader* HQ in Krosno's Polanka Castle was sombre. 60 men –

A *Gruppe* of Ju 88s *en route* to the target in tight formation was an impressive sight

15 complete crews – were dead or missing, and many more had been wounded. The luckless III. *Gruppe* reported 14 aircraft either shot down, written off or severely damaged in crashes, resulting in a casualty rate for the day of exactly 50 per cent! Among the *Geschwader's* dead was the popular Oberleutnant von Wenchowski, the Staffelkapitän of 5./KG 51, whose 'earthy good humour would be sadly missed by one and all'.

Some 110 miles away from KG 51's main base at Krosno, the two *Gruppen* of KG 54, together with Oberstleutnant Otto Höhne's *Geschwaderstab*, all shared the airfield at Swidnik on the outskirts of Lublin. Höhne's crews were also scheduled to fly four missions on this opening day of *Barbarossa*, but their casualties would be far fewer than those suffered by neighbouring KG 51. In fact, just three aircraft were lost – one brought down by enemy fighters and two written off in emergency landings – while four others were damaged but repairable.

The first of the 23 Ju 88s of Hauptmann Richard Linke's I./KG 54 lifted off from Swidnik at 0230 hrs. They were followed by the machines of II./KG 54 under the command of Major Erhart Krafft von Dellmensingen. Carrying a mix of 250 kg HE bombs and smaller fragmentation bombs – the standard load of most Ju 88 units on this first day of the campaign in the east – each *Gruppe* was assigned three target airfields, which were presumably to be attacked on an individual *Staffel* basis. Although several enemy fighters were encountered, they did not press home their attacks with any vigour and all KG 54's aircraft returned safely to base. The defenders were up in greater numbers during I. *Gruppe's* second mission of the morning. Some 30-40 fighters engaged the eight Ju 88s targeting Nielisk airfield but again the latter got back unscathed, claiming one I-153 biplane shot down and one probable.

II./KG 54's second mission, flown about an hour later, did not go so well, however. Having bombed the airfields at Luck and Kolki, crews flew back at low level, ground strafing knots of enemy troops on the way. They received a rude surprise. For the first time they experienced the Red Army's disconcerting habit when under fire, not of diving for the nearest available cover, but of standing its ground and letting fly with every weapon that could be brought to bear. The net result was two aircraft so badly damaged by small-arms fire that they were forced to crash-land behind enemy lines. Both machines were from 4. *Staffel*, including that of the *Kapitän*, Oberleutnant Günther Seubert who, although wounded, made his way back to friendly territory along with two of his injured crew.

By day's end Luftwaffe units had submitted claims for an incredible 1811 Soviet aircraft destroyed – 1489 on the ground and 322 brought down in combat or by flak. If anywhere near accurate, these figures would make 22 June 1941 the most disastrous day for any air force in the history of aerial warfare. At the time they seemed so excessive that even Hermann Göring, the Luftwaffe's flamboyant Commander in Chief and himself no stranger to exaggeration, demanded that they be checked. Subsequent investigation showed that the totals were on the conservative side!

Others accepted the figures at their face value. That same evening the Chief of the General Staff of the Luftwaffe recorded in his diary, 'The timing of this air assault on the Russian airfields on the first day of the campaign was a total success. These attacks pave the way for

operations against the whole of the Soviet Air Force'. Even some of the enemy shared the same view. A Soviet Army commander taken prisoner in the early stages of the fighting in the east is on record as saying, 'Our losses in the air in the first days were horrendous. Our air force will never recover from them'. It is debatable, however, whether the general believed this, or whether he was telling his captors what they wanted to hear.

Although they pale into insignificance against the casualties suffered by the Soviets, the Luftwaffe's own losses on 22 June were far from light. Some 167 aircraft were reported destroyed or damaged from all causes. Of the 61 machines lost as a direct result of enemy action, almost a third – 21 in all – were Ju 88s. The bulk of these were accounted for in the trouncing inflicted by the Russians upon the unfortunate KG 51. But now another, far more invidious, cause of loss had come to light. Those bombers that had inexplicably exploded in mid-air while over German-held territory had not been the victims of friendly fire as at first thought. They had been brought down by their own bombs.

The culprit was the 10 kg SD 10 fragmentation bomb which, although intended primarily as an anti-personnel weapon, was used in great numbers and to devastating effect by the *Kampfgruppen* in their early raids on the Soviet frontier airfields. Unfortunately the SD 10 had a dangerous flaw. Carried in the Junkers' fuselage bomb-bays, usually in bundles of four, an individual bomb could sometimes get caught up in the bomb-bay upon release. Fully armed, it then took just the slightest jolt to detonate it. The resultant explosion was the equivalent of a direct flak hit, and almost invariably led to the loss of the bomber. Once this was discovered, orders were given that the *Kampfgruppen* were no longer to include the SD 10 in their weapons loads. Henceforward, it would be employed only by Stuka and ground-attack units, where it was carried externally underwing and would be sure of falling free when released.

Despite these difficulties, the pace of operations did not slacken. On the southern sector KG 51's losses were hastily made good, and the two Ju 88 *Kampfgeschwader* of V. *Fliegerkorps* continued their attacks on the enemy airfields standing in the path of *Panzergruppe* 1's advance on Kiev. Machines of the *Korps'* reconnaissance *Staffel* had located no fewer than 62 such fields situated ahead of Army Group South's forces. These were grouped mainly in the Kiev, Stanislau and Odessa areas, and reports stated that 51 of them appeared to be occupied by 1270+ aircraft.

Over the course of the next few days KGs 51 and 54 mounted a series of raids on Soviet air bases. These resulted in several hundred more

Fighter pilots were not the only ones to beat up their home airfield on returning from a successful mission. Individual bomber crews often did the same – especially if one of the gunners had shot down an enemy machine

Red Air Force machines being destroyed on the ground. But the attackers had to pay a price too. On 25 June, the day KG 51 bombed the Soviet airfield at Tarnopol, the *Geschwader* lost 16 aircrew killed or missing. Major Walter Marienfeld, the *Kommandeur* of III. *Gruppe*, was lucky not to be among them. With both engines shot up, he managed to pull off an emergency landing on a sand bank in the River Bug from which he and his crew were rescued by a squad of infantrymen. KG 54 escaped more lightly on this date too, with just one 4. *Staffel* machine and its all-NCO crew being reported missing north of Kiev.

The enemy's air bases were not the bombers' only objectives. Both *Geschwader* were also called upon to provide more direct support to the forces in the field by carrying out low-level attacks on concentrations of Soviet troops and armour. One such operation was flown on 26 June against a group of 'super heavy tanks of the Red Army' (this was probably a reference to the cumbersome 45-ton T-35, a multi-turreted but relatively thinly armoured 'land battleship' introduced into service in 1933). The Russian behemoths, threatening the open flank of *Panzergruppe* 1, were successfully repulsed, but this time it was KG 54 that bore the brunt of the losses. These included an aircraft of 5. *Staffel*, which crashed on landing back at Swidnik, killing its entire crew and completely demolishing two other machines on the ground.

In fact, such was the alarming rate of attrition being suffered by the two *Geschwader* from light anti-aircraft and small arms fire during these low-level attacks that the GOC of V. *Fliegerkorps*, *General der Flieger* Ritter von Greim, soon ordered a halt to them. From now on the Ju 88s were to operate at medium altitude, releasing their bombs – 50, 250 or 500 kg, depending upon the target – from a shallow dive.

Despite this curtailment of their air support, the armoured divisions of *Panzergruppe* 1 continued to forge ahead. And it was not long before the Ju 88s were also making their first moves forward to keep pace with them. By mid-July the two *Gruppen* of KG 54 had transferred 160 miles south-southeast from Lublin-Swidnik to Dubno, close to the pre-war Polish-Russian border. And almost midway between Lublin and Dubno, the airfield at Wlodzimierz now housed III./KG 51, which had moved up from Lezany on 5 July. But for the other two *Gruppen* of KG 51, those initially based at Krosno, there came a parting of the ways with V. *Fliegerkorps*. Their first move of the *Barbarossa* campaign took them southwards into Rumania, I./KG 51 to Zilistea and II./KG 51 to Balti. Here, they were subordinated to Generalleutnant Kurt Pflugbeil's IV. *Fliegerkorps*, whose area of operations included the southernmost reaches of the Russian front along the Black Sea coastal belt.

A Soviet officer inspects an aircraft of II./KG 54 *'Totenkopf'* that has force-landed behind enemy lines. Note the (now somewhat inappropriate) *Gruppe* badge consisting of a map of Britain with a bombsight superimposed, and the small fairings behind the nose glazing indicating that the machine is an A-6 variant previously equipped with – or intended for – a balloon-cable fender. Might it even be the *Gruppenstab's* 'B3+EC', an A-6 that failed to return to base on 23 June?

Armourers cheerfully tote a load of 50 kg bombs to a waiting machine

Proudly displaying the Geschwader's elaborate 'Edelweiss' emblem, an A-5 of II./KG 51 basks in the Rumanian sunshine shortly after its arrival at Balti just five days into Barbarossa. Note the tarpaulin covers protecting the mainwheel tyres

Meanwhile, on the central sector, the two Ju 88 *Gruppen* of KG 3 had also been performing the twin tasks of attacking the enemy's forward airfields and supporting their own troops on the ground. The forces on this central area of the front formed the very core of Hitler's *Blitzkrieg* offensive against Russia. Their striking power was concentrated in two *Panzergruppen* – Nos 2 and 3, a total of 17 armoured and mechanised divisions in all – closely supported by the Stukas and ground-attack aircraft of *General der Flieger* Wolfram von Richthofen's highly experienced VIII. *Fliegerkorps*. It was these two *Panzergruppen's* parallel advances towards, and subsequent pincer movements around, Minsk – the capital of White Russia and western terminus of the Minsk-Moscow highway – which resulted in the first of the great 'cauldron' battles of the eastern front.

However the Panzers had left a problem in their wake. On the opening day of the campaign, with their sights firmly set on Minsk, they had bypassed the ancient fortified Polish citadel of Brest-Litovsk. Situated on the eastern bank of the River Bug and held by the Red Army, the guns of the fortress were in range of the Germans' main lines of communications and supply. It posed a grave threat, but every attempt to batter it into submission ended in failure. For a week its walls proved impervious to everything thrown at them, from the huge shells of the army's giant 60 cm mortar *'Karl'*, to the 500 kg bombs of VIII. *Fliegerkorps'* Stukas.

On 28 June (some sources put it a day later) von Richthofen's dive-bombers made one last attempt to breach the citadel's defences. Again they were unsuccessful. That same afternoon, between 1740 and 1800 hrs, seven Ju 88s of KG 3 appeared high overhead. Each machine was carrying a single 1800 kg *'Satan'* bomb. These weapons had been specially delivered to the *Geschwader's* airfield outside Deblin for this one mission. Two direct hits were scored on the eastern fort, the citadel's main centre of resistance. Some 400 soldiers emerged and surrendered to the Wehrmacht's 45. Infantry Division. The remainder of the garrison, numbering 7000 men, gave themselves up the following day and Army Group Centre's supply lines were at last secured.

There were to be no such unexpected hazards, nor any great 'cauldron' battles, in Army Group North's sector, but rather a steady – at times even rapid – advance northeastwards through the Baltic States and across northern Russia towards the ground forces' ultimate objective, Leningrad. This did not mean that the eight Ju 88 *Gruppen* of I. *Fliegerkorps* were underemployed. Indeed, for the first few days of the campaign the Junkers kept up their attacks on the Red Air Force's frontline airfields. These raids, flown both during the hours of daylight and under cover of darkness, were proving costly (*Luftflotte* 1 reported another 18 Ju 88 bombers shot down on 23 June). But their intensity soon persuaded the enemy to vacate his forward air bases and

withdraw all his flying units behind the line of the River Dvina.

On 27 June, with local air superiority thus achieved, the aircraft of KGs 1, 76 and 77 began harassing Soviet troops and armour retreating out of Latvia and Estonia. These operations, flown at lower altitudes, inevitably resulted in even lengthier casualty lists for all three *Geschwader*. On the very first day a mission directed against Red Army units withdrawing south of the Latvian capital Riga cost II./KG 1 their *Gruppenkommandeur* when Hauptmann Otto Stams' aircraft was hit by ground fire. Although seriously wounded, Stams managed to nurse the crippled machine back to Powunden, where he was immediately rushed into hospital. Surgeons were unable to save his leg, however, and its amputation spelled the end of his operational flying career.

After the first German troops had entered Riga on 29 June, a number of Ju 88 *Gruppen* were released to attack targets further afield. These were located primarily along the Soviets' rear area lines of supply and included the road and rail routes between Riga and Pleskau (Pskov), close to the southern tip of Lake Peipus, and Velikye Luki, an important junction on the railway line linking the Baltic States to Moscow.

One unit that particularly distinguished itself during these long-range missions was II./KG 77. Commanded by Hauptmann Dietrich Peltz – who was already sporting the Knight's Cross in recognition of operations flown over Great Britain, and who would subsequently rise to high office as the *General der Kampfflieger* – this *Gruppe* undertook a number of 1000-mile and more round trips from their base at Wormditt, in East Prussia, to attack the main Leningrad-Moscow railway line. Its crews specifically targeted stations and marshalling yards along this important stretch, as well as canals and locks in the same area. It is claimed that their pinpoint accuracy often resulted in such installations being out of action for days, if not

III./KG 51 joined II. *Gruppe* at Balti at the end of August fresh from its re-equipment in the Reich. The unit's new A-4s sport the bright yellow trim indicative of a III. *Gruppe*. In KG 51's case this was applied to the front edge of the engine nacelles and as a thin outline to the *Geschwader* badge – compare with the far less apparent red trim adorning the II. *Gruppe* machine pictured on page 14. It is believed that the spinner colours identified the *Staffel* within the *Gruppe*

The losses suffered during the opening days and weeks of *Barbarossa* were not all one-sided. This A-5 of 8./KG 76 – note the jettisoned cabin canopy in foreground – was lucky to make it back to Schippenbeil for a belly landing after being hit by Soviet anti-aircraft fire...

...equally fortunate was this machine of II./KG 1 bellied in at Powunden, the crew's hasty exit evidenced by the cabin canopy lying upside-down on that bullet-holed wing. On this occasion, according to the pilot, the perpetrators were 'a trio of I-18s'

The Ju 88 reconnaissance units faced all of the dangers but received few of the plaudits accorded to the bombers. This aircraft of 5.(F)/122 burns fiercely following a take-off accident at Jürgenfelde, the field it shared with II./KG 76

weeks on end, and that they alone were responsible for significant disruptions to rail and barge traffic between the Soviet Union's two major cities.

Enemy airfields remained high on the list of priorities for I. *Fliegerkorps'* bombers. On 3 July the two *Gruppen* of KG 1 mounted a successful dusk raid on the base at Pleskau, and at 0500 hrs the following morning elements of KGs 76 and 77 attacked the enemy's airfields at Opochka and Idritsa, some 90 miles further to the south.

It was at this juncture that Soviet forces launched a counter-attack aimed at halting the German advance on Leningrad. Having crossed the River Dvina south of Riga on 2 July, the spearheads of *Panzergruppe* 4 had progressed 200+ miles in just three days. On 5 July they established a bridgehead over the River Velikaya, and it was here, around the town of Ostrov, situated between Pleskau and Opochka, that the Russians struck.

KGs 1, 76 and 77 were called upon to help counter this very real threat. Their intervention proved crucial, as once again it was the bombers that were instrumental in averting the danger to a *Panzergruppe's* exposed flanks. Not only did they operate in direct support of the ground troops below, breaking up the approaching Soviet armoured formations, they also bombed enemy airfields in the immediate vicinity and beyond. By the end of the action, for the loss of only two Ju 88s, they had claimed nearly 150 tanks knocked out and 112 aircraft destroyed on the ground.

With one of the last major water barriers successfully negotiated, the way to Leningrad now seemed wide open. The city lay 200 miles away – the distance recently covered by *Panzergruppe* 4 in just 72 hours. But a lot can happen in 200 miles, and Generaloberst Erich Hoepner's armoured divisions were fated never to roll down Leningrad's broad boulevards.

On 5 July, II./KG 1, commanded now by Hauptmann Emil Enderle, transferred forward from Powunden to Riga-Spilve (where it was soon joined by III. *Gruppe*, the latter after a stopover at Mitau, to the southwest of the Latvian capital). This move facilitated raids on Soviet airfields in neighbouring Estonia. In addition, it enabled them to carry out more attacks on road and rail targets between Lakes Peipus and Ilmen, and also to fly armed reconnaissance missions over the Leningrad region.

But despite all the crushing blows they were inflicting upon the enemy, Russian resistance could at times still be fanatical. This was demonstrated on 6 July when 6./KG 1's 'V4+MP' was deliberately rammed by a MiG-3 fighter near Lake Ilmen. It was by no means a unique occurrence. The first such ramming attack had been carried out within an hour of *Barbarossa* being launched, and eight further instances of Luftwaffe aircraft being intentionally rammed had been recorded before the opening day of the campaign against Russia was over.

Such tactics, dubbed *'taran'* attacks by the Soviets, should not be likened to the consciously suicidal kamikaze missions later flown by the Japanese in the Pacific. They were not the result of official policy, but rather made at the discretion of individual pilots and employed as a last resort, often when the attacker's ammunition had been expended. Nor was the Soviet pilot who chose to engage the enemy by *'taran'* automatically seeking his own death. Many *were* killed, of course, but various methods of *'taran'* were employed. The most common was probably the approach from astern, with the attacker attempting to use his propeller to chew up his opponent's tail. The second involved a deliberate mid-air collision, possibly when the Soviet pilot's own machine had already been damaged and was itself about to crash. A third alternative was for the attacker to use one of his wings as a weapon of destruction, either by slicing it into the rudder of his adversary or – while avoiding actual contact – by positioning it close below the wingtip of the enemy aircraft and making use of the airflow to flip it over out of control.

By perfecting one or other of these methods, many Soviet pilots survived a *'taran'*. Some even scored more than one victory by such means, the highest number recorded being four. According to one contemporary report quoting 'far from complete returns', 43 airmen – the majority of whom survived – carried out successful ramming attacks between 22 June and 31 August 1941. By 1 January 1942 that figure had risen to 100+. But as the war progressed and slowly swung in the Soviets' favour, such incidents became understandably fewer. Nevertheless, by its end 200+ *'taran'* attacks are believed to have been carried out.

One such incident involving a Junkers – unfortunately unidentifiable – was described in a booklet produced by the Foreign Languages Publishing House in Moscow in 1942. Despite the clumsy turgidity of the language, it conveys a vivid impression of the times;

'Senior Lieutenant Vlassov was on duty, sitting in the cockpit of his fighting plane at his aerodrome. Suddenly a German "Junkers-88" dived out of the clouds. Vlassov was in the air in a flash. The bomber opened fire and then turned tail. Vlassov overhauled it and began firing at a range of 200 m. The enemy made off as fast as his engines would carry him. Vlassov put on speed, came within 50 m of the bomber, but found that his cartridges had run out. He decided to ram the bomber. He steered his plane to the left and under the Junkers, and thus got out of range of its machine gun, gave a short spurt and rammed it, cut across its rudder, breaking it clean off. Vlassov's plane bounced off the

Hauptmann Dietrich Peltz's II./KG 77 plaster the Bologoye marshalling yards on the Leningrad-Moscow railway

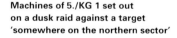

Machines of 5./KG 1 set out on a dusk raid against a target 'somewhere on the northern sector'

enemy plane and listed at an angle of 90 degrees. The fight took place at a height of 4500 metres.

'Dazed by the collision, when Vlassov's mind cleared he found that he was 1500 m from the ground. He tried the steering gear and found that it worked. The engine was silent and the propeller blades were bent. Vlassov was wounded in the right hand and blood flowed from his forehead, over the right eye. He could not see with his left eye as his goggles were smashed. Nevertheless, he landed his plane and then lost consciousness.'

24 hours after Unteroffizier Willi Bukowski and his crew of 6./KG 1 had been brought down by the MiG-3's *'taran'* attack near Lake Ilmen, III./KG 1 almost lost its *Gruppenkommandeur* during a raid on Pernau airfield on Estonia's western coast. Major Walter Lehwess-Litzmann later gave his own account of the incident;

'I could already make out the field from some distance away and could see a number of multi-engined aircraft parked around its perimeter. I put the machine into a shallow dive and gave it full throttle. We released our bombs from a height of 500-600 m and they were bang on target. I pulled up and away in a left-hand curve. We were already out over the waters of the gulf again when the starboard engine began pouring smoke – it had taken a hit. I switched it off and feathered the propeller. The smoke stopped, but I started to lose height. I didn't have the know-how to keep the machine in the air, and realising that I wouldn't make it to Riga, I turned back for the coast. I would have to attempt an emergency landing.

'As I crossed the shoreline I could see a large expanse of open meadows. I immediately decided to belly-land. It wasn't until we were about to touch down that we spotted that the landscape was dotted with numerous large rocks. The flight engineer strapped himself tightly in by my side, while the observer braced himself behind us and prepared to release the canopy roof the moment we landed. And so I made my first belly-landing. It came off. As soon as we hit the ground the observer yanked the canopy jettison lever forward. I switched off the port engine. The ventral gondola was soon torn off and there was an awful juddering and jolting. As we careened across the meadow an enormous great boulder suddenly loomed up in our path. Fortunately the machine came to a halt in the nick of time – there couldn't have been more than half-a-metre separating the glazed nose of our aircraft from the face of the huge rock.

'According to my map we still had to be in territory controlled by the Red Army. A nearby shepherd greeted us in a friendly enough fashion but knew nothing. An approaching cyclist turned out to be the village policeman who – like many in this area – could speak a few words of broken German. He confirmed that we were indeed in Estonia, that the Russians had made off northwards only two hours ago and that the Germans hadn't got here yet – we were the first to arrive!'

Not everybody was as lucky as Lehwess-Litzmann and his crew of 'V4+AD'. On 10 July KG 1 suffered the loss of three more Ju 88s, including another destroyed in a *'taran'* attack by an I-16. The following day three machines of KG 77 failed to return, and on 12 July KG 76 lost one. By mid-July the three *Kampfgeschwader* of I. *Fliegerkorps* had lost 59 aircraft. That represented almost 30 per cent of their serviceable strength at the start of *Barbarossa*, or the equivalent of the then current combat strength of one entire *Geschwader*. Despite this heavy rate of attrition, the Ju 88s kept up the pressure. High on their list of targets by this stage of the hostilities was the main railway line running eastwards out of Estonia, which they subjected to near constant bombardment in an effort to prevent Red Army units from escaping back into Russia proper.

While I. *Fliegerkorps'* units were thus engaged, the northern sector's only other Ju 88 *Gruppe* was waging what almost amounted to a private war of its own against Soviet shipping in the Baltic. The minelaying mission off Kronstadt flown by Hauptmann Emig and his crews of KGr 806 on the first day of the campaign established the basic pattern of operations for the weeks ahead. With its aircraft usually armed with a single 1000 kg LMB (*Luftmine 'B'*, or Aerial mine 'B') apiece, the *Gruppe* carried out a succession of minelaying sorties against specific targets, primarily Soviet naval bases, in the eastern Baltic and Gulf of Finland. However they also flew armed reconnaissance sweeps of the same areas to monitor enemy shipping movements, mounted anti-submarine patrols and undertook convoy escort duties to protect coastal supply routes.

In addition to this multiplicity of maritime tasks, KGr 806's services would sometimes be called upon for special bombing missions. It was one such, flown on 28 or 29 June, that was to cost the unit its *Kommandeur*.

The target was a set of lock gates close to the entrance of the Stalin Canal, a waterway that connected the eastern Baltic – via Lake Onega – to the White Sea. Armed with BM 1000s (the land-based equivalent of the LMB parachute mine, fitted with a conventional bomb-type tail), the attackers approached in three waves. The first was led by the now Major Hans Emig. In order to ensure the success of the mission, Emig went in at extremely low level. The lock gates were destroyed, but so too was Emig's aircraft, which took the full force of the blast. Hauptmann Erich Seedorf, the *Staffelkapitän* of 1./KGr.806, ordered the two following waves to bomb from a height of 100 m, and these escaped without further loss.

Under new *Kommandeur* Major Richard Linke, KGr 806 continued its anti-shipping activities over the Baltic. On 18 July two Soviet destroyers made a daring attempt to intercept a small German supply convoy heading for Daugavgriva, the Latvian port at the mouth of the River Dvina below Riga. The warships were unsuccessful and all the merchantmen reached harbour safely. Now the hunters became the hunted. The two destroyers reversed course and sought to escape from the confined waters of the Gulf of Riga, but 24 hours later they were caught in the narrows east of the island of Saaremaa by the Ju 88s of KGr 806. The 1686-ton *Serdity* was so badly damaged that, despite a three-day battle to save her, she finally had to be scuttled on 22 July.

As the first month of *Barbarossa* came to a close, German forces were advancing on all fronts and the Luftwaffe had gained near undisputed mastery of the air. All the signs pointed towards another successful *Blitzkrieg* campaign in the making. But this was just the beginning.

'M7+GH' was an A-6 of 1./KGr 806, the unit assigned to the *Fliegerführer Ostsee* for minelaying and other maritime missions over the Baltic. The *Gruppe* frequently used airfields in Finland as a forward base, and the aircraft is seen here here at Utti, northeast of Helsinki

BARBAROSSA – DECISION DEFERRED

It was Werner Baumbach, arguably the best known Ju 88 pilot in the Luftwaffe, and certainly one of its most highly decorated, who suggested that the first ten months of the air war in the east could be divided into four separate phases. The first of these, from 22 June to 21 July, saw the Luftwaffe wrest air superiority from the Soviets and support the first of the great 'cauldron' battles on the central sector. Next, from 22 July to the beginning of October, came the 'diversions to north and south, while the central sector remained temporarily quiescent'. Then, on 2 October, the main emphasis was switched back to the Moscow front with the launching of the ground offensive against the Russian capital, which was to last a further two months. Finally, from early December to the spring of 1942, a major enemy counter-offensive in the Moscow area, coupled with the first withdrawals of Luftwaffe units from the Russian to the Mediterranean theatre, dashed any last hopes of a speedy and successful conclusion to the campaign in the east.

But Baumbach's assertion that the central sector became 'quiescent' after 22 July seems to ignore the fact that it was on this very date that the Luftwaffe opened its strategic bombing offensive against Moscow. In fact, to add extra weight to the assault, *Luftflotte* 2 was even reinforced by four additional *Kampfgruppen* from the west. The only Ju 88 units that appear to have been involved in the raids on Moscow, however, were the Air Fleet's resident I. and II./KG 3.

Several sources maintain that elements of KG 54 were detached from neighbouring *Luftflotte* 4 in order to participate in the initial assault on Stalin's capital, but this is not borne out by the unit's history, which has both its *Gruppen* fully engaged in the Poltava-Cherkassy areas on 21 and 22 July.

The Soviets had long been expecting the Germans to launch an all-out aerial offensive against Moscow. The 195 bombers that participated in the first raid on the night of 21/22 July faced formidable

A victim of Moscow's ferocious anti-aircraft defences, 'F6+AK' of 2.(F)/122 lies broken-backed in a birch plantation outside the Soviet capital under the watchful eye of an armed local militiaman

defences – a belt of 300 searchlights 18 miles in front of the city, backed up by anti-aircraft batteries, both heavy and light, plus 170 fighters. It is not known how many of the attackers fought their way through to the target – certainly more than the 'ten or fifteen' noted in one Soviet publication, for another admitted heavy losses among the city's civil population. The Luftwaffe clearly failed in its stated aim of reducing the Kremlin to rubble, although one crew did come close – a single bomb crater in Red Square caused 'quite a stir among the locals the following morning'.

Despite the strength of the defences, this first raid resulted in the loss of only six bombers. A second flown on the night of 22/23 July cost the 115-strong attacking force five of its number, including three Ju 88s claimed by I-16s. The attacks were to continue on a nightly basis for some time to come, but they quickly declined in intensity – 100 raiders on the third night, 65 on the fourth, until the assault finally petered out in mid-September. Moscow suffered neither a single devastating blow such as that inflicted on Belgrade, nor was it subjected to a sustained aerial *Blitz* of the type endured by London. It has been estimated that of the 76 night raids flown against Moscow in 1941, all but 17 were little more than pinpricks carried out by small groups of from three to ten aircraft.

If Ju 88 activity on the central sector during this period was minimal, the same could not be said of the northern and southern fronts.

For the units of I. *Fliegerkorps* in the north it remained very much business as usual, but now that business was being conducted from Russian soil. On 14 July, III./KG 1 had made the move from Riga-Spilve to Pleskau. Nine days later II./KG 1 also vacated Riga. Their destination was Saborovka, where they were then joined by Oberst Karl Angerstein's *Geschwaderstab* and by III. *Gruppe* early in August. For very nearly the next three months this forward landing ground on the eastern shore of Lake Peipus was to serve as KG 1's main operating base.

By the end of July all three of the *Korps' Kampfgeschwader* were targeting Soviet supply lines into Leningrad as part of the softening-up process prior to an assault on the city. Although combat losses were not high during these missions, they did include a Ju 88 of 7./KG 76 downed by an I-16 ramming attack over Krasnogvardeisk on 27 July.

However the troops on the ground had run into difficulties. Having cleared much of the Baltic territories, they had now come up against the so-called Stalin Line. Stretching from the Gulf of Finland in the north to the Black Sea in the south and roughly paralleling, albeit some distance to the rear of, the Soviet Union's pre-1939 western borders, this was not a heavily fortified position in the sense of the French Maginot Line, but more a defensive zone of considerable depth combining man-made strongpoints with natural barriers such as lakes and rivers. Nevertheless, it was sufficient to bring a temporary halt to the momentum of advance.

The only Ju 88 *Kampfgruppen* to participate in the initial raids on Moscow were I. and II./KG 3. A machine of the former unit (note white background shield to the red lightning bolt) is seen here undergoing a major engine overhaul – the starboard powerplant has been removed – with what appears to be two 250 kg bombs nestling beneath turf in the foreground

A contemporary newspaper cutting illustrating one of the earliest Knight's Crosses to be awarded to a Ju 88 pilot on the eastern front. It is being presented to Stabsfeldwebel Rudolf Nacke of III./KG 76 by Reichsmarschall Göring outside the latter's private train, in which he was making a whistlestop tour of Luftwaffe airfields. But, like the other half-dozen or so such awards first made in Russia, Nacke's decoration (announced on 23 July) was primarily for service prior to *Barbarossa*. With 130 operational missions already under his belt, Nacke was one of KG 76's most experienced pilots. He ended the war flying Me 262s and Ar 234s jet bombers with EKG 1

'3Z+AB' of the *Gruppenstab* I./KG 77. Officially, Luftwaffe regulations decreed that an aircraft bearing the individual letter 'A' should be flown by the unit commander, be he the *Geschwaderkommodore*, *Gruppenkommandeur* or *Staffelkapitän*, although this was not always the case in practice. Here, however, the rules are being followed, for 'AB' is also flying a *Gruppenkommandeur's* pennant in front of the windscreen, indicating that it is indeed the mount of Hauptmann Joachim Poetter

Loaded with what appears to be a 1000 kg SC 1000 bomb – nicknamed the 'Hermann' after you know who – on the starboard inner rack and a pair of SC 250s to port, this aircraft from KG 77 runs up its engines prior to a mission. Note the crudely applied black camouflage paint on the machine's undersides, particularly visible on the open ventral gondola entry hatch

While troops paused to collect their strength in preparation for the assault on the Stalin Line, the Ju 88 *Gruppen* offered indirect support. For III./KG 1 this meant attacking Soviet positions along and to the immediate rear of the defences, while II./KG 1 – whose aircraft were still configured to Category 'B', indicating that they had retained their rearmost fuselage fuel tank – flew longer range missions against rail traffic tasked with bringing up reinforcements and supplies from the enemy hinterland.

On 10 August, after a two-day delay due to bad weather, the armoured divisions of *Panzergruppe* 4 started to smash their way through that sector of the Stalin Line running along the lower Luga from Lake Ilmen to the Gulf of Finland. The Ju 88s were now required to provide much more direct support, flying ground-attack sorties against Soviet bunkers, artillery emplacements, tank concentrations and the like.

As the Panzers' advance on Leningrad slowly began to gather pace again, the *Kampfgruppen* reverted to the safeguarding of the ground forces' flanks. On 16 August KG 77 helped break up a dangerous Red Army counter-attack developing around Staraya Russa near the southern tip of Lake Ilmen. On that same date KG 1 succeeded in severing the railway line leading to the town of Luga midway between the northern shore of the lake and the sea. But on 25 August the unfortunate KG 76 suffered yet another loss to a *'taran'* attack near Krasnogvardeisk. This time it was a machine of 6. *Staffel* which had been rammed by a Yak-1.

On 15 September the Germans closed the ring around Leningrad. This heralded the start of an epic 900-day siege. During its early weeks the bombers of I. *Fliegerkorps* found themselves in constant demand. Not only were they assigned targets within Leningrad itself, they were also called upon to attack a number of fighter airfields in the surrounding areas in an effort to reduce the city's air defences. The 19 September raid on Kommandantskoye, which reconnaissance reported to be crowded with 100+ enemy aircraft, was particularly successful. The Ju 88s also dive-bombed ships of the Soviet Baltic Fleet berthed at Leningrad and Kronstadt, which were using their heavy armament to bombard German troops on shore. The ex-Czarist battleship *Oktyabrskaya Revolutsiya* suffered several near misses. Russian naval anti-aircraft fire made such operations expensive, and they were soon called off – Army Group North had more urgent tasks for the Luftwaffe's bombers.

One such task involved the planned offensive to be launched across the River Volkhov southeast of Leningrad. Its aim was to capture the town of Tichwin, an important junction on the main supply route for Soviet forces holding the southern shore of Lake Ladoga, and also eastern terminus of the tenuous air bridge into Leningrad itself.

Air support for this undertaking was to be provided by a specially activated task force – the small but grandiosely titled *Luftwaffenkommando Tichwin*. It was commanded by Oberst Johann Raithel, the *Geschwaderkommodore* of KG 77, whose Ju 88s constituted the *Kommando's* main striking power. However the misuse of the aircraft in low-level ground-attack sweeps led to heavy losses, and these in turn drew forth a strong protest from Hauptmann Dietrich Peltz,

This aerial shot purports to show part of Kronstadt naval base. If this is indeed the case, could that large broad-beamed warship in the inner basin be the *Oktyabrskaya Revolutsiya*? Note the bomb splashes straddling the mole and the column of black smoke close alongside the vessel

the highly experienced *Kommandeur* of II./KG 77. It has been suggested that Peltz's vociferous demands for a change in both tactics and leadership were the reason for his subsequent removal from the frontline. Although his remarks may have struck a chord somewhere along the line, it was more likely to have been his expertise that led to his posting. His next appointment was as CO of a newly created training *Staffel*, which was then expanded into the influential Bomber Unit Leaders' School.

Nor were KG 77's losses solely the result of their own actions. The Red Air Force was slowly but surely recovering from the blows inflicted upon it at the start of *Barbarossa* and was now beginning to hit back. A number of the *Geschwader's* Ju 88s were destroyed when Soviet Il-2s carried out a surprise raid on their Siverskaya base on 6 November.

By this time Russia's autumn mud had given way to winter snow and conditions were deteriorating rapidly. Some flying units were more badly affected than others. In mid-September II./KG 1 had been recalled to Insterburg, in East Prussia, to re-equip with the new Ju 88A-4. When crews returned to Saborovka a month later the first snows had already fallen, and their field – little more than a grass strip full of bumps and hollows, and not ideal at the best of times – was now all but unusable. On 17 October the *Geschwaderstab* and III./KG 1 moved up to Dno. They were joined there by II. *Gruppe* the following week. Although Dno was bigger than Saborovka, it offered little improvement and was crowded with other units. II./KG 1 was ordered to take its Ju 88A-4s further forward still, to Staraya Russa, where it prepared to sit out the winter.

In the period from the beginning of *Barbarossa* on 22 June up until 31 October 1941, I. *Fliegerkorps* reported the loss of no fewer than 162 of its

The aftermath of a Soviet air attack on Siverskaya. The Ju 88 on the left has had its port wingtip well and truly clipped

Below
Bent and buckled, and with a tarpaulin replacing the jettisoned cabin canopy, 8./KG 76's 'F1+AS' is back on its feet after a forced landing in treacherous conditions

Bottom
An unpleasant surprise – I./KG 77 gets to grips with its first taste of a Russian winter

Ju 88s. KG 1 had suffered the lowest casualty rate with 39 machines of its machines destroyed. KG 76 had lost 53, but KG 77 had been hit hardest of all with 70 aircraft shot down or written off to other causes.

Throughout the ground forces' advance on Leningrad, KGr 806 had been continuing its anti-shipping operations over the Baltic. Much of its time and energy was spent adding to the three major minefields designed to keep the Soviet fleet penned up in the Gulf of Finland. But on 6 August the *Gruppe* had deprived the Russians of another of their destroyers when its aircraft bombed the 1354-ton *Karl Marx* in Loksa Bight near Estonia's seaport capital Reval (Tallinn). As with the *Serdity*, the vessel's crew struggled desperately to save their ship, but the old destroyer, which dated back to before World War 1, finally went down two days later.

It was shortly after this that the Germans began their nine-day battle to take Reval, which also served as a major Soviet naval base. The bombers of KG 1 were to play a major supporting role in its capture. However it was the Russians' attempts at a seaborne evacuation after its fall that was to bring KGr 806 its greatest successes. On 28 August enemy vessels began to stream out of the shattered port. The aircraft of KGr 806, together with elements of KG 77, fell upon them while they were still west of '*Juminda*' – the first of the extensive minefields blocking their passage back into the 'safety' of the Gulf of Finland.

Among the Ju 88s' victims on the 28th were the 2250-ton former Latvian naval icebreaker *Krisjanis Valdemars*, now serving as a Soviet auxiliary, and three transports, the 2414-ton *Skrunda*, the 1423-ton *Atis Kronvaldis* (both ex-Latvian ships) and the 2317-ton *Lake Lucerne*. The 2026-ton *Vironia*, a former Estonian steamer taken over by the Soviet navy as a staff vessel, suffered only superficial bomb damage, but then struck a mine off Cape Juminda and sank with heavy loss of life including 'many leading Communist officials escaping from the Baltic States'.

The Ju 88s resumed their attacks the next day, 29 August, by which time most of the fleeing vessels had safely negotiated the *'Juminda'* field. But three more were caught and sunk on this date – the 1270-ton *Lensoviet* (*Leningradsoviet*), a naval navigational and hydrographic training ship and two transports, the 3974-ton *Vtaraya Piatiletka* and the 2190-ton *Kalpaks*, the latter another ex-Latvian auxiliary. Two other transports – the 3974-ton *Ivan Papanin* and the 1270-ton *Saule* (also requisitioned from the Latvians) – were severely damaged by bombs, as was the 5920-ton naval repair ship *Serp-i-Molot*. However, all three vessels managed to beach themselves on the Finnish island of Suursaari. A fourth naval auxiliary transport, the 3309-ton *Kazakhstan*, was likewise badly hit. But after making for another Finnish island, Seiskari, where she put ashore 2300 of the 5000 troops she was carrying, the ship limped into Kronstadt, only for her captain – despite having been wounded and blown overboard during the bombing – to be summarily executed for cowardice.

28 August had also witnessed another raid on the locks of the Stalin Canal, an operation that was to be repeated on 5 September. Just over two weeks later *Fliegerführer Ostsee* was reinforced by the arrival in Riga of the 14 Ju 88s of Hauptmann Josef Sched's 1./KGr 506. By this stage, however, plans for an all-out assault on Leningrad had been shelved, with Hitler decreeing in his War Directive No 35 that the city should instead simply be 'encircled more closely'. With the Soviet Baltic Fleet now effectively bottled up, this brought an end – albeit a premature one – to most of the Luftwaffe's anti-shipping operations in the area.

On 27 October the staff of the *Fliegerführer Ostsee* was disbanded and its component units deployed to other fronts. For Major Richard Linke's KGr 806 this meant a transfer, first to southern Finland and thence to the Mediterranean theatre, where it would subsequently be incorporated into KG 54 as that *Geschwader's* III. *Gruppe*. Finland was also the initial destination for the Ju 88s of Hauptmann Josef Sched's 1./KGr 506.

The dissolution of the *Fliegerführer Ostsee* may have indicated a belief on the part of the Luftwaffe leadership that the anti-shipping air war in the Baltic had come to an end. However on the southern sector a comparable campaign against the Soviet navy's Black Sea Fleet was far from over. Among the major protagonists of that campaign would be the Ju 88s of KG 51.

Unlike KGr 806 to the north, KG 51's activities were not confined to maritime missions alone. Its crews were also required to continue their support of the

Its unknown pilot grinning cheerfully from the cockpit, this A-4 of KG 77 bears a striking similarity to the machine pictured in the bottom photograph on page 22. It displays the same unit badge, of course – a device based on the banner and motto of Germany's medieval knights (see *Combat Aircraft 17,* page 57) – but note too the spinner markings. In fact, the only obvious difference is in the surroundings, the baked expanse of turf in the previous photo having given way to snow piled high against that wooden hangar just visible behind the tailplane

ground forces of Army Group South, but now that I. and II./KG 51 were operating from Rumania, the beneficiaries of that support was no longer *Panzergruppe* 1, which during this late summer of 1941 was still advancing on Kiev – but rather the troops of Generaloberst *Ritter* von Schobert's 11. *Armee*, whose objective was the Crimea.

The terrain below may have been new to crews of the two *Gruppen*, but the opposition they faced in the air was all too familiar. As in the north, Red Air Force units along the southern sectors were also beginning to recover from the early days of *Barbarossa* and were slowly starting to strike back. On 30 July, during an armed reconnaissance of the Odessa area, the pilot of a 4. *Staffel* machine was killed instantly when hit in the head by a round from an I-16. What happened next is described in a message from the GOC IV. *Fliegerkorps*, Generalleutnant Pflugbeil:

'Due to the narrow confines of the Ju 88's cockpit, the other members of the crew were unable to lift the pilot's body from its seat. The dead pilot's weight meant that the rudder remained on full lock. In addition, an engine had been damaged and was running irregularly. The autopilot had also been hit and was no longer functioning. Despite these enormous difficulties the navigator, Obergefreiter Bernhardt of 4./KG 51, took control of the aircraft. Although the air battle was still in progress, he flew it safely back over our own lines, at times through thick banks of cloud, and carried out a smooth belly landing near Racsani.

'His actions thus saved the remaining crew members and the aircraft.

'For this outstanding deed, performed with circumspection and bravery, I extend to Bernhardt my most sincere appreciation.'

Generalleutnant Pflugbeil did more than send this letter of thanks. He promoted Bernhardt to the rank of unteroffizier with immediate effect and invited the surviving members of the crew to dine with him at Air Fleet HQ northeast of Bucharest.

Just over a fortnight later a crew of 3. *Staffel* survived an almost equally harrowing experience, as pilot Leutnant Heinz Unrau recounts:

'While attacking a convoy off the west coast of the Crimea on 15 August we were ourselves attacked by four fighters. As we pulled out of the dive at a height of 800 m, a well-aimed burst of fire from our wireless-operator/air gunner, Feldwebel Winter, forced the pilot of the fighter on our tail to bail out, but the now pilotless machine continued to head straight for us, ramming our tail and causing the right half of the tailplane to break off. What remained of the left half was bent upwards at an angle of about 20 degrees.

'After a lot of initial vibration the machine became very tail heavy. Despite exerting all the pressure I could on the stick – using both hands and one of my feet – the machine continued to climb at a rate of 2-3m/sec at an airspeed of

Back to the heat of a Rumanian summer, made all the hotter by the fire that has broken out in the port engine of this machine of KG 51 at Focsani, and which the field's fire crew is busy smothering with foam. Note the extremely tall ring sight on the weapon mounted in the nose glazing

300 km/h. I was able to counter a simultaneous swing to the left by sideslipping to the right without using the rudder, which had also been damaged and distorted.

'After about 30 minutes I found that I could keep to an altitude of 3000 m by throttling back the engines. Five minutes before reaching the Rumanian coast south of Akkermann the rear fuselage twisted another 20 degrees to an angle of 40-50 degrees. As I now had to reckon with the entire tail unit breaking off at any moment, I gave the order to prepare to bail out.

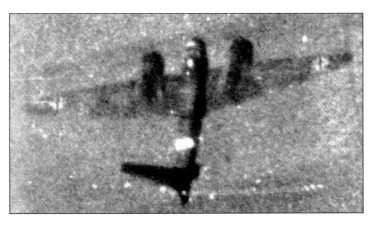

Although of very poor quality, this shot clearly shows the damage done to the tail of Leutnant Heinz Unrau's aircraft

'As a slight westerly wind was blowing, I tried to keep going as far west as possible. But when more pieces of the tail broke away and a violent shaking and juddering of the stick warned me that the whole tail unit was finally about to part company with the rest of the machine, I ordered the cockpit roof and ventral hatches to be jettisoned. The crew exited the aircraft through the ventral gondola hatch. I was about to follow them when what was left of the tail flew off and the way was clear for me to get out via the roof hatch.

'After what I estimated to be about 20 seconds in free fall, I found that I could move my arms and legs, but as parts of the tail unit were whirling through the air above my head, I delayed opening my parachute until they had fallen past me. The jerk of the canopy's opening was cushioned by my life-jacket, and the shock was quite bearable.

'I made a very soft landing. The rest of the crew came down after me within an area some two kilometres square. The attitude of the local farmers who came hurrying towards us was friendly, and that of the Rumanian soldiers who arrived shortly afterwards very courteous.'

Having survived this incident, Unrau also survived the war. At its close he held the rank of major and was *Gruppenkommandeur* of I./KG 51, flying Me 262s. He would also be one of the last Luftwaffe bomber pilots to be awarded the Knight's Cross, which he received on 1 May 1945.

After nearly six weeks spent busily re-equipping at Wiener Neustadt, III./KG 51 joined the rest of the *Geschwader* in Rumania at the end of August. They took over from II. *Gruppe* at Balti, the latter departing in early September for Wiener Neustadt, where it was to remain for the best part of the next three months. During that time I. and III./KG 51 bore the brunt of bomber operations on the southernmost sector of the front.

One of KG 51's most important contributions to the fighting in this area had been its support of 11. *Armee* as it forced a crossing of the lower Dnieper at Berislav. European Russia's second largest river, the Dnieper is more than 750 yards wide at this point, and the pontoon bridge constructed under heavy artillery fire by German Army pioneers became one of the most hotly contested structures of its kind of the whole war.

The Berislav bridgehead was the jumping-off point for the offensive aimed at capturing the Crimea, and it was to the area between Berislav and the Perekop Isthmus, the narrow tongue of land leading from the

Ukraine down on to the Crimean Peninsula, that the crews of I. and III./KG 51 next turned their attention. Targets included road and rail communications, armoured trains, troop columns and airfields. Despite this support from the air, it would take ground forces a full month to bludgeon their way through the formidable Perekop defences, and by that time KG 51's priorities had changed yet again.

On 13 September – the day Generalfeldmarschall Erich von Manstein assumed command of 11. *Armee* – the *Geschwader* carried out a raid on the Black Sea port of Odessa. The whole of Russia's southwestern front was now on the point of complete collapse. On its right-hand flank the great 'cauldron' battle east of Kiev was at its height. This would end in disaster for the Red Army, with over two-thirds of a million of its troops going into captivity. On the left-hand flank the major Soviet naval base at Odessa had been surrounded and cut off by the Rumanians. Here, the defenders had a means of escape – by sea. To avoid further crippling losses, the Soviet Black Sea Fleet mounted a large-scale evacuation. During the first half of October some 70,000 troops and 15,000 civilians would be transported from Odessa to ports on the Crimea.

KG 51, led since 1 September by Oberst Paul Koester, was tasked with interrupting this traffic. To help it do so, the *Geschwader's* two *Gruppen* were moved forward out of Rumania to two airfields in the Ukraine situated on either side of Odessa. I./KG 51 was transferred to Tiraspol, 60 miles northwest of the port, on 10 October, and III./KG 51 went to Nikolayev, much the same distance to the northeast, two weeks later.

Despite their proximity to the target area, the Ju 88s do not appear to have achieved any spectacular anti-shipping successes, although they did mount raids on Odessa and the ports of disembarkation on the Crimea, including Sevastopol and Feodosia – severe damage was done to docks and other harbour facilities. On 2 November, however, they scored two direct hits on the stern of the modern 8000-ton cruiser *Voroshilov*, berthed at Novorossisk, on the Caucasus coast. The vessel was duly towed further south to Poti, another Soviet Black Sea naval base closer to the Turkish border, where it was to remain under repair until February 1942.

KG 51 would also stay *in situ* on their two Ukrainian airfields for much of the winter of 1941/42. At the beginning of December the *Geschwaderstab* and III. *Gruppe* were joined at Nikolayev by II./KG 51 fresh from re-equipment in Austria. Meanwhile I./KG 51 continued to fly missions out of Tiraspol, weather permitting, until it too was withdrawn from operations early in the new year to rest and re-equip. However, there was to be no return to the Reich and accompanying welcome respite from the harsh conditions of the Russian front – just the short hop down to Odessa, which had finally fallen to the Rumanians on 16 October and was now serving as a 'rear area' base.

Meanwhile, what of the two *Gruppen* of KG 54 that had been operating alongside KG 51 as part of V. *Fliegerkorps* at the start

A machine of I./KG 51 emerges from the cloud of smoke billowing from the burning Soviet Army HQ on the Perekop Isthmus, which was attacked by the unit on 24 September 1941

of *Barbarossa*? After little more than a month of hostilities, during which time it had transferred forward from Dubno, in Poland, to Berdichev, in the Northern Ukraine, I./KG 54 had handed its aircraft over to II. *Gruppe* and retired by rail to Ohlau, in Silesia, to receive new Ju 88A-4s.

This left just II./KG 54 as the sole Ju 88 unit supporting *Panzergruppe* 1's continuing advance on Kiev. II./KG 54 had preceded I. *Gruppe* from Dubno to Berdichev in mid-July. As the two Berdichev fields, east and west, were both relatively small – which meant that machines could only take off with reduced bomb loads – part of II./KG 54 had subsequently moved up to Byelaya Zerkov, to the south-southwest of Kiev. Here, they were ideally situated not only to support local ground operations, but also to fly long-range bombing missions against Soviet lines of supply.

These activities resulted in growing casualty lists among both men and machines. Ironically, however, it was not over the Ukraine but back in the homeland that KG 54 came closest to losing its *Kommodore*. Oberstleutnant Otto Höhne was one of the passengers aboard the *Geschwaderstab's* Heinkel He 111D transport machine when it crashed on take-off from Ohlau for a flight to Berdichev on 15 August. Höhne sustained severe injuries. During his lengthy recuperation the position of *Kommodore* was filled by Major Krafft von Dellmensingen, the *Gruppenkommandeur* of II./KG 54. In the event, Oberstleutnant Höhne was not to return to the *Geschwader*. He would be appointed instead to a number of staff and training posts, spending the latter part of the war as CO of the Luftwaffe's Air Warfare Academy at Fürstenfeldbruck.

By now the battle for Kiev was approaching its climax. On 25 August, the day *Panzergruppe* 2's armoured divisions swung down from the central sector to form the northern pincer of the ring of steel closing behind the Ukrainian capital, II./KG 54 transferred to Zhitomir. A major counter-offensive launched by the Soviet 5th Army in an effort to outflank and cut off the advancing German spearheads was brought to a halt on the afternoon of 28 August when the *Gruppe's* aircraft destroyed the pontoon bridge thrown across the River Desna to the northeast of Kiev. By the following morning, however, the desperate Russians had repaired the bridge, and tanks and motorised infantry were again pouring across it. It took two further attacks by II./KG 54 on 29 August before the Red Army finally abandoned the attempt.

The following day II./KG 54 left Zhitomir for Kirovograd-North. For the next two weeks it was engaged primarily against railway targets, but on 13 September it resumed ground support activities by flying a series of missions aimed at Soviet troop positions near Lubny, southeast of Kiev, only to lose two 6. *Staffel* machines which collided in mid-air when diving too close alongside each other.

It was also near Lubny that leading elements of *Panzergruppen* 1 and 2 made contact just 24 hours later. Kiev was thus encircled, and with it the major

A smiling Hauptmann Hans-Joachim Grundmann, *Staffelkapitän* of 6./KG 51, checks the work being carried out on the starboard propeller mechanism of his A-4. Behind him on the steps of the maintenance platform, the unit's *Spiess*, or 'Chiefy' – note the cuff bands ('piston rings' in Luftwaffe jargon) on his greatcoat – is no doubt relieved that all is well

A captured Soviet Caterpillar tractor is put to good use at Kirovograd-North hauling II./KG 54's aircraft to and from the workshops

part of five Soviet armies. It was these latter, trapped in a vast area to the southeast of the city, which precipitated the largest 'cauldron' battle of the 1941 campaign. At its end, on 27 September, 665,000 Red Army troops had been marched into captivity, leaving behind them 900 armoured vehicles, 3700+ artillery pieces and untold amounts of other war material.

By this time II. *Gruppe* had already reverted to its attacks on the Ukrainian rail network, targeting stations, junctions and marshalling yards in a wide arc stretching from Kharkov down to Krivoi Rog.

On 1 October it was joined by I./KG 54, which flew in to Kirovograd-East after nearly eight weeks spent re-equipping in Silesia. As the month progressed the two *Gruppen* broadened the scope of their bombing raids. As many as three or four sorties a day were flown against local objectives such as enemy strongpoints and other obstacles threatening to hold up Army Group South's progress. But the Ju 88s were also continuing with their medium-range bombing missions aimed at disrupting the enemy's lines of supply, including the rail links between Kharkov, Byelgorod and Izyum. During the latter half of October they began to penetrate even further to the southeast, carrying out raids on Rostov, Taganrog and other targets on the Sea of Azov, as well as on ports and harbours on the eastern Crimea and in the Caucasus. Among the successes claimed during these latter attacks was an unidentified 1500-ton merchantman sunk at Kerch and a floating dock damaged at Novorossisk.

Operations on this scale inevitably resulted in casualties, but their numbers differed markedly between the two *Gruppen*. A 6. *Staffel* Ju 88, brought down by anti-aircraft fire west of Kharkov on 1 October, was the only total loss suffered by II./KG 54 throughout the entire month. By contrast, I. *Gruppe* lost five of its new Ju 88A-4s. More significantly perhaps, two of the five were being flown by *Gruppenkommandeure*.

On 10 October Hauptmann Walter Freimann's B3+EB failed to return from an attack on the Kharkov-Izyum railway line. It was later established that the *Kommandeur's* aircraft had been set upon by Soviet fighters. Freimann was forced to make an emergency landing far behind enemy lines. All four members of the crew managed to escape from the burning machine, but were quickly rounded up. Freimann's replacement, Hauptmann Hans Widmann, lasted exactly a fortnight. The actual cause of his loss remains unknown, he and his crew disappearing while attacking the railway line near Byelgorod.

During Hauptmann Widmann's brief tenure of office I./KG 54 had been transferred from Kirovograd down to Dniepropetrovsk. They were not destined to remain here for long. On 17 November came the order to return to the Reich for further re-equipment. This was no reflection on their recent performance in the east, however, and their new destination was not Ohlau, but Memmingen, in Bavaria. Here, an issue of tropical kit gave more than a hint of where they would be heading next. Just over four weeks later the first of the *Gruppe's* Ju 88s touched down on Sicily.

Having been withdrawn from combat on 9 November, II./KG 54 had also initially been scheduled for service in the Mediterranean. Hopes of exchanging Russian snow for Sicilian sunshine were dashed by the worsening situation on the central sector of the eastern front. After spending seven weeks converting onto the Ju 88A-4 at Landsberg, the *Gruppe* moved back up to Königsberg-Neuhausen on 31 December for 'winterisation' prior to returning to Russia.

It was during this phase (or phases, if one accepts Werner Baumbach's chronology) of the air war in the east – from mid-July 1941 until the onset of winter – that the first Knight's Crosses were awarded to members of Ju 88 units on the Russian front. The earliest examples, however, were conferred mainly in recognition of the recipient's previous performance in the night *Blitz* on Britain. The first relating to a specific incident in the war against the Soviets was that awarded posthumously on 21 August to Major Hans Emig, the *Kommandeur* of KGr 806, who had lost his life in the attack on the lock gates of the Stalin Canal two months before.

The first of September's three awards also resulted from one particular incident that was described in detail in a magazine article at the time. Oberfeldwebel Wilhelm Bender had been piloting a Ju 88 of 5./KG 3 on the central sector back in July when, as he was about to dive on the target, his machine was hit by an anti-aircraft shell. The missile came up through the floor of the cockpit, and although it failed to explode, the round ripped open Bender's back and tore off the roof of the canopy as it exited. With the pilot slumped lifeless over the controls, the bomber tipped over onto its right wing and began to plunge earthwards.

After 30 long seconds Bender regained consciousness. His first thoughts were for his crew. 'Don't bail out! It's alright', but only the gunner was there to hear him. The navigator and wireless-operator had both been sucked out of the cockpit when the roof flew off. The gunner tried to staunch the bleeding with a field dressing. It was hopeless. Blood from the gaping wound in Bender's back, stretching from spine to right shoulder, quickly saturated his flying suit. The horrified gunner could only stare at the torn muscles and shattered shoulder blade as the life drained out of his pilot.

But Bender, his face now chalk white, continued to fly the machine with his left hand. At last they reached friendly territory. As they approached the nearest landing ground, Bender's head again fell forward on to his chest. The gunner grabbed the stick and held it steady. With one final

Having returned to the Reich, and from there fully expecting to follow I./KG 54 to the Mediterranean, II. *Gruppe* was instead hastily 'winterised' and sent back to the eastern front. Little wonder that these two 'black men' – Luftwaffe parlance for groundcrew in a reference to their black work overalls – look less than pleased as they warm up the starboard engine of one of their charges at a snowbound Orsha-South in early 1942

Another magazine cutting, another Knight's Cross award ceremony – but one with a difference. A hospital nurse helps Oberst Wolfgang von Chamier-Glisczinski, *Kommodore* of KG 3, adjust the ribbon of the Knight's Cross around the neck of Oberfeldwebel Wilhelm Bender

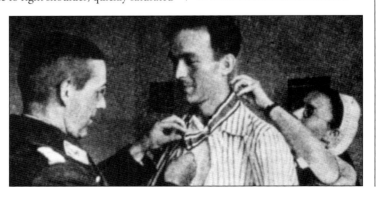

effort Bender took control again and somehow managed to make a wheels-up landing before finally passing out. He was still recovering in hospital when his *Geschwaderkommodore*, Oberst von Chamier-Glisczinski, presented him with the Knight's Cross on 8 September.

Nine days later Oberleutnant Ernst Petzold, *Staffelkapitän* of 5./KG 54, was awarded his Knight's Cross for a series of highly successful bombing raids in the east, culminating in the destruction of a bridge over the River Dnieper which effectively cut off the escape of large numbers of retreating enemy troops. On 19 September Hauptmann Richard Linke was similarly decorated for his leadership of I./KG 54 in the opening weeks of *Barbarossa*, during which time his *Gruppe* was credited with destroying 240+ aircraft on the ground, together with numerous armoured vehicles. Having been appointed as replacement for the fallen Hans Emig, Linke was actually serving as the *Kommandeur* of KGr 806 at the time of his award. But the future Major Linke would find himself back within the ranks of KG 54 a year hence when his command was redesignated to become that *Geschwader's* new III. *Gruppe*.

The next three Knight's Crosses all went to *Geschwaderkommodores*. Oberst *Dr.Ing.* Ernst Bormann of KG 76 was decorated on 5 October, with KG 77's Oberst Johann Raithel being likewise honoured 12 days later. Oberstleutnant Walter Marienfeld received his Knight's Cross on 27 November, just four days after taking the place of the badly injured Oberstleutnant 'Onkel Otto' Höhne at the head of KG 54.

On 18 December KG 51 celebrated its first Knight's Cross winner of the war when Oberleutnant Matthias Schwegler, the *Kapitän* of 1. Staffel, was decorated for his cumulative anti-shipping successes both in the Mediterranean and the Black Sea. A series of damaging raids, the first of them in the night skies of Great Britain and the more recent ones over northern Russian – where he was twice forced to land behind enemy lines and twice returned safely on foot with his crew – won Leutnant Dieter Lukesch of 7./KG 76 his Knight's Cross on 20 December.

But the final decoration of the year went to someone no longer serving on the eastern front. The outspoken Hauptmann Dietrich Peltz was already wearing the Knight's Cross when made *Gruppenkommandeur* of II./KG 77 back in March 1941. For his outstanding achievements in the first months of *Barbarossa* Peltz received the Oak Leaves on 31 December 1941, by which time he was leading the embryonic *Verbandsführerschule Gen. d. Kampfflieger* (Bomber Unit Leaders' School) in Kitzingen.

The first six months of the air war in the east had seen only a handful of Knight's Crosses issued to pilots and commanders of Ju 88 units. However, as the tide turned against the Luftwaffe and the enemy became stronger and operations entailed ever greater dangers, many more such awards would be won, either through exemplary service or by individual acts of courage.

KG 51's first Knight's Cross winner, Oberleutnant Matthias Schwegler, smiles down from his cockpit at a group of well wishers (including at least one civilian – or perhaps an officer in mufti, if the natty headgear at bottom right is anything to go by). 'Teddy' Schwegler would be killed over the Reich just three weeks prior to the end of the war

ARCTIC CONVOYS

hile the three Army Groups on the main sectors of the eastern front were scything their way through vast tracts of Russian territory, a very different kind of war was being waged above the Arctic Circle. Here, there were no sweeping advances, no armoured pincer movements and no huge cauldron battles involving thousands of troops. The fighting in the far north was to remain virtually static for much of the war. The main features of this campaign were not towns and cities that were captured, held and then lost again, but defensive bunkers and extensive trench systems. It was altogether reminiscent of an earlier conflict. Indeed, replace the Arctic tundra with Flanders mud and the men of General Eduard Dietl's mountain corps (the later 20. *Armee*) could well have been fighting World War 1 all over again.

The background to the air organisation in the northern theatre also differed markedly from that on the main fronts, where each of the three Army Groups had its own attendant Air Fleet providing support. In the north *Luftflotte* 5 was responsible for the whole of German-held Scandinavia. With its units based predominantly in Norway, this Air Fleet's operations had hitherto been directed mainly against the United Kingdom, but with the launching of *Barbarossa*, *Luftflotte* 5 suddenly found itself involved in its own two-front war. In order to discharge its manifold responsibilities it would be divided into three separate territorial *Fliegerführer*. It was one of these, the *Fliegerführer Nord (Ost)*, which was charged with setting up a special operational staff to support the ground units engaged in the assault on northern Russia.

The *Einsatzstab z.b.V. Kirkenes* was, in effect, a small task force. It initially comprised a mix of units, mainly of *Staffel* strength or less, but its striking power was provided by a *Gruppe* of Stukas and the Ju 88s of II./KG 30. The *Einsatzstab's* units were based on a clutch of airfields – some already established, some newly constructed – in northern Norway and Finland. For many, these bases were to become semi-permanent. During the opening stages of *Barbarossa*, aircrews in the Arctic would share none of the heady excitement experienced by their counterparts on the main fighting fronts as they leapfrogged forward from one hastily abandoned Soviet airfield to the next in their efforts to keep pace with the rampaging *Panzergruppen*.

However for II./KG 30 at Banak the movement, or otherwise, of the troops on the ground was of little significance. The *Gruppe's* main targets were the port of Murmansk and the railway running southwards from it down into the heart of the

Aircraft of II./KG 30 ('4D+EN' in the foreground) climb away from Banak *en route* to the Soviet fighter airfields around Murmansk on 22 August 1941

Soviet Union. Unlike Archangel on the shores of the White Sea to the east, which was iced up during the winter months, Murmansk was ice-free all year round. The Russians were only too well aware of the strategic importance of Murmansk – their 'gateway to the outside world' – and the port and its surroundings were well defended both by fighters and a heavy concentration of anti-aircraft guns. In such a relatively small area, the barrage these latter could throw up was truly ferocious, and Murmansk quickly gained the reputation of being a 'thoroughly unhealthy place to be'. One Ju 88 pilot famously remarked that he would rather fly three missions to London than one to Murmansk.

This well-known photograph has been described in the past as the aircraft that gave future Soviet ace Boris Safonov his first victory. However, the picture does not fit the facts. Safonov's victim, a machine of 6./KG 30 piloted by Unteroffizier Reinhard Schellern, reportedly went down into the Kola Inlet, killing the entire crew. The aircraft shown here has clearly come down on dry land (but only just – see photograph below), with the jettisoned cabin canopy seeming to suggest the crew's survival...

Not that the crews of II./KG 30 had any say in the matter. After bad weather had disrupted operations on the opening day of *Barbarossa*, 6. *Staffel* spent much of 23 and 24 June mining the approaches to Murmansk. By the end of those two days they had suffered their first total loss, and every other machine bar one had been damaged by flak.

The *Staffel's* sole casualty had not fallen victim to the port's anti-aircraft batteries. On 24 June Unteroffizier Reinhard Schellern had been sent out on a solo reconnaissance mission to the area northeast of Murmansk. He was sighted near the Russian airfield of Vaenga and a rocket-armed I-16, flown by future Soviet ace Boris Safonov, had been scrambled to give chase. After a laborious climb, the Russian attacked out of the sun, damaging the Ju 88 with one of its rockets. Schellern tried to escape by diving towards the sea, but the I-16 clung to his tail and a burst of machine gun fire sent the bomber into the waters of the Kola Inlet.

...obviously the same machine – note the bent starboard propeller blade and the dorsal dinghy hatch cover resting on the port tailplane – this wider view shows the site selected for the skilfully executed belly-landing to be a spit of sand and shingle between two bodies of water. A Soviet marine stands guard as intelligence officers inspect their prize. The only questions remaining – exactly where and when was this?

II./KG 30's other principal objective, the Murmansk railway, proved far less dangerous a target. Many pilots even confessed to enjoying attacking the Russians' supply line, aiming not merely to destroy a section of track but also to find and derail a train at the same time. The line's anti-aircraft defences were nowhere near as concentrated as those ringing Murmansk, but there *were* a number of Soviet fighter airfields located along its route. Due to the haphazard workings of the enemy's warning system, however, the fighters were often unable to get off the ground in time to intercept the approaching bombers. On these occasions the I-16s – in groups of anything up to 50 machines – would instead be reduced to chasing after the Ju 88s 'like an angry swarm of bees', ready to pounce on any bomber that showed signs of being in trouble and beginning to straggle.

Despite their near obsolescence, a Polikarpov in capable hands could prove more than a match for the Luftwaffe's most modern bomber.

Hauptmann Eberhard Roeger, the *Gruppenkommandeur* of II./KG 30, was brought down by one near Vaenga on 3 July, but his loss was not allowed to interfere with the tempo of operations. The *Gruppe* continued its strikes against Murmansk, its railway line and the surrounding enemy airfields. Crews were also sent out to attack the Soviets' coastal convoys and their Northern Fleet naval escorts. On 20 July machines of 5. *Staffel* caught and sank the 1660-ton destroyer *Stremilteny* in the Kola Inlet.

By early August II./KG 30 had been joined at Banak by I. *Gruppe*. The former then returned to Stavanger, in southern Norway, where it flew operations over the North Sea until the end of September. It then retired to Gilze-Rijen, in Holland, to re-equip with Ju 88A-4s before being sent to Orsha on the central sector of the eastern front late in December.

Meanwhile, I./KG 30 was being introduced to the rigours of the Arctic air war the hard way. One of the four Ju 88s lost on 9 August was a machine of 3. *Staffel* claimed by rapidly rising Soviet ace Boris Safonov as his eighth victory. Very soon the *Gruppe* would be confronted by an entirely new enemy – or, to be more accurate, one familiar of old. With his pre-war pact of non-aggression with Hitler rendered meaningless by *Barbarossa*, Soviet dictator Josef Stalin had no hesitation in signing a new pact of mutual assistance offered by Great Britain. In practical terms this 'assistance' was to consist of shipments of war material being despatched to the Soviet Union. It would not be long in coming forth.

On 21 August, less than six weeks after the pact had been signed, a small trial convoy, code-named 'Dervish', set sail from Hvalfjord in Iceland. All seven ships reached Archangel safely ten days later. They had blazed the trail for the first of the now famous 'PQ' convoys that were to follow in their wake in September. That same month two squadrons of RAF Hurricanes arrived at Vaenga to operate alongside the field's resident Red Air Force fighter units.

By this time the midnight sun, which had never dipped below the horizon during the opening weeks of *Barbarossa*, and had thus allowed round-the-clock operations, had given way to the first snowfalls of the year. The Arctic winter was setting in and all flying would soon be severely curtailed. One of the last major engagements of 1941 took place on 6 October during yet another Ju 88 raid on Murmansk. The defenders reported eight of the 25 attacking bombers destroyed, with claims being submitted by anti-aircraft gunners, as well as by both Soviet and RAF fighters. In fact, I./KG 30 recorded the loss of just three Ju 88s.

Throughout the long winter months the PQ convoys continued to deliver their cargos, initially to Archangel and then, when that port became blocked by ice, to Murmansk. The 'only' dangers they faced during this period were the atrocious weather conditions and

A formation of I./KG 30 machines silhouetted against the featureless tundra

the occasional U-boat. They would not be subjected to Luftwaffe attacks until the following spring. By then, however, several changes had taken place in northern Norway and Finland. The *Einsatzstab z.b.V. Kirkenes* had been disbanded and the *Fliegerführer Nord (Ost)* had assumed direct control of air operations in those areas. Also, I./KG 30 – whose strength had sunk to just seven aircraft in January – was reinforced early in 1942 by the arrival at Banak of Hauptmann Hajo Herrmann's III./KG 30.

But when the two *Gruppen* began their anti-shipping operations in earnest in March, one of the first missions flown was to be directed not against Allied merchantmen, but a warship of the Royal Navy. Convoy PQ 12 had departed Reykjavik on 1 March bound for Murmansk. British intelligence was aware that the German battleship *Tirpitz* had been ordered to put to sea to intercept the 16-vessel convoy. Capital ships of the Home Fleet were therefore shadowing it in support, hoping to bring the *Tirpitz* – sister ship of the ill-fated *Bismarck* – to bay and send her to the bottom too. To counter this perceived threat, aircraft of KG 30 were sent out from Banak on 9 March with orders to sink HMS *Victorious*, the only aircraft carrier included in the British task force. Despite poor weather, three Ju 88s managed to find her but failed to achieve any hits.

KG 30 was to have more success towards the end of the month after a Bv 138 reconnaissance flying boat reported sighting the next Allied convoy on the morning of 27 March. Weather conditions had since gone from bad to worse and PQ 13 had already endured 36 hours facing the full fury of an Arctic storm. This had resulted in the vessels splitting up into small groups, and was no doubt a contributory factor to 'Unlucky 13's' becoming the first Arctic convoy to be severely mauled (during the 12 previous convoys only one ship had been lost, sunk by a U-boat). Five of PQ 13's 19 merchantmen would fall victim to enemy action, two of them being despatched by aircraft of III./KG 30.

It was shortly after midday on 28 March that they caught and sank a solitary straggler, the Panamanian-registered *Raceland*. Seven hours later, in the last of the day's twilight, they chanced upon another singleton. Having made good progress despite the storm, the *Empire Ranger* was the leading ship of the scattered convoy. It went down only 200 miles north-northwest of the Kola Inlet. Nor did PQ 13's torment end there. Two of the convoy's survivors, the *Empire Starlight* and the *New Westminster City*, would be destroyed in bombing raids after reaching Murmansk.

The Allied convoys were now being given priority over all other targets in the Arctic theatre. The importance attached to the disruption of this vital seaborne supply route was underlined by the return of II./KG 30 to Banak in late March. For the first time *Geschwaderkommodore* Major Erich Bloedorn had all three *Gruppen* of his command together in the far north as the Luftwaffe awaited the next convoy. But of the 24 ships of PQ 14 that left Iceland on 8 April, 16 were forced to turn back due to ice and weather. Of the remaining eight, only one was sunk (by a U-boat), while five Ju 88s were lost in several unsuccessful attacks.

The Arctic convoys were organised to operate in 'pairs', however, with the return sailing of ships that had arrived earlier in Russia and had since discharged their cargos being timed to coincide with the despatch of an outbound convoy. Thus, the 16 ships of PQ 14's 'paired' convoy left Murmansk just 48 hours after the former had left Reykjavik, in Iceland.

An aircraft of II./KG 30 runs up its engines at Banak. Despite the amount of ordnance lying scattered around, it has been suggested that all-white fuselage codes such as those carried by this A-4 were used to identify machines engaged primarily on maritime reconnaissance duties

The returning vessels, sailing as QP 10, were not to escape so lightly, losing four of their number.

Two of the four were claimed by the Ju 88s of KG 30. II. *Gruppe* bombed and sank the *Empire Cowper* just a day out of Murmansk, but paid heavily for this success. Three of their machines were shot down by anti-aircraft fire from the convoy's naval escorts. Others were damaged, including that of the *Gruppenkommandeur*, Hauptmann Sigmund-Ulrich *Freiherr* von Gravenreuth, who was seriously wounded. Two days later, on 13 April, another Ju 88 scored a direct hit on the stern of the *Harpalion*. Rendered unmanageable by the loss of her rudder, she had to be sunk by gunfire from an escort vessel. It was a sad end for the two vessels, for both were survivors of the earlier punishment – natural and man-made – that had been meted out to PQ 13.

Another ship that had survived PQ 13, although only just, was the Royal Navy's 8000-ton cruiser HMS *Trinidad*. By an ironic twist of fate she had managed to torpedo herself during a surface engagement with three German destroyers on 29 March. The cause of this unfortunate incident was variously attributed to a faulty torpedo circling back on itself, or the toppling of the gyro that controlled the weapon's direction system as it passed through a shell splash. After makeshift repairs in Russia, *Trinidad* – with an escort of four destroyers – sailed for Iceland on 13 May. A Luftwaffe reconnaissance machine spotted the small force the following day and it was attacked late that same evening by Ju 88s of KG 30 and by He 111 torpedo-bombers of KG 26.

It was while the cruiser's anti-aircraft gunners were concentrating their fire on the eight low-flying Heinkels emerging from the glare of the midnight sun that a lone Junkers dived out of the thin cloud overhead to release its full load of four bombs. These had a devastating effect, starting numerous fires and tearing off the temporary plates that had been attached to the ship's port side. Belching smoke, she began to settle by the bow. After surviving members of her crew had been taken off, one of the attendant destroyers put three torpedoes into *Trinidad's* starboard side, sending the blazing cruiser to the bottom in the early hours of 15 May.

Two PQ convoy battles would be fought in May. In the first of them PQ 15 lost three merchantmen, but all were credited to KG 26's torpedo-carrying He 111s. The only 'success' that KG 30 could lay claim to was a near miss, which damaged the naval trawler *Cape Palliser* on 3 May. For the next three weeks (apart from the attack on *Trinidad*) the *Geschwader* directed most of its energies against land targets, adding the power station at Murmashi, southwest of Kola, to its usual list of objectives.

Then, on 25 May, aerial reconnaissance reported the approach of the next convoy. The 35 ships of PQ 16, which had put out from Reykjavik four days earlier, constituted the largest Arctic convoy to date. It elicited a swift and equally strong response from the Luftwaffe, although this time it was the torpedo-bombers of KG 26 that made up the bulk of the initial attacking force. They got a hot reception. Not a single Heinkel scored a hit and one was lost to a Hurricane launched from a CAM ship. The half-dozen Ju 88s of III./KG 30 fared marginally better. Although two of the Junkers were brought down by the concentrated barrage of anti-aircraft fire that greeted them, a near miss immobilised the American merchantman *Carlton*, which had to be towed back to Iceland.

Sporadic air attacks on the convoy during 26 May proved ineffective. But it was to be a different story 24 hours later when PQ 16 was subjected to an assault by wave after wave of German aircraft. The vast majority of these were Ju 88s of KG 30. Records indicate that the *Geschwader* in fact flew 100+ individual sorties on 27 May. By now the ships were southeast of Bear Island. The day was fine and clear, with a light westerly ruffling the surface of the sea – a far cry from the Arctic storm that had battered PQ 13 two months before. Although the main cloud base was at 3000 ft, a thin veil of stratus at half that height sufficed to hide the diving Ju 88s from the vessels until they were almost on top of them.

Their first victims were the Russian freighter *Stary Bolshevik* and one of the escorting destroyers, the Polish *Garland*, which they attacked at around midday. Although damaged, the two ships would survive. Not so the American merchantmen *Alamar* and *Mormacsul,* caught by a second wave of bombers about an hour later. Both went down. Next, a vic of three Ju 88s hit the *Empire Lawrence*, the CAM ship whose Hurricane had claimed the Heinkel two days earlier. The stricken vessel, already starting to settle, was then blown apart by a stick of four more bombs from another Junkers that appeared out of the clouds just minutes later. These attacks also damaged the *Empire Baffin* and the American *City of Joliet*, the latter so badly that she was briefly abandoned, and then re-boarded, only to sink in the early hours of the following morning.

The last ship of PQ 16 to succumb to KG 30's bombs was yet another of the British Ministry of Shipping's 'Empire' vessels, the *Empire Purcell,* which blew up with a tremendous explosion at around 2000 hrs.

It was while the convoy's anti-aircraft gunners were focusing their attention on the Ju 88s that a small group of wave-hugging He 111s achieved their only success of the day, putting two torpedoes into the *Lowther Castle,* which burned for eight hours before also exploding.

KG 30's parting shot of 27 May left another merchantman, the *Ocean Voice,* badly damaged, but eventually able to continue on her way. Bad weather the following day kept air operations to a minimum. The few missions that *were* flown produced no results, and three separate attacks by KG 30 on 29 May proved equally fruitless.

By this time PQ 16 had split into two, with the larger group making for Murmansk and the smaller

The 7457-ton CAM ship *Empire Lawrence*, which was sunk during the PQ 16 convoy battle. Note the disruptive camouflage on her foredeck and the Sea Hurricane I sitting on the bow catapult

contingent heading further east to Archangel, which, with the break up of the winter ice, was now open to navigation again.

On 30 May, while the Archangel group steamed on down into the White Sea completely unmolested, the ships bound for Murmansk were subjected to three last dive-bombing attacks by the Junkers of KG 30. None of the vessels was hit, but two Ju 88s were reported lost on this date. It is possible that one of them – or maybe even both – had fallen to the guns of Boris Safonov. The Soviet ace was certainly in action against a formation of Ju 88s that was harassing a group of ships off Kola Inlet on the morning of 30 May – in fact, he was heard over the radio claiming three of the bombers shot down before he himself disappeared (it is believed that Safonov was forced to ditch with a damaged engine). At the time of his loss Boris Safonov was credited with 26 kills (including six shared) over the Arctic, of which 12 (three shared) had been Ju 88s.

The six-day battle of PQ 16 did not end there. Luftwaffe forces next concentrated on trying to prevent the supplies that had been delivered to Murmansk and Archangel from being transported any further. On 1 June a series of small-scale raids on vessels unloading in Murmansk harbour resulted in the sinking of two ships (one a much-bombed veteran of the earlier PQ 13). Magnetic mines were also air-dropped in and around Murmansk, these resulting in the destruction of at least two more Arctic convoy survivors before June was out. KG 30's crews also targeted the railway system carrying the supplies to the south, 17 Ju 88s bombing the station at Louhi, close to the shores of the White Sea, on 13 June. However the strengthening of Soviet fighter defences along this important stretch of line was making such missions increasingly hazardous. Another attack by KG 30 on a railway bridge in the same area two days later led to a running battle in which one Ju 88 was downed and two others seriously damaged.

It was not long before the first reports of the next convoy began coming in. The 36 merchantmen, most of them American, that made up PQ 17 had sailed from Iceland's Hvalfjord on 27 June. All but eight of them were bound for Archangel, as Murmansk was 'almost at a standstill' after recent heavy bombing. On 18 June, in an operation aimed at incapacitating the port's work force, some 12,000 incendiary bombs had been showered on the town, reducing almost half of it to ruin.

At first the convoy's progress followed a familiar pattern. After five days spent ploughing eastwards, PQ 17 suffered its first attack from the air on the evening of 2 July. This was delivered by nine torpedo-carrying He 115 floatplanes, but failed to inflict any damage. The ships reaped the benefit of low-lying fog for much of the next 24 hours. Then, early on the morning of 4 July, the He 115s found them again, this time putting a torpedo into a US merchantman. This vessel would later be sent to the bottom by a U-boat, a fate awaiting many of the ships damaged by air attack in the days ahead. That same evening, just after 2000 hrs, He 111 torpedo-bombers of I./KG 26 claimed three successes. A simultaneous dive-bombing attack by Ju 88s of KG 30 produced no hits at all, however. This air assault had undoubtedly been a blow, but it was hardly a fatal one. Yet two hours later the convoy was ordered to scatter. Why?

It was the result of a decision that had been taken in London, and one that remains controversial to this day. The Admiralty firmly believed that PQ 17 was in imminent danger of surface attack from a powerful German

Boris Safonov was squadron commander of 72nd SAP of the Northern Fleet Air Force at Vaenga airfield. The leading ace on the northern front during the first year of the war, he had been credited with 26 victories by the time he perished in combat on 30 May 1942. Most of these successes came in the I-16, and his tally included no fewer than 12 Ju 88s destroyed

battle group led by the battleship *Tirpitz*. Their Lordships consequently despatched three brief but startling signals. The first effectively denuded the convoy of its main naval support force. Timed at 2111 hrs, it read: 'Secret and Most Immediate. Cruiser force withdraw to westward at high speed'. Although the Royal Navy warships were being ordered to reverse course in order to engage the enemy presumed to be bearing down on the convoy – and to do so 'at high speed' to minimise the danger from lurking U-boats – their hasty departure did little to instil confidence in the crews of the merchantman (in fact it aroused extremely bitter feelings, not least the charge of 'turning and running').

A second signal received 12 minutes later only served to fuel the flames. 'Secret and Immediate. Owing to threat from surface ships convoy is to disperse and proceed to Russian ports.' 30 minutes later still came the even more alarming 'Secret. Most Immediate. Convoy is to scatter'. The smaller naval vessels of the close escort were still with the convoy, and it was this last message that resulted in the senior officer's hoisting the visual signal to scatter at about 2215 hrs. After some initial reluctance, the masters of the merchant ships began to comply.

Some five hours later the Admiralty came close to admitting that it had blundered with a further signal. 'It is presumed enemy ships are north of Tromsö, but it is not, repeat not, certain they are at sea'. By then it was too late. Convoy PQ 17 as such was no more. Although well past Bear Island when the order to scatter was given, Archangel still lay some 800 miles away. Therefore, most ships – with the exception of a small group that opted to head north into the pack ice and sit it out until the reported danger had passed – chose to set course east-southeast at top speed, either singly or in twos and threes, and head for the large island of Novaya Zemlya, which was a good 200 miles closer.

Air reconnaissance soon reported the astonishing fact that the convoy appeared to be breaking up. It was now that the three *Gruppen* of Major Erich Bloedorn's Banak-based KG 30 came into their own. Throughout 5 July they were in the air almost without pause, flying one mission after the other in the hunt for individual ships.

One of their first victims was the elderly American freighter *Pankraft*, which was quickly discovered amid the loose floes bordering the pack ice. A near miss from a high-altitude bomb brought her to a stop. She was then set on fire by low-level strafing. Abandoned by her crew, the *Pankraft*, which had 5000 tons of TNT in her holds, burned for nearly two days before blowing herself apart. In mid-afternoon of 5 July another group of Ju 88s found and attacked two more US merchantmen. The *Fairfield City* went down almost at once, but the *Daniel Morgan* escaped into the mist lying to the east. She was not to survive for long, being pounced upon by yet more marauding Ju 88s. Although the vessel's gun crew claimed to have downed two of her five attackers, she was herself badly damaged and then finished off by a shadowing U-boat .

These last two American ships had already made it nearly halfway to Novaya Zemlya. At about the same time as they went under, but much further to the northwest, the *Earlston* was attracting the attention both of a *Staffel* of KG 30 machines and a trio of U-boats. The lone British merchantman stood no chance. A near miss by one of the former caused multiple fractures in the vessel's pipework, and a torpedo from a surfaced

U-boat broke her cleanly in two. Two hours after this, at about 1700 hrs, four Ju 88s made a high-altitude bombing run on the *Peter Kerr*. The US Liberty ship took three direct hits and exploded within minutes.

Meanwhile, back close to the edge of the pack ice, 200 miles north of where the *Peter Kerr* met her end, a group of three merchantmen was coming under attack from machines of III./KG 30. The American *Washington* was lifted clear out of the water by the force of the bombs detonating in the sea all around her. As she began to go down, her crew took to the boats. Like those of the *Peter Kerr*, they were able to pull away before she blew up. Now it was the turn of the other two ships. The British *Bolton Castle* erupted as a direct hit turned her into an inferno. Incredibly, her crew also escaped without a single loss, as did those of the Dutch *Paulus Potter*, which was disabled by several near misses to be left a smoking, drifting wreck. The *Bolton Castle* soon joined the *Washington* on the bottom, but the abandoned hulk of the *Paulus Potter* remained afloat for eight days before being despatched by a prowling U-boat.

The last two ships to be claimed by KG 30 on this incredible day were not merchant vessels. The *Aldersdale* was a fleet oiler (although on this voyage part of her cargo of oil was intended for the Russians). On the evening of 5 July she was attacked by four Ju 88s, one of which laid a stick of bombs across her stern. While efforts were being made to take her in tow, bombs from another Junkers straddled a smaller vessel nearby. This was the *Zaafaran*, one of the three rescue ships that had sailed with the convoy for the express purpose of picking up survivors. Now she herself was going down. Luckily, all but one of her crew and the many merchant seamen she had already rescued were saved. In the meantime the *Aldersdale* had had to be abandoned. Two days later her derelict hulk became yet another of KG 30's victims sent to the bottom by a U-boat.

6 July again found the crews of KG 30 out over the Barents Sea searching for merchantmen. One they chanced upon was the American *Pan Atlantic*, steaming south at full speed for the entrance to the White Sea. A single Ju 88 dived on the vessel, placing a bomb in one of her forward holds. Her cargo of cordite exploded, blowing her bows off. Within three minutes the *Pan Atlantic* had disappeared beneath the waves. Not far away, other Ju 88s found and attacked two Russian ships, damaging the tanker *Donbass* and sinking a small naval patrol vessel.

By this stage most of the surviving ships of PQ 17 were at last nearing Novaya Zemlya. Their intention was to hole up for the time being in Matochkin Strait – or 'Funk Creek' as it was soon dubbed – the narrow stretch of water that bisected the island. The ruse clearly worked, for finding no more ships at sea the Germans concluded that the convoy had been totally annihilated. On 7 July KG 30 reverted to the bombing of Murmansk and its surroundings.

But when the merchantmen sheltering in Matochkin Strait decided to risk the final dash down along the coast of Novaya Zemlya into the White Sea, they were quickly spotted by patrolling U-boats and the aircraft of KG 30 were ordered out after them again. The bombers' task was made easier by the fact that an extensive ice field was blocking the direct approach to the White Sea. In order to circumnavigate this obstacle, the vessels were forced to steer a southwesterly course, bringing them ever closer to the Luftwaffe's bases in northern Norway and Finland.

KG 30 utilised the situation to the full, sending out nearly 50 machines to scour the edges of the ice field. The merchantmen had nowhere to hide. Their only option was to fight it out, which is exactly what the leading group of five ships tried to do after being detected by a formation of Ju 88s. It was an unequal contest, with the bombers attacking in waves, each one coming in at a different angle from the last in order to fragment the defenders' fire. Three bombs exploded close alongside the American *Hoosier*, which slowly started to go down. Shortly afterwards, at about 0200 hrs on 10 July, the Panamanian-registered *El Capitan* was also near-missed. She struggled on, only to be hit by a single Ju 88 hours later. Now disabled, she too – like the *Hoosier* – gradually began to sink on an even keel. Both vessels, barely afloat, would later succumb to U-boat torpedoes.

They were the last ships of PQ 17 to be lost. Although aircraft of KG 30 flew further search missions on 10 July, and were out again the following day, all they could claim were two vessels damaged during a sustained attack by a dozen or more bombers on a small group of ships around midday on 11 July.

One final mission was mounted later that same afternoon, only to run into long-range fighters of the Red Air Force. Although the Ju 88s had already seen action against the Russian navy – having damaged two Soviet destroyers that had put to sea to guide in a previous group of survivors 24 hours earlier – they were caught off-guard by the unexpected appearance of the twin-engined Petlyakov Pe-2s. In the fight that ensued 1./KG 30 lost their *Staffelkapitän*, Hauptmann Eberhard Schröder. His was the last of ten Luftwaffe machines reportedly shot down during the PQ 17 battle.

In Germany the battle was hailed as an overwhelming success. It received banner headlines in the newspapers and dramatic footage of exploding and sinking ships filmed by the crews of KG30 was shown in cinema newsreels throughout the Reich. The *Geschwader's* performance also resulted in a flurry of awards, among them Knight's Crosses for Hauptleute Konrad Kahl and Erich Stoffregen, *Gruppenkommandeure* of I. and II./KG 30, respectively (III. *Gruppe's* Hajo Herrmann was already wearing the coveted decoration, which he had won in October 1940). *Staffelkapitän* of 5./KG 30, Hauptmann Willi Flechner, was similarly honoured.

In London the repercussions from PQ 17 were very different. Although it had been a catastrophe largely of its own making, the

Following the successful PQ 17 action, a ceremonial parade was held at Banak to honour KG 30's three new Knight's Cross winners. Seen here in the centre of the photograph saluting the assembled ranks, they are Hauptmann Konrad Kahl (leading the trio), Hauptmann Erich Stoffregen (almost completely hidden behind Kahl) and Hauptmann Willi Flechner (right). Also just visible on the extreme left is Generaloberst Jürgen Stumpff, GOC *Luftflotte* 5, and (third from left) Oberstleutnant Erich Bloedorn, the *Geschwaderkommodore* of KG 30

Ju 88A-4 '4D+CP' of 6./KG 30, pictured while on detachment to Nurmoila, in southeast Finland, during the late summer/early autumn of 1942

Admiralty decreed that no further convoys would be sent to Russia until summer's round-the-clock hours of daylight began to give way to the darkness of autumn. It would thus be nearly two months before the next convoy braved the passage to Archangel.

KG 30 was to spend much of this intervening period attacking ground targets. Almost from the very start of *Barbarossa*, elements of the *Geschwader* had operated out of central Finland in a series of temporary deployments, either to attack the southerly stretches of the Murmansk railway or in support of local actions by German and Finnish troops.

On 19 August II. *Gruppe* was transferred in its entirety from Banak down to Kemi. The purpose of the move was to carry out a fire-raid on Archangel similar to that which had earlier destroyed much of Murmansk. The White Sea port had not been subjected to any major air raids in the past because of the distances involved, and its defenders were therefore taken by surprise when the 19 Ju 88s of II./KG 30 arrived overhead during the night of 25/26 August. All the bombers returned to Kemi, reporting that their incendiaries had caused widespread fires. However two machines despatched 48 hours later to assess the exact extent of the damage failed to return. The crew of one, which had force-landed deep in enemy territory, returned on foot. The other, flown by recent Knight's Cross winner Willi Flechner, was rammed by a Soviet fighter.

Exactly a week later the next Arctic convoy set sail. In an attempt to hoodwink the Germans, who were closely watching Iceland, most of the 40 ships of PQ 18 departed from Loch Ewe, in northern Scotland. Another innovation was the inclusion, for the first time, of an aircraft carrier as part of their escort. HMS *Avenger* was no large fleet carrier, but a light escort carrier, a class of vessel created by affixing a flightdeck atop the hull of a merchant ship. Her complement of aircraft comprised just six Sea Hurricanes and three Swordfish anti-submarine biplanes. Although few in number, this was a distinct improvement on the single, expendable Hurricane perched on the catapult of a CAM ship. Despite displaying the inevitable signs of inexperience associated with any pioneering venture, *Avenger* would play a large part in breaking up attacks on the convoy, both from the air and from under the sea.

She would have her work cut out, for changes had also been taking place among the ranks of the Luftwaffe units poised in northern Norway. Arguably the most important of these was the arrival at Banak early in September of III./KG 26, equipped with torpedo-carrying Ju 88s.

Here is yet another instance where available sources of reference differ widely. Some maintain that the torpedo-armed Junkers had been sent to the Arctic much earlier, and that they had already participated in the attacks on PQ 17 – and even PQ 16. This seems doubtful, as the III./KG 26 of summer 1942 (the third such unit, incidentally, to operate under this designation) was a standard *Kampfgruppe* that was to be renumbered at the beginning of July to become I./KG 1. The newcomer to the Arctic is much more likely to have been the ex-KGr 506, previously a coastal unit, which was withdrawn from service to re-equip and retrain for the torpedo role. Indeed, it was this *Gruppe* that was redesignated as the fourth, and final, III./KG 26 while under training in July.

Whatever their past history, the arrival of Hauptmann Klaus-Wilhelm Nocker's Ju 88s could not have come at a more opportune moment –

The escort carrier HMS *Avenger* with her full complement of six Sea Hurricanes from 883 Naval Air Squadron embarked. Note the special 'Arctic' camouflage applied to her flightdeck for the PQ 18 operation. *Avenger* was sunk by U-boat U-155 during the early hours of 15 November 1942 while escorting convoy MKF 1(Y) off the Portuguese coast. A single torpedo hit the ship's bomb room and ignited the munitions stored there, causing numerous secondary explosions. With her back broken, the carrier sunk in under five minutes, taking 68 officers and 446 ratings with it

although this might well have been the result of Luftwaffe foresight rather than pure chance. The doubling of numbers of torpedo aircraft in the far north also heralded a role reversal for KG 30. The crews that had been largely instrumental in 'annihilating' PQ 17 would find themselves acting as little more than a back-up force in attacks on PQ 18, flying high-altitude bombing missions to disrupt the convoy's defences while KG 26's torpedo-bombers went in at low level.

The battle for PQ 18 opened on the morning of 13 September with two merchantmen being sent to the bottom by U-boats. An attack by KG 30 early that same afternoon produced no results other than the launching of several of *Avenger's* Sea Hurricanes in an abortive attempt to see them off. It was the massed assault an hour later by the torpedo-bombers of KG 26 (28 He 111s and 18 Ju 88s in all), supported by high-altitude bombing runs by aircraft of KG 30, that did the damage. In the space of less than 15 minutes no fewer than eight of the remaining 38 merchant ships had been sunk or were sinking. It is not possible to state with certainty which had fallen victim to Heinkels and which to the Junkers. What is known, however, is that five of the attackers were lost.

14 September began very much as the day before, with another merchantman being claimed by a U-boat in the early hours. But it was to end with just one further vessel sunk in a series of air attacks that cost the Luftwaffe 17 aircraft destroyed and nine seriously damaged. Hardest hit was III./KG 26, which had specifically targeted *Avenger* shortly after midday. 11 of the Gruppe's Ju 88s failed to return from this mission. A machine of KG 30 was also brought down during a dive-bombing attack not long afterwards.

Then, at 1405 hrs, two more waves of torpedo-aircraft from KG 26, this time 22 Heinkels and another 18 of III. *Gruppe's* Junkers, attacked the convoy head-on. Split up by a fierce anti-aircraft barrage from the forward escorts and chased by four of *Avenger's* Sea Hurricanes – three of which were shot down by 'friendly fire' from the merchant ships' gunners – the carefully coordinated attack came apart at the seams. Many aircraft dropped their torpedoes at random, some did not release at all. A single

Laden with ammunition, the American Liberty ship *Mary Luckenbach* 'erupted with an enormous explosion, sending a huge column of flames and smoke towering into the sky'

missile sped down between the columns of merchantmen before hitting the *Mary Luckenbach*, which 'erupted in an enormous explosion, sending a huge column of flames and smoke towering into the sky'.

Intermittent air attacks continued over the next three days, but it was not until shortly after 0600 hrs on 18 September that the Luftwaffe claimed its last victim, the *Kentucky* going down after being hit by a torpedo and two bombs. KG 26's torpedo-bombers were subsequently credited with ten of the 13 merchant ships sunk during the battle for PQ 18. But this success was offset by the loss of 38 of its own aircraft. KG 30's casualties totalled six.

If PQ 17 had been the high point of the Ju 88's anti-shipping war in the far north, then PQ 18 was to be its swansong. Never again would the Arctic theatre witness such sustained and violent action. In the wake of the PQ 18 battle all three *Gruppen* of KG 30 gathered at Kemi with the intention of resuming the raids on Archangel. Worsening weather put paid to these plans, and on 24 September III./KG 30 was transferred back to Nautsi, southwest of Petsamo. Poor conditions kept the *Geschwader's* machines on the ground for much of the time during the next four weeks, but news of another convoy apparently assembling in Iceland prompted I. and II./KG 30's return to northern Norway on 20 October.

In the event, convoy PQ 19 was never despatched. Instead, between 29 October and 2 November, in what was known as 'Operation *FB*', individual merchantmen were sent out from Iceland at approximately 12-hour intervals to make the voyage to Russia some 200 miles apart. Incredibly, many got through, but luck did not favour one Soviet vessel. The *Dekabrist*, a veteran of PQ 6, was sunk by Ju 88s of I./KG 30 on 4 November. Aircraft of II. *Gruppe* damaged two other ships.

Events far removed from the icy wastes of the Barents Sea would now come to bear. On 8 November Anglo-American forces landed in northwest Africa. German countermeasures included stripping *Luftflotte* 5 of almost its entire bomber strength. Within days the two *Gruppen* of KG 26, together with II. and III./KG 30, were *en route* for the Mediterranean. This left just I./KG 30 to maintain some semblance of an offensive posture in the far north by mounting smaller-scale raids on the *Geschwader's* 'traditional' targets in and around the Murmansk area.

Having to shoulder the full burden of the bomber war above the Arctic Circle, I./KG 30 was often called upon to deploy its individual *Staffeln* on airfields far apart. December saw the *Gruppe's* strength divided between Kemi, Kemijärvi and Nautsi. By mid-January 1943 1. and 3. *Staffeln* were both at Kemi, while 2. *Staffel* had made the short hop from Nautsi up to Petsamo.

By this time, however, the regular Arctic convoys had started running again (albeit under a new designation system, the first of the new series being sent to Russia as JW 51 and the corresponding return convoy being coded RA 51). So when, on 23 January 1943, air

Anti-aircraft bursts pockmark the sky and debris rains back down into the sea as a tremendous explosion marks the end of yet another PQ 18 merchantman

reconnaissance reported sighting a group of more than a dozen eastbound vessels – this being convoy JW 52 six days out of Loch Ewe – all three *Staffeln* of I./KG 30 were immediately rushed back up to Banak. They then proceeded to carry out a series of attacks on the heavily escorted merchantmen over the course of the next two days. But none was successful, and the *Gruppe* was lucky to escape with only one aircraft lost.

II./KG 30 returned to Petsamo early in February, only for a Bv 138 reconnaissance flying boat to discover and report the next Russia-bound convoy on the 23rd, exactly one month after the last. Again the Ju 88s at Banak were sent out to attack the merchant ships, but convoy JW 53 had been provided with an even stronger escort. The ten bombers that dived through the inferno of anti-aircraft fire on 25 February nonetheless claimed a near miss on one British merchantman. A follow-up attack 24 hours later had to return empty-handed. On 5 March a dozen Ju 88s struck at the homebound RA 53. This attack also foundered in the face of an intense anti-aircraft barrage. However a raid on Murmansk the next day inflicted extensive damage on one of the recent JW 53 arrivals. In another raid on the port a week later, aircraft of KG 30 finally sank the *Ocean Freedom*, a seasoned veteran of the 'Kola Run' that had somehow survived the *Geschwader's* attentions during the historic PQ 17 action.

The Arctic convoys were suspended for the next nine months, with JW 54 not departing Loch Ewe until mid-November 1943. By then I./KG 30 would no longer be on hand to contest its passage. In the aftermath of JW 53 the *Gruppe* had continued to mount sporadic attacks on the convoy's vessels as they unloaded at Murmansk. On 4 April a Ju 88 scored a direct hit on the merchantman that had suffered the near miss at sea back on 25 February. The elderly *Dover Hill* seemed to bear a charmed life, however. The bomb failed to explode, and she would finally end her days as one of the blockships sunk off the Normandy beachhead shortly after D-Day to form part of the vast 'Mulberry' artificial harbour.

I./KG 30's next priority was, as usual, to prevent the supplies that had been landed at Murmansk from being transported any further. In an attempt to accomplish this they carried out a number of small raids on the railway leading south out of the port. Included among their targets were the station at Kandalaksha and the many Soviet fighter airfields that now protected this vital stretch of track skirting the shores of the White Sea. But the *Gruppe's* days in the far north were already numbered, for even as its Ju 88s were bombing the Murmansk railway, the last Axis troops were surrendering in North Africa. When Anglo-American forces invaded Sicily on 10 July, I./KG 30's time had finally come. Within hours they vacated Banak for Trondheim on the first leg of their long flight south to join the rest of the *Geschwader* in the Mediterranean.

The departure of I./KG 30 meant that the sole remaining Ju 88 presence in the Arctic was

Two of III./KG 30's Arctic aces, *Gruppenkommandeur* Major Werner Baumbach (left), wearing the Oak Leaves with Swords presented to him on 18 August 1942 (the first member of the bomber arm to receive the award), and Oberleutnant Helmut Weinreich (right), sporting the Knight's Cross won on 22 January 1943. Weinreich duly retrained as a *Wilde Sau* nightfighter pilot in the early autumn of 1943, being appointed *Geschwaderkommodore* of JG 301 in October. He was killed on 18 November 1943 when his Fw 190, damaged in combat with an RAF bomber, exploded in the air as he approached to land at Frankfurt/Rhein-Main

being provided by a handful of meteorological and long-range reconnaissance machines.

That was not quite the end of the story. Over a year later, in the late autumn of 1944, two *Gruppen* of Ju 88s were transferred to the far north for the specific purpose of resuming the campaign against the Russian convoys. By this late stage of the war KG 26 had long been established as a fully-fledged torpedo-bomber *Geschwader*. After service in the Mediterranean and operations against the Allied landings in both Normandy and southern France, it had been withdrawn to Germany to rest and refit. It was from here that the two *Gruppen* were deployed up into northern Norway, I./KG 26 to Bardufoss and II./KG 26 to Banak. It was not long, however, before the latter unit was on the move again, being ordered down to Trondheim, in central Norway, to conduct operations over the North Sea.

Thus, when convoy RA 62 was sighted on 10 December 1944 leaving the Kola Inlet for the return run to Scotland, it fell to the Ju 88s of I./KG 26 to mount an attack. About 15 of the *Gruppe's* machines lifted off from Bardufoss on the morning of 12 December, only to become separated in bad weather. One by one the crews managed to locate the 28-ship convoy, but their single uncoordinated torpedo strikes held out little hope of success. None of the vessels was hit and two Ju 88s were lost, one going down on fire and the other being seen to ditch.

The following day's mission, flown by ten aircraft, was reportedly more successful. The convoy was found near Bear Island, a concerted attack was carried out and hits were claimed. In all, four attacks would be made during the five days that RA 62 was within range of the Bardufoss-based Ju 88s, the last by just five machines. Further claims resulted, but British records indicate that all 28 merchantmen reached port safely.

This was to be I./KG 26's last major action of the war. Early in February 1945 the *Gruppe* was disbanded, although most of the aircrew remained at Bardufoss for incorporation into the newly arrived II./KG 26. The latter's place at Trondheim – and its responsibility for North Sea operations – was in turn taken over by III./KG 26, which had flown up from Germany after completing re-equipment on Ju 188s.

February was also to witness the final confrontations between the Arctic convoys and the Luftwaffe's bomber forces in northern Norway. As always, events were set in motion by a reconnaissance sighting. This occurred on 6 February when a routine meteorological flight chanced upon convoy JW 64 three days out from Scotland. The following morning 25 machines of II./KG 26 prepared to take off from Bardufoss. However they were not after the merchantmen; on the express orders of Reichsmarschall Göring they were to target the aircraft carrier reported to be sailing in the middle of the convoy.

Ever since the HMS *Ark Royal* fiasco in the very first month of the war (see *Osprey Combat Aircraft 17 - Ju 88 Kampfgeschwader on the Western*

The Allied landings in North Africa in November 1942, code-named Operation *Torch*, resulted in the wholesale withdrawal of Luftwaffe bomber units from the Arctic and elsewhere. The only *Kampfgruppe* remaining in the far north following Operation *Torch* was I./KG 30, one of whose machines is seen here at a wintry Banak in December 1942

Machines of 2./KG 30 – '4D+HK' in the foreground – over Banak in June 1943, just one month before I. *Gruppe's* transfer to the Mediterranean

For more than a year after the departure of I./KG 30, the only regular Ju 88 presence in the far north was that of *Luftflotte* 5's long-range reconnaissance and meteorological units. This Ju 88D reconnaissance machine attracts the curiosity of a horse-drawn mountain artillery troop plodding past the runway at Alakurtti, in northern Finland, in August 1943. Although coded 'G2+EH', which would indicate its being part of 1.(F)/124, the aircraft is wearing the 'midnight sun' badge of the *Aufklärungskette Lappland* beneath its cockpit

Front), Göring had been obsessed by the fact that 'his' Luftwaffe had not managed to sink a single one of the Royal Navy's aircraft carriers. Now was probably its last chance. In fact, JW 64 was enjoying the protection of *two* escort carriers – HMS *Campania* and HMS *Nairana* – although neither vessel was in the body of the convoy, but part of the accompanying escort.

The Ju 88s of II. *Gruppe* may not have found their carrier, but the carriers' Wildcat fighters found them. Attacked from the air and faced by a curtain of defensive fire from the merchant ships and their naval close escorts, the torpedo-bombers failed to get through. Three aircraft were shot down and many more were damaged. The following day, 8 February, the Ju 188s of III./KG 26 flew in to Bardufoss from Trondheim-Vaernes. The two *Gruppen* were to mount a combined assault – attack the convoy *and* sink the carrier. Take-off was timed for 0830 hrs on 10 February. First, the 14 remaining serviceable Ju 88s of II. *Gruppe*, and then the 18 Ju 188s of III./KG 26 30 minutes later.

It was no easy task to coordinate an attack by two different types of aircraft approaching a target over 300 miles away from two different points of the compass. Perhaps not surprisingly, the assault on the convoy did not go according to plan, with the two waves attacking separately. This time five crews were lost and yet more machines suffered damage. However III./KG 26 did claim one merchantman sunk and both *Gruppen* also reported hits on a number of other vessels, including several warships. In reality, no ships were sunk, and certainly no aircraft carrier – a fact that was not lost on an aggrieved Göring, who immediately fired off a teletype addressed to both *Gruppenkommandeure*. 'I demand that you now finally sink an aircraft carrier as well'.

KG 26's torpedo-bombers had not managed to inflict any serious damage on JW 64. Their next operation, an attack flown on 20 February by 40 aircraft from both *Gruppen* against the returning RA 64, met with an equal lack of success. Moreover, six of their number were shot down by Fleet Air Arm Wildcats. Three days later – three days of gale-force winds and mountainous seas – 19 machines of KG 26, sent out to try to re-establish contact with the westbound convoy, stumbled instead upon a lone straggler. The outcome was inevitable and the hapless *Henry Bacon*, a 7177-ton US Liberty ship, has the dubious distinction of being the last Allied vessel to be sunk by Luftwaffe torpedo-bombers in World War 2.

Shortly after this 'success', the Ju 188s of III./KG 26 returned

to Trondheim. March remained quiet, as did most of April, but towards the end of that month radio intercepts warned the Germans that another convoy was assembling in the Kola Inlet. Once again III. *Gruppe* was ordered up to Bardufoss, but the planned strike by II. and III./KG 26 against RA 66 – the penultimate homebound Allied convoy of the campaign – was called off at the very last moment. The Ju 188s promptly flew back to Trondheim, but within the week they were on the move again – this time not northwards, but southwards. On 8 May 1945 Germany surrendered, and both *Gruppen* were instructed to gather at Oslo-Gardemoen. Here, on the morning *after* the official capitulation, they were briefed for one final mission.

Another Ju 88D – this time of *Wekusta* 1/Ob.d.L, a meteorological *Staffel* – about to go down off the coast of Norway on 22 November 1943. Although this particular machine, 'D7+BH', had fallen foul of an RAF Mosquito, its final moments mirror a fate shared by many Arctic-based Ju 88 crews

For months past tremendous efforts had been made to rescue as many as possible of the untold thousands of Wehrmacht personnel and civilian refugees trapped in the east by the advancing Red Army. Most of those saved had been evacuated by sea from the many ports along the Baltic coast. Now, although having formally surrendered, German naval and Luftwaffe units were being granted one day's extension by the Western Allies to carry on with their humanitarian task.

The largest body of German troops cut off behind the Russian front was on Latvia's Courland Peninsula, where more than 200,000 men of the 16. and 18. *Armeen* had been holding out since October 1944. And it was to Libau, on the peninsula's western coast – ironically, one of the ex-Soviet airfields targeted in the opening hours of *Barbarossa* – that the aircraft of KG 26's two *Gruppen* were now being sent with orders to bring out all the wounded they could carry. The date was 9 May 1945, and they had until 2000 hrs to complete their task, as this was the deadline set by the Allies for the unarmed torpedo-bombers to take-off from Libau for the flight back, either to Oslo or to Lübeck-Blankensee.

Some 40 machines were serviceable and able to take part in the mission. Each was permitted a crew of just two – a pilot and wireless-operator. They succeeded in rescuing 300+ men, returning with as many as eight wounded packed together in cockpits that were a squeeze for a normal crew of four. Upon landing, crewmen and wounded alike were taken into British captivity.

So ends the story of the totally separate war that was fought between the Arctic convoys and the Luftwaffe's two foremost anti-shipping *Kampfgeschwader*. It is time now to return to the Ju 88 bombers on the main sectors of the eastern front during that bitter first winter of 1941/42.

Ju 88s and Ju 188s of KG 26, the majority of them having very likely taken part in the recent Courland rescue operation, collected at Oslo-Gardemoen to await destruction by the victorious Allies in the summer of 1945

1
Ju 88A-5 'V4+KS' of 8./KG 1, Eichwalde, East Prussia, June 1941

2
Ju 88A-4 'V4+FR' of 7./KG 1, Pleskau-South, Northern Sector, May 1942

3
Ju 88C-6 'V4+DT' of 9.(Eis)/KG 1, Dno, Northern Sector, February 1943

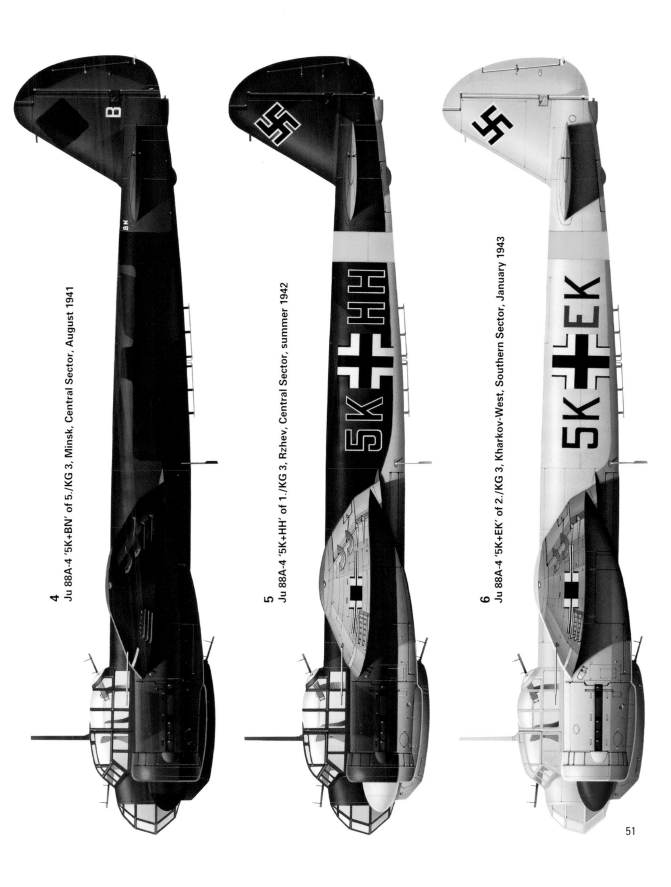

4
Ju 88A-4 '5K+BN' of 5./KG 3, Minsk, Central Sector, August 1941

5
Ju 88A-4 '5K+HH' of 1./KG 3, Rzhev, Central Sector, summer 1942

6
Ju 88A-4 '5K+EK' of 2./KG 3, Kharkov-West, Southern Sector, January 1943

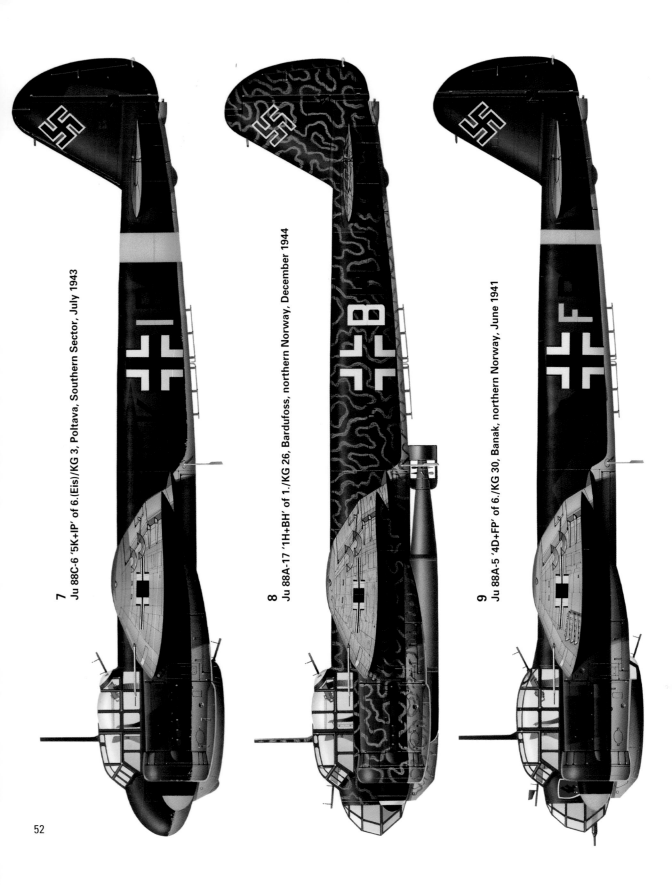

7
Ju 88C-6 '5K+IP' of 6.(Eis)/KG 3, Poltava, Southern Sector, July 1943

8
Ju 88A-17 '1H+BH' of 1./KG 26, Bardufoss, northern Norway, December 1944

9
Ju 88A-5 '4D+FP' of 6./KG 30, Banak, northern Norway, June 1941

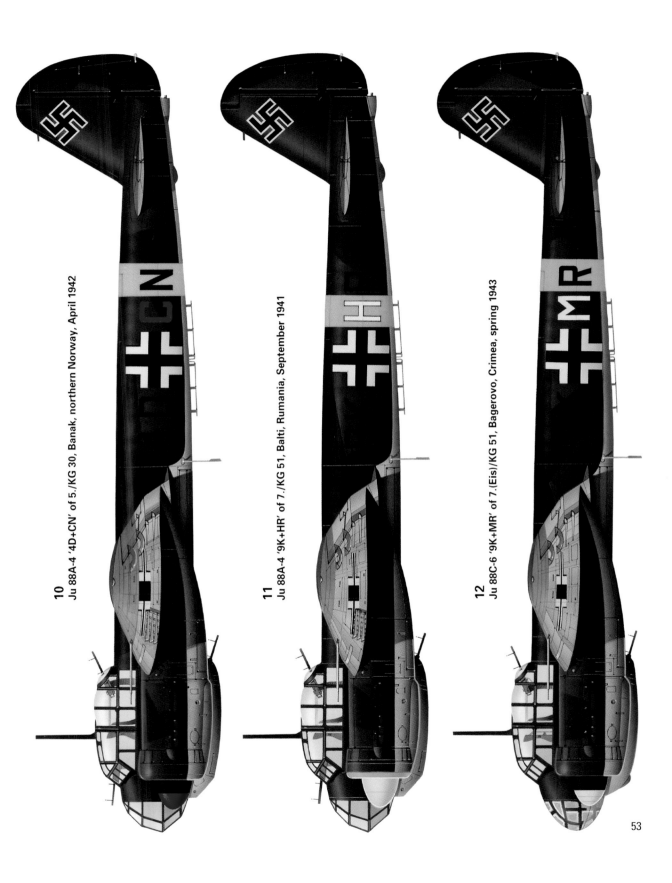

10
Ju 88A-4 '4D+CN' of 5./KG 30, Banak, northern Norway, April 1942

11
Ju 88A-4 '9K+HR' of 7./KG 51, Balti, Rumania, September 1941

12
Ju 88C-6 '9K+MR' of 7.(Eis)/KG 51, Bagerovo, Crimea, spring 1943

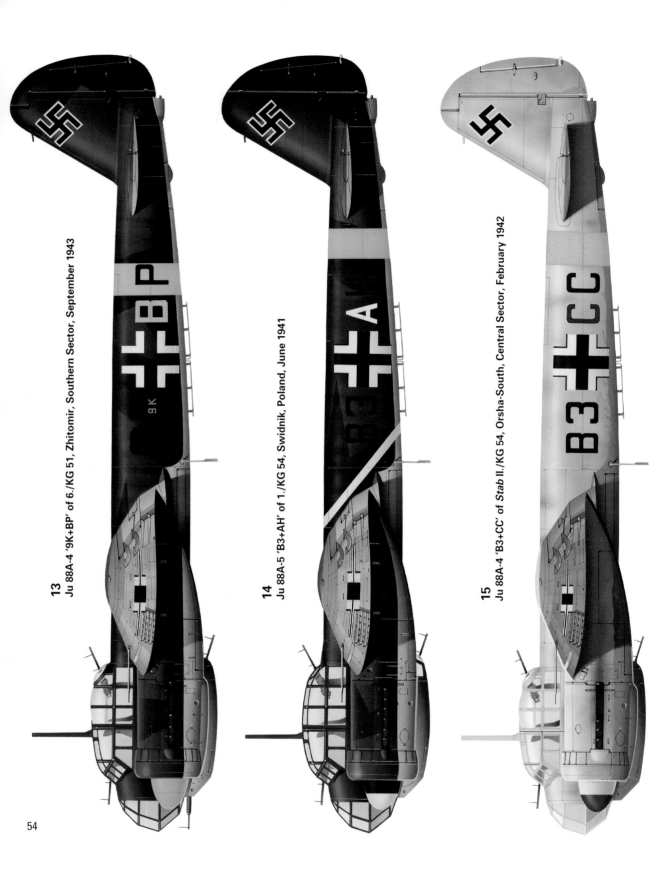

13
Ju 88A-4 '9K+BP' of 6./KG 51, Zhitomir, Southern Sector, September 1943

14
Ju 88A-5 'B3+AH' of 1./KG 54, Swidnik, Poland, June 1941

15
Ju 88A-4 'B3+CC' of *Stab* II./KG 54, Orsha-South, Central Sector, February 1942

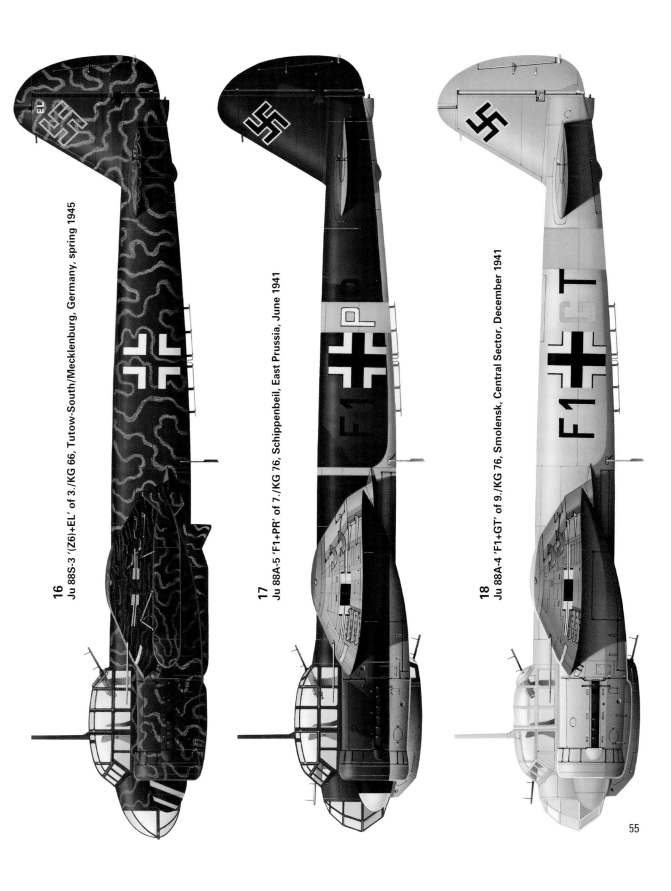

16
Ju 88S-3 '(Z6)+EL' of 3./KG 66, Tutow-South/Mecklenburg, Germany, spring 1945

17
Ju 88A-5 'F1+PR' of 7./KG 76, Schippenbeil, East Prussia, June 1941

18
Ju 88A-4 'F1+GT' of 9./KG 76, Smolensk, Central Sector, December 1941

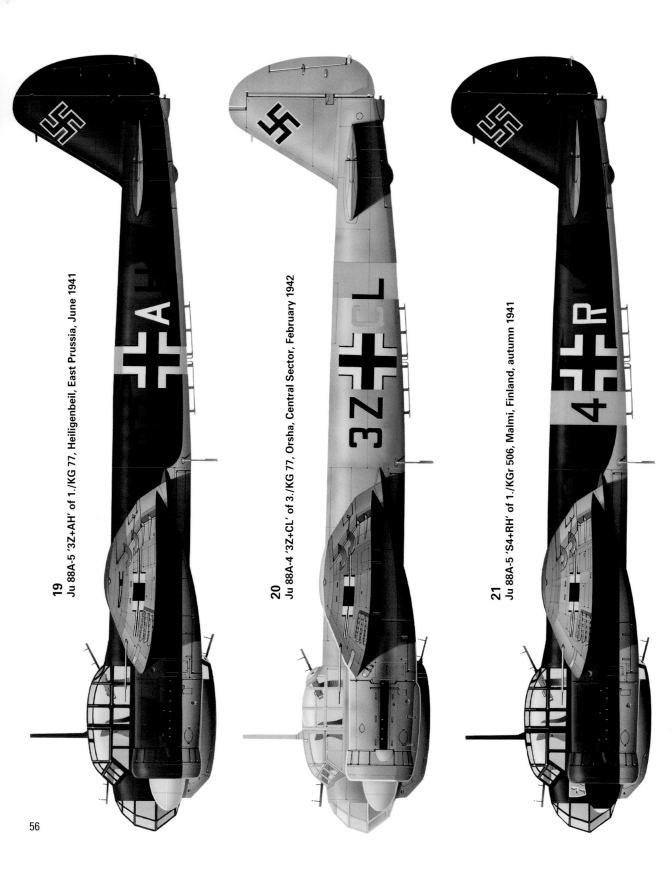

19
Ju 88A-5 '3Z+AH' of 1./KG 77, Heiligenbeil, East Prussia, June 1941

20
Ju 88A-4 '3Z+CL' of 3./KG 77, Orsha, Central Sector, February 1942

21
Ju 88A-5 'S4+RH' of 1./KGr 506, Malmi, Finland, autumn 1941

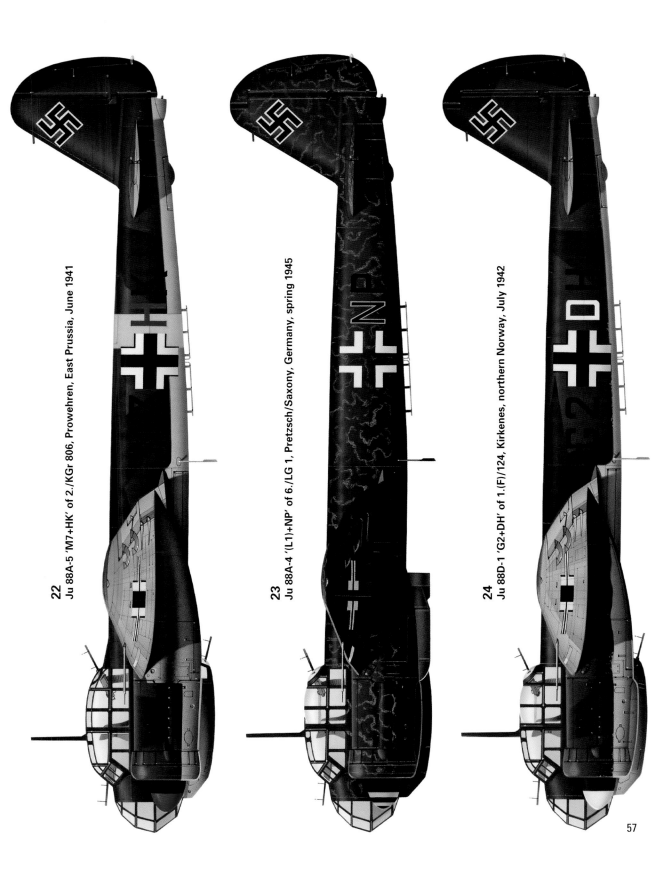

22
Ju 88A-5 'M7+HK' of 2./KGr 806, Prowehren, East Prussia, June 1941

23
Ju 88A-4 '(L1)+NP' of 6./LG 1, Pretzsch/Saxony, Germany, spring 1945

24
Ju 88D-1 'G2+DH' of 1.(F)/124, Kirkenes, northern Norway, July 1942

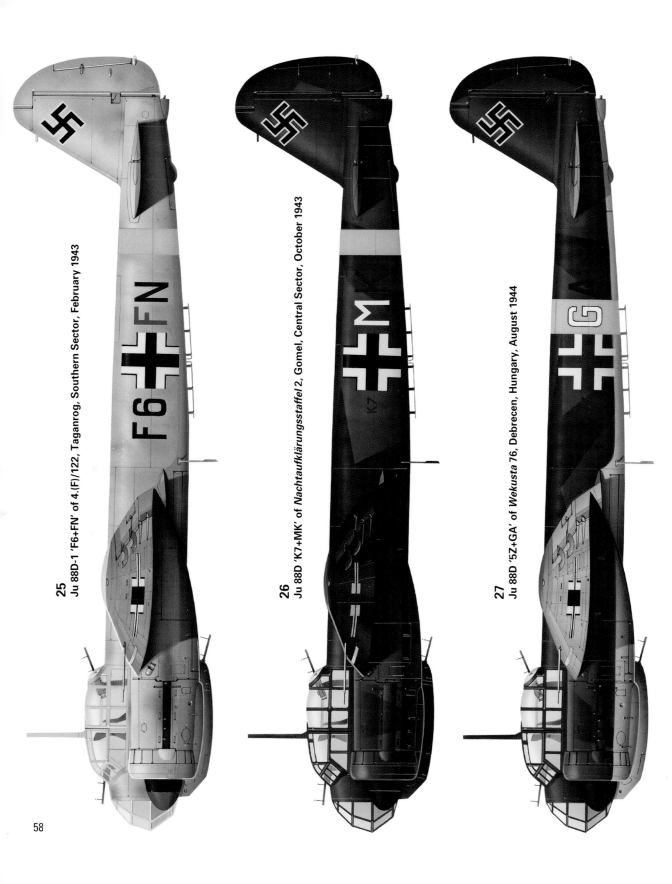

25
Ju 88D-1 'F6+FN' of 4.(F)/122, Taganrog, Southern Sector, February 1943

26
Ju 88D 'K7+MK' of *Nachtaufklärungsstaffel 2*, Gomel, Central Sector, October 1943

27
Ju 88D '5Z+GA' of *Wekusta 76*, Debrecen, Hungary, August 1944

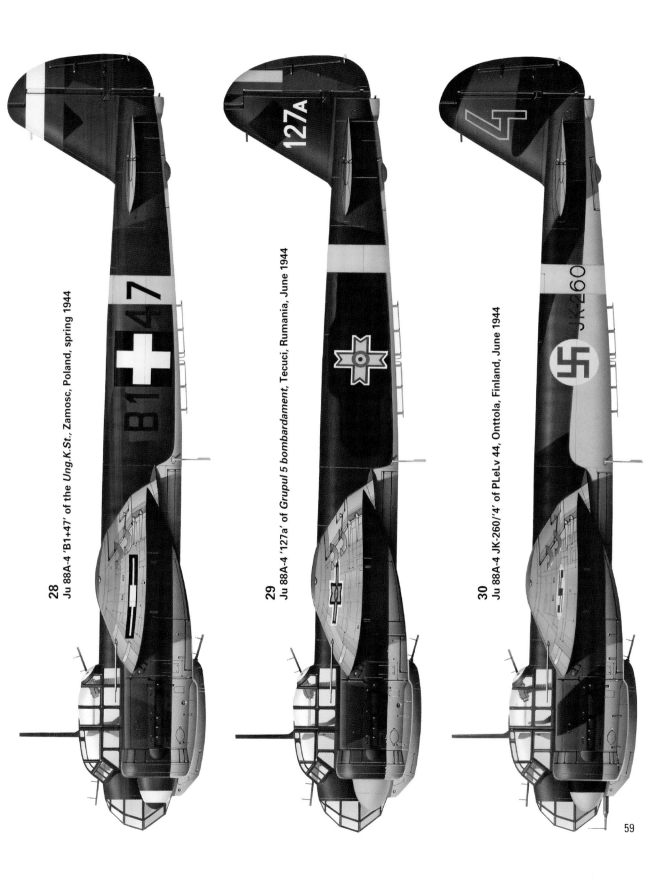

28
Ju 88A-4 'B1+47' of the *Ung.K.St.*, Zamosc, Poland, spring 1944

29
Ju 88A-4 '127a' of *Grupul 5 bombardament*, Tecuci, Rumania, June 1944

30
Ju 88A-4 JK-260/'4' of PLeLv 44, Onttola, Finland, June 1944

STALINGRAD AND AFTER

The Wehrmacht's failure to destroy the Red Army in the field before the onset of winter 1941 came as a devastating blow to Hitler. The German leader had gambled on a speedy and decisive *Blitzkrieg* in the east. Now that gamble had been lost and he was powerless to rectify the situation in the short term. His forces were ill prepared and ill equipped to fight a winter war. He acknowledged this in his Directive No 39 of 8 December 1941;

The first winter of the war in Russia took a heavy toll on men and machines alike. Here, a seemingly endless line of railway flatbed wagons has been loaded with damaged Ju 88s for transportation to the rear for major repair work

'The severe winter weather, which has arrived surprisingly early in the east, compels us to abandon immediately all major offensive operations and go over to the defensive.'

Less than four months later, however, he was drawing up plans for a renewed offensive in the east. Directive No 41 of 5 April 1942 stated;

'As soon as the weather and the state of the terrain allow, we must seize the initiative again. The armies of the central sector will stand fast, those in the north will capture Leningrad, while those on the southern flank will break through into the Caucasus.'

Among the original aims of *Barbarossa*, as first set out in December 1940, had been the occupation of Leningrad and the capture of Moscow 'which would represent a decisive political and economic success'. However the *Führer* now had more material prizes in mind. He wanted control of the industrial and mineral basins of the Dnieper and Don rivers, and the oil of the Caucasus. The main focus of operations on the Russian front in 1942 would therefore be in the south. But the renewal of the offensive called for by Hitler in April would not be launched until the summer. For the opening months of the year German forces on all three sectors – north, central and south – would have to conduct what, in modern parlance, might be termed damage limitation exercises. They had to attempt to repel all Soviet counter-offensives or, at the very least, restrict the enemy's territorial gains to a minimum.

THE NORTHERN SECTOR

The changeover from the offensive to the defensive affected German ground and air forces alike. In fact, the Luftwaffe's task was made all the more difficult by the start of the wholesale withdrawal of its units from the

Russian front for service in other theatres. The first such transfers had already taken place before the end of 1941, and would ultimately result in a marked reduction in the number of Ju 88 bomber units in the east. This was particularly true of the northern sector where, of the eight Ju 88 *Kampfgruppen* that had made up I. *Fliegerkorps* at the beginning of *Barbarossa*, only two remained by January 1942.

During the early winter months KG 77 had returned to the Reich for re-equipment prior to deployment

Another *Kampfgruppe* whose intended transfer to the Mediterranean was deferred by the worsening situation on the eastern front was I./KG 77. Bundled up against the cold, a group of mechanics are in the process of changing the engine on this 1. *Staffel* machine

to the Mediterranean, but only two of its *Gruppen* were subsequently to make the flight south. Events on the eastern front led to I./KG 77 being moved up to Heiligenbeil, in East Prussia, for 'winterisation' before then being returned to Russia, albeit not to the northern sector. I. *Fliegerkorps* also lost the services of Oberst *Dr.Ing.* Ernst Bormann's KG 76. He took two of his *Gruppen* to the central sector, leaving I./KG 76 to retire to the Reich for rest and refit. This meant that by early 1942, the sole Ju 88 bomber presence on the northern sector was being provided by II. and III./KG 1, and even they would be temporarily withdrawn from the area on deployment to both the central and southern sectors during the year.

In the winter of 1941/42, operations on the northern front were still dominated by the siege of Leningrad. The first week of the new year saw the two *Gruppen* of KG 1 (together with the He 111s of KG 4) attacking the now famous 'ice road', the perilous route across the frozen surface of Lake Ladoga used by Soviet truck convoys to ferry supplies into the beleaguered city. Then, in mid-January, a major Russian counter-offensive between Lakes Ladoga and Ilmen drove German forces back across the River Volkhov. The two *Gruppen* of KG 1 were immediately called upon for support. They bombed the advancing Red Army units and attacked the rail supply lines to the enemy's rear.

Soon the whole northern sector was ablaze. The lack of Luftwaffe numbers in the area was quickly laid bare as KG 1's Junkers were

Could this aircraft about to be bombed up also belong to I./KG 77? Although the unit badge has been thoroughly obliterated, the size and position of the defaced area closely approximates the emblem still being worn by the machine above. The snow-covered background offers no clues, but note that both aircraft have a similar additional machine gun installed in the lower nose glazing

forced into a series of 'fire brigade' actions, rushing from one area of danger to the next in their attempts to stem the Soviet flood tide. By late January the Red Army had broken through the front south of Lake Ilmen, cutting off two large bodies of German troops at Demyansk and Cholm. The battle for these two pockets would rage for very nearly three months before ground contact was re-established and the surrounded units were at last reached by reinforcements.

Some *Gruppen* spending winter on former Soviet airfields enjoyed the luxury of hangar space for essential maintenance and repairs. Although such structures kept the worst of the elements at bay, the temperatures within were still sub-zero – note the layers of snow clinging to this aircraft's canopy and engine nacelle

The struggle overhead was no less ferocious as Luftwaffe and Red Air Force machines fought for mastery of the skies above the twin battlefields. In one particularly confused melee over the Cholm perimeter on 28 February, 4./KG 1 lost its *Staffelkapitän*. Oberleutnant Johannes Brandenburg, who had won the Knight's Cross while serving with KG 30 in the west, was killed when his aircraft exploded in mid-air after being struck by a bomb from another machine diving above him.

By mid-March KG 1's crews were flying as many as six sorties a day in support of the ground troops in and around the Demyansk pocket. Operations of such intensity inevitably resulted in further casualties. Two *Kapitäne* of 5. *Staffel* were reported missing in the space of just three days – Oberleutnant Hans Sumpf on 26 March and Hauptmann Peter Runkel on the 29th – both failing to return from missions to the northeast of Demyansk. Coincidentally, the latter date also saw II. *Gruppe* fly its 4000th operation since the start of the war (with III./KG 1 clocking up its 5000th just 48 hours later).

In early April the two *Gruppen* enjoyed – if 'enjoyed' be the right word – a brief respite from the fighting for the two pockets when they participated in a large-scale attack on major units of the Soviet Baltic Fleet. These included the elderly battleship *Oktyabrskaya Revolutsiya* and the heavy cruiser *Maksim Gorky*, both of which were still locked fast in the ice of Leningrad's River Neva. Running the gauntlet of the city's legendary flak defences, the bombers claimed numerous near misses, causing minor damage to the two capital ships and several other vessels.

The spring thaw may not yet have reached Leningrad, but it was already turning KG 1's base at Dno into 'one huge lake'. On 11 and 12 April the two *Gruppen* therefore moved to Pleskau-South in order to continue their operations over the two pockets. A corridor through to the 95,000 men trapped at Demyansk was finally opened on 21 April. It was on this day that III./KG 1 was ordered back to the Reich for refit, leaving just II. *Gruppe* to fly the ground support missions that would help free the much smaller Cholm pocket on 5 May. Major Hans Keppler's III./KG 1 returned to Pleskau-South on 22 May, and three days later it was the turn of II. *Gruppe* to head for Germany and four weeks rest and re-equipment.

By this time Lake Ladoga's 'ice road' to Leningrad had melted away and the lake's flotilla of small merchant vessels would soon be sailing again. One of III./KG 1's early missions after its arrival back from Insterburg, in East Prussia, was a raid flown on 28 May against the ships' ports of departure on the far shore of Lake Ladoga. This attempt to disrupt the city's surface lifeline cost 8. *Staffel* one of its new Ju 88A-4s. On 1 June the *Gruppe* made the short hop from Pleskau-South to Raskopolye, a small landing ground nearby, before returning to a now thoroughly dried-out Dno nine days later. For much of the rest of the month crews would be primarily engaged in attacking the surviving units of the Red Army force that had breached the Volkhov defences back in January and were now surrounded and trapped at Lyuban, 55 miles south-southeast of Leningrad.

On 22 June II./KG 1 flew back in from Germany to rejoin III. *Gruppe* at Dno. During the first few days of July the two units carried out several anti-shipping sorties over the Gulf of Finland. Then, on 7 July, a dangerous Soviet armoured thrust on the central sector resulted in

III./KG 1 being rushed down to Bryansk, about 250 miles southwest of Moscow. It was followed by II. *Gruppe* 72 hours later. KG 1's bombing attacks on the enemy's armoured spearheads and rear area lines of supply clearly helped to contain the threat, for on 27 July both *Gruppen* were sent back to Dno.

From here they turned their attention to Leningrad again, taking part in the raid of 2 August that was reportedly the heaviest experienced by the city for almost a year. The defending fighters' claims for 27 of the attackers shot down were wildly optimistic. KG 1's actual casualties were just three crewmen wounded by machine-gun fire, but the *Geschwader* was to suffer far more grievous losses before the month was out.

Within hours of the Leningrad raid another major Soviet counter-attack on the central sector saw the two *Gruppen* quickly transferred down to the danger area. Operating initially out of Shatalovka-East against troop movements to the southeast of Rzhev, they were then deployed to Bryansk again on 9 August, where they were to perform more of the 'fire brigade' duties that they had undertaken along this selfsame stretch of front only weeks before. This time it was to cost them dear.

KG 1's long-serving *Geschwaderkommodore*, Generalmajor Karl Angerstein, had only recently relinquished command of the unit upon being appointed GOC of the Luftwaffe's bomber and reconnaissance schools. His replacement, Oberstleutnant Peter Schemmel, was to last less than a month. The new *Kommodore* and his crew were lost when their 'V4+AA' was shot down by Soviet fighters northeast of Rzhev on 14 August. The *Gruppenkommandeur* of II./KG 1, Major Herbert Lorch, was immediately named acting-*Kommodore* in his stead, but his tenure of office proved to be even shorter, for he too fell victim to enemy fighters just five days later.

On 27 August the two *Gruppen* returned north to Dno. During its brief deployment to the central sector KG 1 had lost some half-dozen aircraft and crews (including the two *Geschwaderkommodores*). In the same period it had gained three new Knight's Cross winners. The first of these was Oberleutnant Otto von Ballasko, the *Staffelkapitän* of 9./KG 1, who was decorated on 13 August. The second award, announced exactly one week later, was posthumous. It honoured Oberleutnant Hans Sumpf, one of the two *Kapitäne* of 5. *Staffel* lost over Demyansk back in March. The third recipient was the *Kommandeur* of III. *Gruppe*, Major Hans Keppler. He received his Knight's Cross on 21 August, and ten days after that was appointed *Geschwaderkommodore*, by which time KG 1 was back on the northern sector.

Fate had one last trick to play. Just *three* days after assuming command of the *Geschwader*, Major Keppler and his crew were killed when their Ju 88 was involved in a mid-air collision with a Bf 109 of III./JG 54 south of Lake Ladoga.

With three *Kommodores* having been lost in fewer than as many weeks, it would be 18 September before Hans Keppler's successor was announced. Major Heinrich Lau was doubly fortunate. Not only did he survive his six months at the head of KG 1, he was also the first *Kommodore* in more than two-and-a-half years to command a full *Geschwader* complement of three *Gruppen*, for on 8 September II. and III./KG 1 had been joined at Dno by a brand new I./KG 1.

The last *Gruppe* to bear this number had parted ways with the *Geschwader* upon being redesignated III./KG 40 back in March 1940. The new *Gruppe* was created in a likewise manner when III./KG 26, then based at Lübeck-Blankensee and flying He 111s, had been redesignated to become I./KG 1 early in June 1942. The following three months had been spent re-equipping with the Ju 88 and training, both in Germany and France, before the unit was finally transferred to the eastern front.

I./KG 1's arrival at an already overcrowded Dno led to II. *Gruppe's* moving up to Siverskaya, closer to Leningrad, a week later. From here II./KG 1 continued to fly missions over the Lake Ladoga area, while the two Dno-based *Gruppen* spent the latter half of September operating against enemy forces exerting pressure on the Demyansk sector of the front south of Lake Ilmen. Then, early in October, the *Geschwader* was put on standby for another move. This was to take it not just across the Army Group boundary into the central sector, but much further south. By 7 October Major Lau's three *Gruppen* found themselves deployed on the two fields at Morosovskaya, just 125 miles away from Stalingrad.

The crews were not impressed with their new surroundings, claiming that the accommodation in Morosovskaya's earthen bunkers was 'primitive in the extreme', but they soon had other things to worry about. On 10 October KG 1's Ju 88s took part in a major raid on the oil refinery at Grozny, deep in the Caucasus, from which a machine of 1. *Staffel* failed to return. They would lose at least eight more aircraft during their four weeks on the Stalingrad front, where their main targets were pockets of resistance within the ruins of the city itself, as well as Soviet artillery positions and lines of supply on the east bank of the Volga and beyond.

Early in November III./KG 1 was instructed to return to the Reich for refit. At the same time the rest of the *Geschwader* was transferred up to Orsha-South on the central sector. Intelligence had revealed that the Red Army was about to launch another large-scale counter-offensive in this area and, despite the sudden onset of winter in the region, KG 1's two *Gruppen* were tasked with disrupting the build-up of supplies. An attack on two important marshalling yards to the enemy's rear on 10 November was particularly successful, crippling the movement of all traffic for several days. After this the Ju 88s concentrated on the Soviet infantry and armoured formations' assembly points around Rzhev and Bjely.

'V4+EL', a winter-camouflaged Ju 88A-4 of 3./KG 1, returns from a mission to the Rzhev area in November 1942

In spite of all their efforts, a powerful force of enemy tanks managed to smash through the German front southeast of Rzhev on 28 November. Although the weather was appalling, the Junkers were ordered into the air. It was to be one of the blackest days in the *Geschwader's* history, as although the crews involved somehow succeeded in sealing off the breach, it cost them 11 aircraft lost and many more damaged. In ever more atrocious conditions – snowstorms, freezing fog and low-lying cloud – I. and II./KG 1 continued to fly in support of the hard-pressed ground forces. On 8 December II. *Gruppe* lost its *Kommandeur* when the Ju 88 of Hauptmann Heinz Laube iced up and crashed. He and his crew would be the final casualties of the year. Two weeks later the still leaderless II./KG 1 returned home to join III. *Gruppe* at Königsberg-Neuhausen.

Meanwhile I./KG 1 had been transferred down to the southern sector again, staging from Orsha, via Bryansk and Kharkov, to Urasov, where it was placed under the control of *Luftwaffenkommando Don* (the renamed I. *Fliegerkorps* – see below). It would spend the closing days of 1942 in action against a triumphant Red Army that was surging westwards past an already encircled and doomed Stalingrad.

The instructions contained in the *Führer's* Directive of 5 April 1942 that the forces on the northern sector 'will capture Leningrad' had clearly not been fulfilled. As far as Ju 88 numbers were concerned, the sector that had had two *Kampfgruppen* within its area of command at the beginning of 1942 ended the year with none. So how had the forces on the central sector fared during the same period – had they been able to follow Hitler's orders to 'stand fast' in 1942?

HOLDING THE CENTRE

In terms of aerial strength, the central sector had been the hardest hit by the withdrawal of units to other theatres. Towards the end of 1941 the whole of *Luftflotte* 2's staff organisation, together with one of its two subordinate *Fliegerkorps*, had been transferred *en bloc* to the Mediterranean. This left just one *Korps* – General Wolfram *Freiherr* von Richthofen's close-support VIII. *Fliegerkorps* – solely responsible for the approximately 400 miles of front that made up the central sector.

But the sector's two 'resident' Ju 88 *Kampfgruppen*, although hitherto part of II. *Fliegerkorps*, had not been included in the mass exodus to the Mediterranean. They had been retained on the Moscow front, where they would be joined by a large number of other *Kampfgruppen*. Together, these would provide von Richthofen with a powerful longer-range strike force. By early 1942 he controlled no fewer than 13 such *Kampfgruppen*, eight of which were equipped with Ju 88s.

These were all organised into one special battle group, or aerial task force, the so-called *Gefechtsverband Bormann*. As its name indicates, this force was commanded by Oberst *Dr.Ing.* Ernst Bormann, the *Geschwaderkommodore* of KG 76, who had brought two of his *Gruppen* down from the northern sector. Another incomer from the north, via a brief period of 'winterisation' in the Reich, was I./KG 77. Like the latter, II./KG 54 had also initially been scheduled for transfer to the Mediterranean, only then to be 'winterised' and returned to the Russian front. Coming from further afield, II./KG 30 had previously operated in the Arctic and – finally – I. and II./KG 3 were joined

1./KG 77's '3Z+DH' looking decidedly the worse for wear – victim of a Soviet air raid, or an accident while bombing up? Oddly, the port mainwheel tyre seems to have escaped the mayhem

Coming down from the Arctic, midwinter on the central sector must have felt positively balmy to the crews of II./KG 30. Note the captured British Army Scammell heavy artillery tractor being employed to tow 5. *Staffel's* white-camouflaged '4D+BN'

The Ju 88C heavy fighter carried a crew of three. In the original of this wartime magazine illustration showing an aircraft of 6.(Eis)/KG 3 at Orsha-South in the spring of 1942, II. *Gruppe's* white lightning bolt and its red shield background can both be clearly made out. But note too the small white disc on the nose of the machine. This bears the black 'songbird on a tree branch' motif, which was II./KG 3's original badge dating back to the days before the war

by III. *Gruppe*, which had recently completed conversion from the Dornier Do 17 on to Ju 88s.

During the early weeks of 1942, based on the airfields of the large Orsha complex and others in the surrounding areas close to the main Minsk-Moscow highway, the *Gefechtsverband's* units were engaged primarily in bombing the salients punched into the German frontlines by the Red Army's winter counter-offensives. Given the Soviet troops' unfailing habit of letting loose with every weapon that they could bring to bear against any enemy aircraft daring to fly overhead, it could be a risky business. KG 76 reportedly lost six machines to ground fire during a mission close to the hotly contested town of Rzhev on 8 January.

Nor were the Russians the only enemy that had to be faced. The appalling conditions and freezing temperatures were the cause of numerous fatal accidents. Three crew members of another KG 76 machine were killed when their aircraft skidded off the icy runway upon landing back at Orsha after a mission and smashed head-on into the solid wall of snow banked up high alongside.

Other targets during January included the Soviets' lines of supply. Major Sigmund-Ulrich *Freiherr* von Gravenreuth's II./KG 30 scored a spectacular success during one attack on a marshalling yard on the Tula-Orel railway line when a 1000 kg bomb completely demolished the station buildings and started a conflagration among trains loaded with fuel and munitions. Furthermore on 27 January II./KG 3, commanded by Major Waldemar Krüger, carried out a raid on an airfield being used by the Russians to drop airborne troops into the Vyazma area. Huge damage was done, the field's fuel store set ablaze and a dozen elderly four-engined Tupolev TB-3 paratroop transports destroyed on the ground.

As January gave way to February it was the Red Army in the field that continued to suffer most at the hands of the *Gefechtsverband's* Ju 88s. On 13 February machines of II./KG 54 strafed an enemy ski column, virtually wiping it out. However the following day two of its Ju 88s – one flown by the *Kommandeur*, Hauptmann Heinz Gehrke – failed to return from a mission sent out against Russian troop movements on the Toropez road. It may well have been the Soviet frontline soldier who was feeling the full weight of the Junkers' attacks, but it was undoubtedly *his* ground fire in return that was inflicting the greatest number of casualties upon the Ju 88 units. For although the Red Air Force was now beginning to mount retaliatory raids on the bombers'

Orsha airfields, mainly under the cover of darkness, these were, by comparison, causing very little damage.

On 4 March II./KG 54 lost three more aircraft during low-level strikes against road convoys in the vicinity of Rzhev. Two crews survived and returned safely to base. The third, that of Oberleutnant Günther Seubert, the *Staffelkapitän* of 4./KG 54 and acting *Gruppenkommandeur*, was posted missing. Later in the month the *Gefechtsverband's* units started to focus their attention on the enemy's lines of supply in those regions astride the boundary between Army Groups Centre and North. A resurgence of activity in the north – not least the heavy fighting around Demyansk and Cholm – had already led to the temporary detachment of both I./KG 3 and I./KG 77 to the *Luftflotte* 1 area.

Throughout April and into May, although still occasionally called upon to bomb the now much more quiescent enemy salients, the central sector Ju 88 units concentrated their efforts mainly on railway traffic deeper to the Russian rear. To help them in their task they had already received a small number of cannon-armed Ju 88C heavy fighters which, in the right hands, proved effective train busters. No longer having to confront the ground fire thrown up at them by frontline troops, casualty figures among the bombers' crews fell considerably during this period.

They did not disappear altogether, of course. On 21 May Knight's Cross wearer Oberleutnant Ernst Petzold, the *Staffelkapitän* of 5./KG 54, was severely wounded by an anti-aircraft burst while dive-bombing the railway station at Yukhno. And just 24 hours later Leutnant Horst Deutschbein, who had taken over leadership of the *Staffel* in Petzold's absence, was himself shot down by a LaGG fighter during an attack on another station in the same region. A second victim of 22 May's anti-railway operations was Major Waldemar Krüger, *Gruppenkommandeur* of II./KG 3, who was shot down by anti-aircraft fire along a stretch of track southeast of Vyazma.

Coincidentally, this same date also saw the last of the three Knight's Crosses awarded to Ju 88 crew members during the spring 1942 campaign on the Moscow front. The first had been presented on 16 April to the *Gruppenkommandeur* of I./KG 77, Hauptmann Joachim Poetter, and the second to Oberleutnant Horst Müller of II./KG 76 on 3 May. That won on 22 May went to one of Poetter's veteran NCO pilots, Oberfeldwebel Horst Henning, who had flown 300+ missions and whose successes included the destruction of 23 trains.

By this time significant changes were taking place on the eastern front. The *Gruppen* of the *Gefechtsverband Bormann* can be said to have fulfilled their purpose inasmuch as they had helped the ground forces on the central sector to 'stand fast' – as per the *Führer's* orders – in the face of heavy Soviet pressure. The Red Army's winter counter-offensives had been largely repulsed (or had simply run out of steam, depending upon the historical viewpoint one chooses to subscribe to). Now the main weight of operations was about to switch to the southern sector.

Generaloberst von Richthofen's close-support VIII. *Fliegerkorps* had been transferred down to the Crimea at the beginning of May. The command now responsible for the central sector was the newly created *Luftwaffenkommando Ost* (more accurately, the retitled V. *Fliegerkorps*). The *Gruppen* of the erstwhile *Gefechtsverband Bormann*, their work done, were already dispersing. II./KG 30 had long since departed for the

In January 1943 one of III./KG 3's *Staffeln* was also re-equipped with C-6's for train-busting operations. The machine seen here carries both the III. *Gruppe* badge (red lightning bolt on a yellow shield) and the device chosen by the *Staffel* in question, 9.(Eis)/KG 3, to reflect its new role: the 'Winged wheel' emblem of the *Reichsbahn*, or German State Railways. The officer pictured is Leutnant Udo Cordes, the *Staffel's* most successful '*Loktöter*' ('Loco-killer'). In the first five months of the unit's existence he destroyed no fewer than 77 locomotives – 41 in one three-week period alone on the River Donetz sector. This performance would earn him the Knight's Cross on 25 May 1943

A pair of accordionists, a solo violinist and an unseen drummer provide the musical accompaniment as the *Staffel* chef cuts the cake to celebrate the 200th mission of 5./KG 3's Oberfeldwebel Friedrich Kralemann (centre). Kralemann flew his 260th, and last, mission on 10 September 1942 when, despite severe injuries that were to cost him his left eye, he managed to bring his crippled machine – minus cabin roof canopy and ventral gondola – back to base. Over a year later, on 29 October 1943, Kralemann was awarded the Knight's Cross, before finally succumbing to his wounds on 1 December 1943. The machine in the background of this photograph from happier times also carries both the II. *Gruppe* 'lightning' badge and the earlier 'songbird' emblem in the small white disc ahead of it

Netherlands, where it would re-equip before returning to the far northern theatre. I./KG 77 was likewise to head west – to Creil, in France – for re-equipment and its subsequent redesignation as I./KG 6. Three *Gruppen* were ordered down to the southern sector, II. and III./KG 76 to the Crimea during May, and I./KG 54 to Kharkov in June.

This left just Oberst Heinrich Conrady's KG 3 to continue operations on the central sector of the frontline as the sole Ju 88 *Kampfgeschwader* assigned to *Lw.Kdo.Ost*. Throughout the coming summer months KG 3 would keep up the campaign against the Soviets' rear area road and rail networks. These activities were interspersed with other missions flown in more direct support of the troops on the ground. In June, for example, I./KG 3 would again see action on the northern sector, this time assisting KG 1 in the reduction of the Lyuban pocket. And later the following month a renewed enemy counter-offensive in the Rzhev area – intended primarily to relieve pressure on the southern front – would see KG 3 committed against a now numerically far superior Red Air Force.

Flying as many as four sorties a day, Conrady's crews suffered accordingly. On the last day of June alone the *Geschwader* lost eight of its aircraft. During July and August KG 3 would lose more than 30 machines in all, and suffer many more damaged. This may not seem unduly excessive at first glance, but it was higher than any other Ju 88 *Kampfgeschwader* then serving on the eastern front. When measured against the unit's average serviceability figures of just 16 aircraft per *Gruppe*, it represented a casualty rate of very nearly 65 per cent.

Yet as hard as KG 3 may have been finding it on the central sector, it was to the south that the main battle was now being fought.

ADVANCE IN THE SOUTH

At the beginning of 1942 the only Ju 88 bomber unit on the southern sector was KG 51, whose three *Gruppen* were based at Tiraspol, Zaporozhe and Nikolayev, respectively. The south had not escaped counter-attack by the Red Army during the winter months, and elements of Oberst Paul Koester's *Geschwader* had already covered the withdrawal of German troops from Rostov back to the River Mius line during the closing weeks of 1941. Now Soviet amphibious landings around Kerch, on the easternmost tip of the Crimea, were jeopardising German operations elsewhere on the peninsula, which had still not yet been fully conquered.

In order to help alleviate the situation, the Luftwaffe hastily set up the *Sonderstab Krim* (Special Staff Crimea) in mid-January 1942. Tasked primarily with 'the interdiction of Soviet supply and troop movements on to the Crimea by sea and by ice road and the bombing of troop assemblies and concentrations, particularly around Kerch, but also in the rear areas', the *Sonderstab's* striking power comprised two *Stukagruppen* and three *Kampfgruppen*, one of the latter being the Nikolayev-based III./KG 51.

A celebration of another kind. Not the 60th operation of another II./KG 3 aircraft as might at first glance be supposed, but the 600th machine repaired and restored to service by a field maintenance unit, whose members have gathered around to mark the occasion

The history of the *Sonderstab* was to be brief and undistinguished. Among the main factors it had to contend with were the appalling weather conditions over the eastern Crimea at this time. Heavy snowfalls alternating with low cloud or extensive ground fog severely hampered operations. The intense cold and snow also played havoc with the poorly equipped ground organisation. Serviceability figures plunged alarmingly. At one point III./KG 51 reported just four of its machines operational.

The *Gruppe's* troubles were further compounded when, after only four days, it was temporarily despatched northwards to help repulse a major Soviet counter-offensive around Izyum, a town on the River Donetz south of Kharkov. When it resumed operations over the Crimea, it did so not from Nikolayev, but from Saki, a small, unprepared strip close to the western coast of the peninsula itself. On 11 February Reichsmarschall Göring ordered the dissolution of the *Sonderstab Krim*, and it was with relief that the crews of III./KG 51 returned to Nikolayev.

It was while III. *Gruppe* was engaged in the Izyum operations that KG 51 won its second Knight's Cross of the war, awarded on 24 January to Feldwebel Georg Fanderl of 1. *Staffel*. Among the long-serving Fanderl's many achievements was a daring low-level attack on an aircraft factory in the UK and the damaging of a large British troop transport in Suda Bay, Crete, the latter despite his Ju 88 having suffered numerous hits and being about to crash (he would spend 17 hours in a dinghy before being picked up). More recently Fanderl had been credited with sinking the Soviet Black Sea Fleet's 6934-ton cruiser *Krasny Krim* in Sevastopol harbour, although Russian records do not substantiate this claim.

On the day of Fanderl's award I./KG 51 was withdrawn from operations for rest and re-equipment at Odessa. In the weeks ahead Oberst Koester's two remaining *Gruppen* would find themselves fully stretched meeting the many demands made upon their services over both the Ukraine and the Crimea. Even after the disbandment of the *Sonderstab Krim* in mid-February, III./KG 51 would continue to operate in and around the area of the Crimea. Their targets were mainly the

A *Staffel* of KG 51 machines in tight formation low over the rolling landscape of the central Crimea

Soviet vessels, naval and merchant, that were supporting and supplying the two Soviet enclaves still holding out on the peninsula, Sevastopol in the west and Kerch in the east.

On 24 February the *Gruppe* was ordered to attack the elderly battleship *Parizhskaya Kommuna* – sister-ship of the Baltic Fleet's *Oktyabrskaya Revolutsiya* – which had been bombarding German coastal positions near Sevastopol. The eight Ju 88s failed to find the 25,464-ton battleship, but did report damaging a heavy cruiser in the same area. Five days later III./KG 51 was in action over the other, eastern end of the peninsula bombing Soviet troops attempting to break out of their Kerch beach-head – a mission from which an 8. *Staffel* Ju 88 failed to return.

Although it was the anti-shipping sorties that were taking up by far the greater part of the *Gruppe's* time and energies, somebody in the corridors of power was clearly not impressed by their performance to date. On 14 March a Ju 88 coded '4D+KM' touched down at Nikolayev. It was the aircraft of KG 30's Hauptmann Werner Baumbach, who had been sent by Oberst Dietrich Peltz to assess III./KG 51's capabilities and, at the same time, impart some of his own knowledge and anti-shipping expertise to the unit. Baumbach wasted little time in familiarising himself with local conditions, flying his first mission with the *Gruppe* over the waters south of the Crimea the very next day.

On 18 March Baumbach accompanied a small formation of Ju 88s led by *Gruppenkommandeur* Major Ernst *Freiherr* von Bibra in an attack on the port of Novorossisk. Despite heavy anti-aircraft fire, they succeeded in damaging a 4629-ton tanker, but an attack on ships in Sevastopol harbour 48 hours later was thwarted by poor weather. A series of raids on Tuapse, however, brought better results. Like Novorossisk, Tuapse was an important Soviet naval base on the Black Sea's Caucasus coastline. The first raid was carried out on 23 March by nine aircraft, with Baumbach in the lead. Their bombs straddled many of the warships berthed in the harbour, although there are conflicting reports on their actual successes. Claims included two minelayers, one motor torpedo boat and one submarine sunk at their moorings, and two other submarines damaged.

The following day a second attack on the same target resulted in the sinking of a tanker and a submarine depot ship. According to one account, this was the last mission in which Baumbach took part – he had seen enough. After returning to the Reich he reported on his findings. Laying the blame for KG 51's recent poor anti-shipping record on the weather and a shortage of equipment, he dismissed any suggestions of lack of resolve on the part of the crews as being totally baseless.

A final raid on Tuapse on 26 March resulted in damage to a large tanker and a harbour tug at the cost of one 7. *Staffel* crew reported missing. III./KG 51 withdrew to Odessa for seven weeks' rest and re-equipment shortly thereafter. At the same time I. *Gruppe*, its period of refit at Odessa completed, moved up to join II./KG 51 at Zaporozhe. It thus fell to these two *Gruppen* to continue anti-shipping operations over the Black Sea. They suffered losses in the process, including a Ju 88 from 5. *Staffel* that failed to return from a mission on 21 April, during which a transport was sunk and a minesweeper damaged.

April had also seen two more Knight's Crosses for KG 51. Both went to pilots with a wealth of combat experience and a string of successful operations behind them. The first recipient, Hauptmann

Rudolf Henne, the *Staffelkapitän* of 9./KG 51, had already amassed 200 missions flying with the *Legion Condor* in Spain. His award was announced on 12 April. 24 hours later Oberleutnant Helmut Klischat of 2. *Staffel* was similarly honoured.

Not all missions ran smoothly. Groundcrew inspect the damage after 6./KG 51's '9K+BP' landed back at base on 21 March 1942 with its port engine nacelle, wing and undercarriage all showing the effects of a near miss from an anti-aircraft shell. Note that the machine's tailwheel is still retracted, and that it has come to rest on the fuel jettison outlet/ emergency tailskid fairing

A stick of bombs from an aircraft of III./KG 51 goes down on Tuapse harbour, narrowly missing a row of eight Soviet submarines. This photograph is believed to have been taken during the raid of 23 March 1942, which resulted in the sinking of the 2121-ton auxiliary minelayer *Nikolai Ostrovsky*, the tug *Veshilov*, a small survey vessel (the GS.13) and an unidentified cutter. Two submarines, the D 5 and the S 33, were also damaged

Important though KG 51's anti-shipping activities undoubtedly were, the outcome of any military campaign – and the eastern front was no exception – is determined and decided by the actions of the armies in the field. So in May 1942, with the opposing sides both preparing for their summer offensives, the emphasis of the ground fighting, and with it the supporting operations of the Ju 88 units, began to shift inland.

By 17 May the last Soviet troops had been driven back off the Kerch beachhead. That same day the Red Army's counter-thrust at Izyum exploded into the ferocious 12-day battle for Kharkov that threatened to endanger the stability of the southern sector. All three of KG 51's *Gruppen* at Zaporozhe (III./KG 51 had flown in from Odessa two days earlier) were thrown into the breach around Kharkov. They were in the air almost without pause from dawn till dusk, logging almost 300 individual sorties in one two-day period alone at the height of the battle.

Also heavily involved over the Kharkov area were II. and III./KG 76, the two *Gruppen* that had formed the nucleus of the now defunct *Gefechtsverband* Bormann. They had been transferred down from the central sector earlier in the month to assist KG 51 in clearing the Kerch Peninsula. Together, the five *Gruppen* of Ju 88s played a significant role in helping to smash the Soviet counter-offensive around Kharkov. 29 Red Army divisions were wiped out in the fighting, together with 14 armoured or motorised brigades. Nearly a quarter-of-a-million enemy troops were taken prisoner and 1250 tanks and over 2000 artillery pieces either captured or destroyed. The threat to Army Group South's left flank had been eliminated and the way was now clear for Hitler's own summer offensive. Yet there was one last potential thorn in his side that had to be dealt with first – the fortress harbour of Sevastopol was still holding out on the southwestern tip of the Crimea.

It was for this very purpose that General von Richthofen's VIII. *Fliegerkorps* had also been brought down from the central sector. To provide additional firepower for his close-support Stukas, von Richthofen's command was to be reinforced temporarily by six *Kampfgruppen*, all but one of which were equipped with Ju 88s. I. and III./KG 51 thus departed Kharkov-West for the Crimea, where they were again to operate alongside II. and III./KG 76. The fifth Ju 88 *Gruppe* assigned to von Richthofen was III./LG 1, which had been in Germany since its withdrawal from the Mediterranean theatre at the end of 1941.

Summer 1942 in the Crimea, and the pilot of 8./KG 51's '9K+GS' runs up his engines and starts to roll. In this excellent close-up shot of the business end of a Ju 88, the additional 20 mm MG FF cannon (painted white) projecting from the ventral gondola is clearly visible

The battle to take the reputedly impregnable fortress of Sevastopol opened on 2 June with the heaviest artillery bombardment yet seen on the eastern front. It was accompanied throughout the hours of daylight by bombing raids flown by every aircraft available to VIII. *Fliegerkorps*. For the four *Gruppen* of KGs 51 and 76 it was a repetition of the Kharkov operations of just two weeks before. The one big difference was that they no longer had to make a 160-mile approach flight to the target area (most of

An armourer of I./KG 51 takes a well-earned breather in the Crimean sun while his charge ('9K+BL') gets a last-minute check-over. The bombs are standard 'SC' (general purpose) types as indicated by the horizontal yellow stripe painted between the fins

their Kharkov missions having been mounted from Zaporozhe). Sevastopol lay little more than 40 miles away from their new Crimean bases around Sarabuz. This meant that the Ju 88s could each fly three or four separate sorties before they needed refuelling. The crews remained in their aircraft the whole time – even during the brief periods on the ground while the machines were being bombed up again – and were able to take a break only in those intervals when the fuel tanks required refilling.

III./LG 1 was also fully committed, its specific task being to maintain standing patrols over the battle area ready to deal with any particularly troublesome anti-aircraft batteries or field artillery positions impeding the advance of the ground troops. Nor did the vessels of the Soviet Black Sea Fleet escape the destruction being rained down on Sevastopol. Ships continued to run the gauntlet to deliver reinforcements and supplies to the fortress's hard-pressed defenders. On 10 June Ju 88s sank the 1686-ton destroyer *Svobodny* and the 4727-ton auxiliary transport *Abkhaziya*, and damaged the small 441-ton 'Tral' class minesweeper T.413.

The one outstanding achievement by a Ju 88 pilot during the battle for Sevastopol was undoubtedly the single-handed sinking of a huge anti-aircraft raft by Oberleutnant Ernst Hinrichs of 2./KG 51. This craft – 'Floating Anti-aircraft Battery No 3', to give it its proper title – was moored in Severnaya Bay, close to the Sevastopol lighthouse on Cape Kherson. Its 164 anti-aircraft guns dominated the south-western approaches to Sevastopol harbour.

A pair of III./KG 51 machines ('9K+DS' in the foreground, '9K+FR' to the rear) pictured above the *Tafelberg* (Table Mountain) near Simferopol in the Crimea

Not unnaturally, most Luftwaffe pilots tried to steer well clear of this hornet's nest. However, on the evening of 19 June Hinrichs and his *Staffelkapitän* took off from Sarabuz with the express intention of putting the flak raft out of action once and for all. Hinrichs was the first to dive on the target, the plan being for him to throw the enemy gunners off their aim and so allow his *Kapitän* a clear run. In the event, Hinrichs himself scored a direct hit. The raft quickly

An aircraft of KG 51 is refuelled between shuttle raids on Sevastopol

An almost vertical shot of Sevastopol harbour taken from a machine of III./KG 76

began to sink and the explosion of the tons of ammunition stored in its magazines did the rest.

There were many witnesses to the series of enormous detonations that marked its end. Among them was General von Richthofen himself, who happened to be aloft nearby in his Fieseler Storch. The General was so impressed by Hinrichs' feat that he immediately recommended him for the Knight's Cross. Quite by chance, it was on this very date that a Knight's Cross was awarded to 4./KG 76's Oberleutnant Benno Herrmann. Oberleutnant Ernst Hinrichs did not have to wait long for his – it was presented to him just over a month later, on 25 July.

The reduction of Sevastopol, which was to have taken only four days, in fact lasted that many weeks and more. Towards its end the problem of supply shortages – especially of bombs and ammunition – was once again becoming acute. So desperate was the situation that the Ju 88s were no longer permitted to salvo their bombs. Each had to be carefully aimed and released singly. This meant that in the course of one day's operations pilots were being required to make as many as 32 separate dives.

Despite such difficulties Sevastopol finally fell on 1 July. By then Hitler's great 1942 summer offensive on the southern sector was all of three days old. Initially code-named 'Fall Blau' ('Case Blue'), it had been launched at 0215 hrs on 28 June. Its aim was the capture of the rich industrial areas along the lower reaches of the Rivers Don and Donetz and the extensive oilfields beyond. The first phase of the operation was completed in little more than a week. Then, in his Directive No 45 of 23 July 1942, the Führer ordered that the main axis of advance be split into two, with one army group being sent due east towards Stalingrad and the other striking southwards down into the oil-rich Caucasus.

The directive contained precise instructions for the Luftwaffe. The units supporting Army Group B were told that 'the early destruction of the city of Stalingrad is of paramount importance', whereas those covering Army Group A's drive south were warned that 'in view of the decisive importance of the oilfields of the Caucasus for the further prosecution of the war, air attacks against their refineries and storage tanks, and against ports used for oil shipments on the Black Sea, will only be carried out if the operations of the army make them absolutely essential'.

This division of ground forces already dangerously thinly stretched was to have dire consequences. For the Ju 88 units on the southern sector, however, it initially entailed little more than further redeployment.

For the first few days of the offensive those *Gruppen* recently involved against Sevastopol were to remain *in situ* in the Crimea, albeit now under the control of IV. *Fliegerkorps*. On 2 July *Gruppenkommandeur* Hanns Heise led his I./KG 76, together with the He 111s of I./KG 100, in a highly successful operation against ports along the Caucasus coast. The Soviet Black Sea Fleet's 2893-ton *Tashkent*, a destroyer flotilla leader that had recently made more than 40 round trips to Sevastopol in her temporary role as a fast transport, was sent to the bottom of Novorossisk harbour, as was the 1660-ton destroyer *Bditelny*. Three transport ships were also sunk, together with several smaller vessels.

A day or two later KG 76 was transferred up to the Voronezh area, where it was to form the nucleus of the newly established *Gefechtsverband Nord* (the 'Nord' in this instance referring not to the northern sector, but to the left-hand, or northernmost flank of Army Group South). Crews were greeted shortly after their arrival by heavy enemy air raids on their airfields. Despite suffering 'considerable losses', they were soon in action targeting rail junctions ahead of the advancing 4. *Panzerarmee*.

Immediately to their south the only unit now in the Kharkov area – jumping-off point for 6. *Armee's* drive on Stalingrad – was Hauptmann Otto Köhnke's II./KG 54, which had flown down from Bryansk, on the central sector, two weeks earlier. They were not to remain at Kharkov for long, however. Indicative perhaps of the growing confusion that was beginning to permeate the Luftwaffe High Command, II./KG 54 unexpectedly received orders on 8 July to transfer to northern France for operations over the UK, but its time at Beauvais was to be equally brief. Staying only long enough to lose four aircraft over southern England, and for Otto Köhnke to be awarded the Knight's Cross (on 1 August), the *Gruppe* was rushed back to the eastern front two weeks later.

The unit returned not to Kharkov, but to Shatalovka on the central sector. It was from here, using the airfields at Vyazma and Bryansk as forward landing grounds, that II./KG 54 conducted its final operations in the east. These were flown mainly in support of Army Group Centre's northern flank where the Russians were making strenuous efforts to break through the German front around Rzhev. Among the many casualties suffered by the *Gruppe* during this period was *Kommandeur* Hauptmann Otto Köhnke himself, who was severely injured in a deadstick landing on 27 September after both his engines had been knocked out by anti-aircraft fire. Köhnke lost a leg as a result of his injuries. He would subsequently hold various staff and training appointments before returning to active service as CO of the now infamous *Kommando* Elbe in the closing weeks of the war (see *Osprey Aviation Elite Units 20*).

II./KG 54 flew its last operation on the Russian front on 9 October. Four days later the *Gruppe* was ordered back to the Reich, prior to rejoining its parent *Geschwader* in the Mediterranean.

The Black Sea looks deceptively tranquil as a Ju 88 returns to base guided by the light of the evening sun

The Red Army made extensive use of armoured trains. This particular example has been put out of commission by a direct hit from a KG 51 bomb. The explosion has blown one of the train's turrets completely off

On the southernmost wing of the 1942 summer offensive 17. *Armee* had been tasked first with retaking Rostov – initially captured by German forces early in November 1941, only to be regained by the Russians before that same month was out – and then pushing on down into the Caucasus. To provide air cover for these operations the *Geschwaderstab* KG 51, under new *Kommodore* Major Wilhelm von Friedeburg, was transferred forward to Stalino, together with I. and III. *Gruppen*, on 10 July. II./KG 51 meanwhile was to remain at Zaporozhe.

This left Hauptmann Hermann Hogeback's III./LG 1 as the only Ju 88 *Gruppe* still operating over the Black Sea area, where it continued to fly anti-shipping missions as part of *Fliegerführer Süd*.

Within two days of its launch *'Fall Blau'* had been renamed Operation *'Braunschweig'* ('Brunswick'). In its early stages all went according to plan. As far as the Ju 88 *Kampfgruppen* were concerned this entailed KG 76 supporting the northern flank of the advance, and KG 51 the southern. Among the latter's early targets were the bridges over the Donetz and Don rivers. It was during one such mission on 12 July that Soviet fighters shot down the aircraft flown by Knight's Cross holder Oberleutnant Helmut Klischat. KG 51 next attacked the enemy's rail network beyond the Don and down into the Kalmyk Steppe of the northern Caucasus. Then, after the fall of Rostov on 23 July, the *Geschwader* began to strike at Soviet lines of communication deeper in the Caucasus.

It was also on 23 July that the hitherto combined southern offensive was divided into two separate and increasingly divergent lines of advance, one aimed at Stalingrad and the other at the oilfields of the Caucasus. As the attack on Stalingrad began to gain in importance, this in turn would lead to KG 51's previously clearly defined areas of operations becoming ever more blurred. One source maintains that the *Geschwader* was diverted from the southern regions to fly its first raid on Stalin's namesake city on 27 July, adding that it celebrated its 15,000th sortie of the war just two days later.

The first week of August brought further redeployment, with I. and III./KG 51 moving from Stalino down to Kerch, on the eastern tip of the Crimea. This placed them much nearer to their targets in the western Caucasus and to the enemy-held ports along its Black Sea coastline. Like most other Ju 88 *Kampfgeschwader* in Russia, KG 51 was now operating a small number of cannon-armed Ju 88C-6 heavy fighters, and these were employed to good effect against Soviet coastal shipping. However the two *Gruppen* were soon on the move again. On 19 August, after just a fortnight at Kerch, they were transferred – via Taganrog – to Tazinskaya, an airfield only 150 miles away from Stalingrad.

This meant that as German ground forces closed in on the city, all four of the southern sector's Ju 88 *Kampfgruppen* – I. and III./KG 51, and II. and III./KG 76 – would be operating in their support. Of the other two *Gruppen*, II./KG 51 was still at Zaporozhe and serving as a quasi maintenance unit for the rest of the *Geschwader*, while III./LG 1 – having been involved in brief action over the Caucasus and then being redesignated III./KG 6 – would be transferred to *Luftflotte* 1 before the end of August and thence back to the Reich for re-equipment.

During KG 51's period of engagement in the Caucasus, Oberst *Dr.Ing.* Ernst Bormann's KG 76 had been tasked with isolating Stalingrad from its rear area bases of supply and reinforcement. On 21 August they had caught two Red Army divisions in the open steppe some 100 miles to the east of the Volga and effectively wiped them out. Two days later, coincident with the launch of the final push on the city, crews of both KG 51 and KG 76 participated in the first major air raids mounted against Stalingrad.

It was during one of the early missions on 23 August that the Ju 88 flown by Major Ernst *Freiherr* von Bibra, the *Gruppenkommandeur* of III./KG 51, was hit by anti-aircraft fire and forced to make an emergency landing in enemy-held territory close to the River Chir. Seeing the Kommandeur's plight, Oberleutnant Werner Poppenburg of 7./KG 51 – von Bibra's old *Staffel* – landed alongside the crashed aircraft, packed its entire crew aboard his own machine and succeeded in taking off again before the Russians could intervene.

On 30 August the leading German troops broke through the ring of defences around Stalingrad. Heavy fighting raged throughout September as the Red Army withdrew into the city. Despite their many missions flown in support of the ground operations during this period, the Ju 88 *Gruppen* suffered remarkably few losses. Stalingrad's anti-aircraft defences were still relatively weak and ill coordinated (unlike the massed batteries that were later to exact such a terrible toll on the transport Ju 52/3ms attempting to airlift supplies into the then besieged city). In the first week of September two members of KG 76 had been decorated for outstanding leadership, Hauptmann Hanns Heise, the *Kommandeur* of I. *Gruppe*, receiving the Knight's Cross on 3 September, and the following day *Geschwaderkommodore* Oberst *Dr.Ing.* Ernst Bormann being presented with the Oak Leaves.

This sudden proliferation of awards – there were to be four in all in September and double that number in October – could not disguise the fact that the Ju 88 *Gruppen* on the Stalingrad front were by now in a parlous state. Worn down by the near constant round of dive-bombing missions and the unhealthy conditions they were living in, the crews of Major von Bibra's III./KG 51 were withdrawn to the Crimea on 28 September for a period of rest and recuperation. They were followed by I./KG 51 a

Crews of 7.(Eis)/KG 51 gather outside the ops room to while away the time between missions. On the original print of this photograph – taken in the Crimea, hence the proliferation of life-jackets – it can be seen that the solid nose of the C-6 heavy fighter in the background has been painted with fake transparencies to make it look like a bomber

III./KG 76 attacks the railway junction at Harlinskaya, north of Stalingrad

One of the early raids on the central railway station district of Stalingrad. Note the west bank of the River Volga running along the top of the picture and the still relatively undamaged state of most of the city's buildings. The strange 'gashes' scarring the street layout below the railway tracks are some of the *balkas*, or natural ravines, that were such a distinctive feature of the Stalingrad terrain

These groundcrew of KG 51 appear to be coping quite well with their second winter on the eastern front as they ready one of the *Geschwader's* aircraft for its next mission, against Rostov-on-Don, on 12 January 1943

week later. To fill the gap left by their departure, KG 1 was flown down from the northern sector.

Towards the end of October Stalingrad gained a brief respite when the Ju 88s redirected their attentions southwards again. On 25 October II./KG 51, which had joined its parent *Geschwader* in the Crimea, was moved down to Armavir in the Caucasus. From here – the deepest penetration KG 51 would make into the Soviet Union – it carried out raids on a number of targets, including Tuapse. Elements of KG 76 were also active in the same area, claiming the sinking of three merchant ships south of Tuapse on 4 November. But at about 2200 hrs that evening a small bomb from a Russian night harassment aircraft chanced to hit the huge fuel dump on the edge of Armavir airfield. The resulting fires quickly spread to the 'more than 100 Ju 88s and He 111s, many fully fuelled and armed', which packed the field. A tremendous amount of damage was caused. Only one machine of II./KG 51 remained unscathed and over the next few days the crews were returned – minus aircraft – to Bagerovo, in the Crimea, to await the arrival of replacements.

Early November was also to witness the end of KG 76's service on the eastern front. The *Geschwader's* sudden withdrawal from Russia was brought about by the Allied landings in northwest Africa on 8 November. With *Geschwaderkommodore* Oberst *Dr.Ing.* Ernst Bormann then recovering from illness, it fell to KG 51's Major Wilhelm von Friedeburg to take his place and lead KG 76 back to Germany for hurried 'tropicalisation' prior to its transfer to the Mediterranean theatre.

KG 1 disappeared from the Stalingrad front at about this same time when Major Hans Keppler was ordered to take his *Geschwader* back to the northern sector. This left just one Ju 88 *Gruppe* operating in direct support of the ground troops struggling to take the city. On 3 November I./KG 51, under recently appointed *Gruppenkommandeur* Major Fritzherbert 'Fritze' Dierich, had flown back in to Tazinskaya after its brief period of rest in the Crimea. However with the onset of winter the conditions that awaited crews – snow, icy winds and freezing temperatures – were even worse than before. They took to the air whenever the weather allowed, but a single *Gruppe* stood little chance of influencing the inevitable course of events. On 22 November two massive Soviet counter-offensives to the north and south of Stalingrad

linked up at Kalach on the Don, completely encircling the city and trapping Generaloberst Friedrich Paulus' 6. *Armee* within its ruins.

On 7 December I./KG 51 retired from Tazinskaya back to Rostov. The large, if underdeveloped expanses of Tazinskaya and Morosovskaya – soon dubbed 'Tazi' and 'Moro' – had been selected as the main termini for the airlift operations that Reichsmarschall Göring had rashly promised would keep the now besieged defenders of Stalingrad supplied with all their needs. During their first few days at Rostov Major Dierich's crews were engaged on missions aimed at helping shore up the crumbling Don front. They were even called upon to drop leaflets to Rumanian army units urging them not to retreat any further, all to no avail.

I./KG 51 was next tasked with supporting 4. *Panzerarmee's* attempt to break through to Stalingrad from the south. This was launched on 12 December and made good progress at first. Despite every effort, including III./KG 51's arrival at Rostov on 20 December to add its weight to the operation, this too ultimately ended in failure. Having fought to within 30 miles of the Stalingrad perimeter, 4. *Panzerarmee* could get no further. The relief effort had to be called off on 24 December. The city's fate was sealed. The newly promoted Generalfeldmarschall Paulus would surrender it, and the surviving 250,000 troops of his 6. *Armee*, to the Russians on 31 January 1943.

By that time, however, I. and III./KG 51 had long been ordered to turn their backs on the unfolding tragedy. They were now responsible for covering the retreat of the German forces streaming northwards out of the Caucasus. In this they were more successful, despite the mounting chaos and confusion that surrounded them. 'Everything went wrong, nothing worked any more. There was a lack of bombs, equipment, spare parts and fuel for the machines'.

Having to fly anything up to five low-level missions a day against Soviet troop columns resulted in a growing number of losses. On 3 January 1943 Oberst Heinrich Conrady had arrived at Rostov to take over the *Geschwader* from the departed Major von Friedeburg. Having spent the previous 14 months at the head of KG 3, Conrady was of the old school of bomber *Kommodores*, and one of the remaining few never to have undergone pilot training. Instead, it had become his custom during pre-op briefings before a mission to choose a crew with whom he would fly in the role of navigator-observer. Unfortunately, the crew he selected five days after assuming command of KG 51 was that of 6. *Staffel's* Oberleutnant

Few, if any, train-busting *Staffeln* took such elaborate care in painting the noses of their C-6 heavy fighters as did 4.(Eis)/KG 76. Here the fake glazing has even been carried down on to the ventral gondola. This somewhat weather-beaten machine also wears the *Staffel* badge, first introduced in 1940 for operations over England, but now decidedly anachronistic in the depths of a Russian winter more than two years later. It depicts a defecating goose wearing a British tin hat, smoking Churchill's cigar and carrying Chamberlain's umbrella, all centred behind a bombsight...

...which can be seen in much greater detail in this close-up shot of one of 4./KG 76's earlier A-5 bombers. The snarling face at the pilot's window was presumably the *Staffel* mascot!

The irrepressible Oberleutnant Alfons 'Ali' Berger, *Staffelkapitän* of 1./KG 51, whose many successes included 'one tank sunk'

Edwin Stöhr, whose '9K+AP' was downed in flames by flak. One source claims that this was the start of a run of 'particularly bad luck, with I. *Gruppe* alone losing 13 crews in the space of just three days'.

One of the last of the month's casualties was the popular Kapitän of 1. *Staffel*, Oberleutnant Alfons 'Ali' Berger, among whose successes was listed 'One tank sunk' – a cryptic reference to a Soviet armoured vehicle bombed while apparently attempting to negotiate the frozen shallows of the Sea of Azov. On 27 January, during a mission flown in support of an SS armoured division, one of 'Ali' Berger's engines was hit as he attacked a group of enemy tanks. Unable to control his machine, he attempted to make a belly landing, only for the aircraft to explode just seconds before he touched down.

AFTERMATH

On 31 January 1943, the day Generalfeldmarschall Friedrich Paulus surrendered Stalingrad, the six Ju 88 *Kampfgruppen* remaining on the Russian front together mustered a total of exactly 88 serviceable aircraft. The battle of Stalingrad has long been regarded as the turning point of the war in the east, but it also marked the beginning of the end of the Ju 88's career as a bomber on the eastern front. For of those six *Gruppen* operational in Russia on 31 January 1943, just one *Gruppe* and one *Staffel* – 20 serviceable machines in all – would remain by year end. The story of the Ju 88's rapid decline is perhaps best and most clearly described if each of the three main sectors is taken in turn.

The northern sector was the first to lose the services of the Ju 88, with *Luftflotte* 1 bidding farewell to the last elements of the long-resident KG 1 in April 1943. After re-equipping in the Reich, Hauptmann Werner Kanther's III./KG 1 had returned to Dno, southwest of Lake Ilmen, in late January. During February it was to operate primarily against the enemy's lines of communication in the Volkhov, Staraya Russa and Cholm areas, before being joined briefly by the *Geschwaderstab* and I. *Gruppe* in the latter half of March. It was at Dno on 18 March that Major Horst von Riesen, hitherto the *Gruppenkommandeur* of II./KG 1, took over command of the *Geschwader* from Major Heinrich Lau.

Throughout March and into April KG 1's units kept up their attacks – mainly by night – on the Soviet rail network, concentrating on the stretch of line between Volkhov and Tichwin. But on 7 April I. *Gruppe* was ordered back to Germany to refit and, less than three weeks later, III./KG 1 was transferred down to the central sector. The latter's departure from Dno on 26 April marked the end of Ju 88 bomber operations in the north.

On the southern sector the Ju 88 would remain in service with *Luftflotte* 4 throughout 1943, albeit only in single *Gruppe* strength during the latter half of the year. After covering the retreat of Axis forces out of the Caucasus back across the lower Don in January 1943, both I. and III./KG 51 had themselves been forced to vacate Rostov on 5 February in the face of the approaching enemy. The two *Gruppen* retired to Zaporozhe to rejoin II./KG 51. Upon their arrival they took over II. *Gruppe's* aircraft, the latter then being withdrawn from service to rest and refit.

Zaporozhe was to provide only a temporary haven from the oncoming Soviet tide. I. and III./KG 51's primary purpose now was to try to halt the advance of the enemy's armoured spearheads. At one point Russian tanks were reported to be less than ten miles from the field's perimeter. When, on 15 February, an SS *Panzerkorps* gave up Kharkov without a fight – and against Hitler's strict instructions – Major Klaus Häberlen's I. *Gruppe* was ordered to support the same corps in recapturing this important industrial and communications centre. It would take a full month, even with the help of I./KG 1 brought down from the central sector especially for the purpose.

Meanwhile III./KG 51 had resumed their activities in support of the ground troops still attempting to extricate themselves from the Caucasus, either by retreating back over the Don or by retiring into the Kuban bridgehead just across the narrow Straits of Kerch from the eastern Crimea. At first III. *Gruppe* continued to operate out of Zaporozhe, only to lose its long-serving *Kommandeur* and recent Knight's Cross recipient Major Ernst *Freiherr* von Bibra, who failed to return from a mission on 15 February. It was therefore under new *Kommandeur* Hauptmann Wilhelm Rath that III./KG 51 transferred down to Bagerovo, in the Crimea, on 27 February.

It was joined there by I./KG 51 just over a month later, and together the two *Gruppen* carried out yet more operations over the Caucasus. The Ju88C-6 heavy fighters of 7. *Staffel* – more accurately 7.(Eis)/KG 51 – were particularly successful against the Soviet rail network in the region. Another weapon to prove its worth during this period was the tiny 2 kg SD 2 'Butterfly' bomb, smaller cousin to the SD 10 fragmentation bomb that had proved such a hazard to Ju 88 crews at the very start of *Barbarossa*. Dropped from higher altitudes in an AB 23 container,

Future Knight's Cross recipient Major Klaus Häberlen, the *Gruppenkommandeur* of I./KG 51, proudly holds the placard indicating his 300th operational mission, flown on 17 April 1943. Life jackets, such as the early kapok style being worn here by Häberlen and two of his crew, were essential items of equipment for overwater operations from the Crimea. Note the 20 mm MG FF cannon mounted in the ventral gondola

One of just six Ju 88 *Kampfgruppen* still operating on the Russian front come January 1943, II./KG 3 was subordinated to *Luftwaffenkommando Don*

Widely dispersed against air attack on a desolate expanse of snow, this shot of III./KG 1 machines early in 1943 – probably at Dno – neatly encapsulates the two enemies faced by the Luftwaffe in Russia – the Red Air Force and the weather. Note the bomb visible beneath the wing centre-section of 'V4+CT' in the foreground. From the unit's loss tables it is apparent that at this time 9.(Eis)/KG 1 was operating both C-6 heavy fighters *and* standard A-4 bombers

Mission completed, smiling crewmen of III./KG 51, wearing a mix of kapok and inflatable life jackets, make their way past the unit standard at Sarabuz, in the Crimea, in May 1943

these 'devilish little devices' inflicted heavy casualties on the Red Army units chasing hot on the heels of the retreating Germans.

Then, on 19 April, I./KG 51 was suddenly sent to Poltava, in the Ukraine. There, after almost three weeks of near inactivity, the *Gruppe* received notice of an even more surprising transfer. On 8 May it was to return to the Reich to begin conversion onto the Me 410.

At the same time both II. and III./KG 51 (the former now back on operations) were despatched up to Bryansk on the central sector. On the way they lost their *Kommodore*. Major Egbert von Frankenberg und Proschlitz had taken over the *Geschwader* from Oberst Conrady back in January. His non-arrival at Bryansk on 9 May raised some questions. Had he fallen victim to enemy action, or perhaps been forced down behind enemy lines by mechanical failure of some sort? A third alternative, that he had deliberately landed in Soviet territory, was at first dismissed out of hand.

Yet within days the good Major's voice was heard on Radio Moscow exhorting German troops not to lay down their lives 'for a criminal regime', but to come over to the Russians and build for themselves a peaceful, socialist life in the east. Any lingering doubts as to where von Frankenberg's true loyalties lay were dispelled when it was learned that he had become one of the founding members of the 'National Committee of Free Germany' and co-founder of the 'Association of German Officers' in the Soviet Union – both of which organisations would later play a major role in establishing the government of post-war East Germany.

KG 51's two *Gruppen* were replaced on the southern sector by I. and II./KG 3, and it was the latter two units which would provide the Ju 88 presence along the southern shoulder of the Kursk salient during Operation *Zitadelle* two months later. However the premature collapse of Hitler's armoured counter-offensive around Kursk in mid-July led to further reduction and redeployment of the *Kampfgruppen* in the east.

Late in August – in the aftermath of the historic battle of Kursk – the *Gruppen* of KGs 3 and 51 again exchanged places, with I. and II./KG 3 returning to the central sector and II./KG 51 resuming operations around Kirovograd in the south. It was not long, however, before this last unit was on the move again. On 18 September II./KG 51 was unexpectedly transferred to Salonika, in Greece, to participate

in the recapture of the Dodecanese Islands in the eastern Mediterranean. This in turn resulted in I./KG 3's hasty recall from the central front to fill the void left by II./KG 51's departure.

The dozen or so serviceable machines of I./KG 3 would thus be the only Ju 88 bombers contesting the Red Army's advance through the Ukraine for much of the last quarter of 1943. It was not until II./KG 51's return from the Mediterranean at the end of November that I./KG 3 was taken off operations for a well-earned rest and refit. II./KG 51's final stint in Russia was to be even briefer than its recent foray down into Greece. After supporting the ground fighting around Zhitomir and Cherkassy during December, Major Herbert Voss's *Gruppe* was pulled back to Vinnitsa on 4 January 1944 and thence – via Lublin, in Poland – to the west, where it joined the rest of KG 51 in converting to the Me 410.

Thus, by the winter of 1943/44, the Ju 88 bomber had disappeared entirely from both the northern and southern sectors of the Russian front, but what of events on the central sector following the loss of Stalingrad?

Since the transfer of *Luftflotte* 2 to the Mediterranean at the end of 1941, the central sector had undergone a succession of command changes. Responsibility for the area had first been assumed by VIII. *Fliegerkorps*, which had in turn been replaced by *Luftwaffenkommando Ost* (the ex-V. *Fliegerkorps*) in April 1942. Four months later a new command – *Luftwaffenkommando Don* (the temporarily redesignated I. *Fliegerkorps*) – had then been inserted into the widening gap between *Lw.Kdo.Ost* and *Luftflotte* 4 to its immediate south. It was not until 6 May 1943, 18 months after the withdrawal of *Luftflotte* 2, that the central sector would again be controlled by an Air Fleet, this being the date when *Lw.Kdo.Ost* was officially retitled *Luftflotte* 6.

At the time of its creation *Luftflotte* 6 had just one Ju 88 *Kampfgruppe* under its command. This was Hauptmann Werner Kanther's III./KG 1, which had flown in to Sechinskaya from the northern sector ten days earlier, but the Air Fleet's Ju 88 strength was soon bolstered by the arrival at Bryansk of both II. and III./KG 51 (on 8 and 10 May respectively) from the south.

Throughout May and June the three *Gruppen* operated mainly over the Kursk and Voronezh areas, flying dusk and night missions against Red Army troop concentrations and their rear area lines of supply. The Ju 88s also took part in several nocturnal raids of a more strategic nature during this period. Among the targets they attacked were the tank factory and iron foundries at Gorki, east of Moscow, on 2 June and the Yaroslavl chemical works north of the Soviet capital 18 days later. A number of crews were reported missing during these operations, and KG 51 was fortunate not to lose its new *Kommodore* in a night raid on Yelets, to the northeast of Kursk, at this time. Major Hanns Heise's aircraft was severely damaged, but he managed to nurse it back to friendly territory before he and his crew took to their parachutes.

As June drew to a close the three Ju 88 *Gruppen* began to mount daylight army support missions over the Kursk-Orel regions in preparation for Hitler's forthcoming counter-offensive. Launched on 5 July, Operation *Zitadelle* was the *Führer's* last great gamble in the east. Most accounts of the Luftwaffe's role in the battle of Kursk rightly concentrate on the activities of the ground-attack units. However from

The summer storm clouds gather as the battle of Kursk approaches. Its outcome will herald the virtual end of Ju 88 bomber operations on the Russian front

The premature ending of *Zitadelle* did not mean an end to the casualties. This partially night-camouflaged machine of III./KG 51 – '9K+XS'? – was lucky to make it back to Krimskaya for a belly-landing after an anti-aircraft burst had mangled its starboard wing and tailplane on 29 July 1943

their bases on the northern flank of the Kursk salient – III./KG 1 having transferred from Sechinskaya to Orel-West on 9 June – the Ju 88 crews played no less important a part in *Zitadelle*, flying day and night against artillery positions, tank assembly areas, troop columns and truck convoys. The Ju 88C-6 heavy fighters of 9.(Eis)/KG 1 and 7.(Eis)/KG 51 proved particularly effective against these latter targets (their performance being mirrored by the C-6s of 6.(Eis)/KG 3 currently operating in similar fashion along the southern shoulder of the salient).

The abandonment of *Zitadelle* after little more than a week of fighting – a move brought about by a combination of events in the Mediterranean and, closer to home, a major Russian counter-attack around Orel on the northern flank of the Kursk 'bulge' – led to all three central sector Ju 88 *Kampfgruppen* retiring to Sechinskaya before July was out. It was only now, at this late stage of the air war in the east, that the decision was finally taken to concentrate the Luftwaffe's bomber forces under one command and employ them 'as an instrument of strategic aerial warfare'. Hitherto, it was estimated, they had been flying 80 per cent of their operations in direct or indirect support of the ground forces over the battlefield. Now three complete *Kampfgeschwader* were to be sent back to rear area bases in Poland for training in their new role.

Ironically, this decision drove another nail into the coffin of the Ju 88's bombing career on the Russian front for the new eastern strategic bomber force was to be composed primarily of units flying the venerable He 111, whereas the remaining Ju 88 *Gruppen* were either to be transferred to other theatres for operations against the western Allies, or temporarily withdrawn from service for re-equipment with newer types of aircraft.

This new policy resulted in fundamental changes on the central sector in the weeks following *Zitadelle*. By the end of August II./KG 51 had been despatched back to the southern sector, and III./KG 51 returned to the Reich for conversion onto the Me 410. Meanwhile, two of III./KG 1's *Staffeln* had departed by rail for Flensburg in northern Germany, where they were to re-equip with the Ju 88P-1.

Armed with a seven-round 75mm Pak 40L anti-tank gun in a large ventral gondola, this variant of the Ju 88 was intended specifically for the tank-busting role. In the event, III. *Gruppe* never completed their planned conversion and KG 1 ended its war flying four-engined He 177s.

To fill the gap thus left on the central front, I. and II. *Gruppen* of Oberst Walter Lehwess-Litzmann's KG 3 were flown back up from the south, and the only *Staffel* of KG 1 still operating out of Sechinskaya, Hauptmann Wilhelm Wölfing's 9.(Eis)/KG 1, was placed under their command. Coincidentally, the then Major Lehwess-Litzmann had led III./KG 1's for the first four months of *Barbarossa*, but the train-busters of 9. *Staffel* had little opportunity to get to know their erstwhile *Kommandeur*, for on 7 September

Oberst Lehwess-Litzmann's machine crashed shortly after taking off from Sechinskaya. Ending up in Russian captivity, he too was apparently 'turned', for he also joined the Soviet-sponsored 'National Committee of Free Germany' and was later an important figure in the development of military and civil aviation in post-war East Germany.

Lehwess-Litzmann's aircraft was just one of a number of Sechinskaya-based machines lost in recent weeks. Most had simply been listed as 'failed to return', but when several were seen inexplicably to explode in mid-air, an investigation was carried out. It was discovered that Soviet partisans had infiltrated the ranks of the many Russian civilian volunteers performing menial duties about the airfield and had been attaching explosive charges, fitted with barometric pressure switches, to the Ju 88s' rear fuselage fuel tanks during the hours of darkness prior to missions.

The *Stab* and I./KG 3 were withdrawn to Terespol, in Poland, later in September to begin training for their new strategic role (the only Ju 88-equipped *Kampfgeschwader* so to do). For the next two months there were thus just four Ju 88 *Staffeln* in action on the central sector – the A-4 bombers of 4. and 5./KG 3 and the C-6 heavy fighters of 6.(Eis)/KG 3 and 9.(Eis)/KG 1. When, in the closing weeks of 1943, the former pair was also ordered back to Terespol, it heralded the end of the Ju 88 bomber on the Russian front.

After spending the first quarter of 1944 in Poland under the *Auffrischungsstab Ost* (literally 'Regeneration Staff East', the command charged with creating the eastern front's new strategic bomber force), some elements of KG 3 did reappear briefly on IV. *Fliegerkorps'* order of battle towards the end of April. Despite this seeming return to operations, however, Major Fritz Auffhammer's *Geschwaderstab* and II./KG 3 were still at Terespol, while I. *Gruppe* had simply been moved to nearby Byala

The Ju 88C-6 heavy fighters of 6.(Eis)/KG 3 were particularly active along the southern flank of the Kursk 'bulge'

Podlaska. The following month these units were all transferred to Baranowicze, in eastern Poland. But it is doubtful whether they were able to conduct any of the strategic missions they had been training for. All indications are that they were instead employed for the next two weeks in support of the retreating ground troops, before being returned to the Reich early in June. Here, III./KG 3 was re-equipped and redesignated to become I./KG 53, and the rest of the *Geschwader* was disbanded.

An even more unlikely Ju 88 presence on the eastern front during April and May 1944 was that of 4./KG 26, whose dozen or so Ju 88A-17 torpedo-bombers had been ordered down from northern Germany to Focsani and Zilistea, in Rumania. The evacuation of

German forces now cut off on the Crimea was currently underway and the mission of Hauptmann Rudi Schmidt's *Staffel* was 'constantly to monitor the sea areas between the Caucasus and the Crimea, and along Rumania's Black Sea coast, and to engage Soviet warships in these areas'.

Despite complying with these orders to the letter by keeping four aircraft in the air at all times, the *Staffel* was unable to claim any successes. Not a single enemy warship was sighted in the prescribed areas, and although there was a lot of Soviet merchant shipping off the coast of the Caucasus, Schmidt's pilots were forbidden to attack these targets due to the severe shortage of torpedoes. They had to content themselves with escorting their own transports during the final stages of the Crimean evacuation until their recall to the German Baltic coast in mid-May.

With the exception of 4./KG 26's short foray down to the Black Sea, and KG 3's equally brief return to frontline service in Poland, the only Ju 88 'bombers' operational on the eastern front in 1944 were not, in fact, bombers at all, but a single *Staffel* of Ju 88C-6 heavy fighters.

In January 1944 the two train-busting *Staffeln* on the central sector, 9.(Eis)/KG 1 and 6.(Eis)/KG 3, had been amalgamated to form 14.(Eis)/KG 3. If the intention behind this move was to create a powerful railway interdiction strike force, it fell far short of expectations. During its ten-month existence the combined *Staffel's* serviceable strength rarely, if ever, reached double figures. It was normally around seven, but at times dropped as low as four. Given these totals it is clear that 14.(Eis)/KG 3 could do little to influence the course of events in the east. Although the crews, hunting singly or in pairs, continued to fly missions 'to the extreme limit of their ranges' deep into the enemy's hinterland, and continued to exact a steady toll of Soviet locomotives and rolling stock, the successes they achieved were purely local and much too limited to bring about any lasting disruption to the Russian rail supply network.

As the ground forces on the central sector retreated in the face of ever growing enemy pressure, so too did 14.(Eis)/KG 3. Based at Orsha, west of Smolensk, at the beginning of the year, it retired to Bobruisk in late March. The *Staffel* remained here until the Red Army's great summer offensive of 1944, unleashed on 22 June, drove them back across the width of Poland. Its 14 machines, exactly half of which were serviceable, last appeared on *Luftflotte 6*'s order of battle based at Graudenz on 15 October.

PIGGYBACK POSTSCRIPT

The operational history of the Ju 88 bomber units on the eastern front had thus lasted precisely one week short of 40 months. During that time the impressive force of Ju 88s gathered for the launch of *Barbarossa* – 18 *Kampfgruppen* in all, totalling 463 serviceable aircraft – had, as described above, dwindled to a single *Staffel* of just seven serviceable machines.

That was not quite the end of the story. In the chaotic closing weeks of the air war in the east the Ju 88 suddenly reappeared over the front. However, it was a very different kind of Ju 88 – unmanned, packed with explosives and with an ungainly trestle arrangement on its back, atop which was perched a single-engined fighter.

This strange contraption went under several names, including *'Huckepack'* ('Piggyback'), *'Vater und Sohn'* ('Father and Son') and *'Beethoven'*, but it was officially and most commonly referred to as the

'*Mistel*' ('Mistletoe') device. The composite aircraft concept was not new. Experiments along similar lines had been carried out in the 1930s in an effort to increase the ranges of passenger and mail aeroplanes, but it took the Luftwaffe to turn it into a weapon of war.

The first *Mistel* combination had been delivered to training *Staffel* 2./KG 101 in May 1944. A number of ambitious schemes had initially been proposed for the strategic employment of the weapon. Among the targets considered was the Royal Navy's anchorage at Scapa Flow, in the Orkneys, Gibraltar, Leningrad and several important power plants and industrial complexes deep inside the Soviet Union. Before any of these could be properly implemented, however, the realities of war intervened. On 1 February 1945 Russian tanks reached the River Oder, northwest of Küstrin, and less than 45 miles from Berlin. Within days the Red Army was massing its forces along the eastern bank of the river in preparation for the final assault on the German capital. There were more than 130 road and rail bridges across the Oder in front of the Berlin sector, and retreating German troops had managed to demolish just 12 of them.

In a desperate attempt to stave off the impending Soviet assault on his capital for as long as possible, Hitler ordered that every means available was to be used to destroy the remaining Oder bridges. The officer first charged with this daunting responsibility was Werner Baumbach – the same Werner Baumbach who had imparted his anti-shipping expertise to KG 51 in the Crimea three years earlier. The *Führer's* order of 1 March 1945 was a model of brevity. 'I authorise Oberstleutnant Baumbach, *Kommodore* of *Kampfgeschwader* 200, to combat all enemy crossings of the Oder and Neisse rivers'.

That same day Göring also appointed Baumbach to the post of *Fliegerführer* 200. This multiplicity of tasks – *Geschwaderkommodore*, then *Bevollmächtigter* (Supreme Commander) of Oder bridge operations and now *Fliegerführer* – was too much for one man to handle. Baumbach needed a deputy to oversee air operations against the river crossing points. This task landed in the lap of ex-Mediterranean Ju 88 bomber ace Oberst Joachim 'Jochen' Helbig, who currently commanded three of the last Junkers *Kampfgruppen* still active in the west – I. and II./LG 1 and II./KG 26. To these were now added the *Mistel*-equipped II./KG 200, plus a miscellany of other *Luftflotte* 6 units, the latter being attached on a temporary basis according to the day's operational requirements. This *ad hoc* force was to be known as the *Gefechtsverband* Helbig.

After a short spell of bad weather the first *Mistel* attack was made on 8 March 1945. It was carried out against two of the bridges spanning the Oder at Göritz, south of Küstrin, by four *Misteln* of the Burg-based II./KG 200. They were accompanied by five Ju 188s and a pair of Ju 88s, whose job was to suppress the bridges' anti-aircraft defences. Although hits were claimed on both structures, with 'wreckage visible in the water', neither was completely destroyed and the

This otherwise anonymous, scribble-camouflaged, Ju 88A-4 – all national markings (and yellow fuselage band?) blacked out for night operations – carries the fuselage code letters 'EH', repeated in small white characters on the exhaust flame damper shroud. Pictured in the winter of 1944/45, it is purportedly a machine of I./LG 1, which was one of the *Gruppen* that took part in the attacks on the Oder bridges during the closing weeks of the war

I./KG 66 employed examples of the improved Ju 88S variant – similar to the S-3 of an unidentified unit seen here late in 1944 – for pathfinding duties during many of the Oder bridge operations

Soviet build-up in front of Berlin suffered minimal disruption.

Over the course of the next three weeks numerous small-scale attacks were mounted against the Oder bridges by the various units assigned to Helbig's command. A wide variety of aircraft were employed in these missions, from single-engined fighters to Do 217s armed with Hs 293 guided bombs. During the night of 22 March eight Ju 88s of II./LG 1 attacked the bridges at Göritz and Neu-Rathstock, but they inflicted only superficial damage. It would be 31 March before the next *Mistel* mission. The target on this occasion was the railway bridge at Steinau, but only one of the six participating II./KG 200 *Misteln* was credited with a hit.

Early in April a second *Mistel* unit was placed under Helbig's control. In November 1944 KG 30, veteran of the Arctic convoy battles, had been redesignated as KG(J) 30. The 'J' indicated the *Geschwader's* intended conversion to a fighter unit. However a number of its pilots were selected to undergo special *Mistel* training at Prague-Ruzyn in preparation for one of the planned deep-penetration raids into the Russian Urals. The situation at the front put paid to this scheme, however, and the KG(J) 30 *Misteln* were now to be employed instead in an attack on targets in Poland to the rear of the Red Army massed along the Oder.

Scheduled for the night of 7/8 April, this complex operation was to be carried out by no fewer than 24 *Misteln*, equally divided between four airfields and supported both by the pathfinding Ju 88s of I./KG 66 and a force of He 111 'illuminators'. Operation *Weichselbrücken* (Vistula Bridges) was to be dogged by misfortune from the very start. On the afternoon of 7 April more than 100 B-17s of the USAAF's Eighth Air Force bombed Parchim airfield. The Americans were after the field's resident Me 262s, but the damage they caused had an added bonus – it prevented the six *Misteln* based there from taking off to attack the bridge over the River Vistula at Thorn (Torun).

Then, at two of the other bases, Oranienburg and Peenemünde, the leading *Misteln* were involved in take-off accidents, which blocked the runways and kept both the Deblin and Tarnow contingents firmly on the ground. Only at Rechlin did five of the six *Misteln* targeting Warsaw succeed in lifting off. One of these reportedly fell victim to a nightfighter *en route* to the objective, and three of the other pilots were forced by mechanical malfunctions to take to their parachutes. Just one pilot, a young oberfähnrich, managed to get through to the target area. He aimed the explosive-laden Junkers beneath his fighter at one of Warsaw's bridges – and missed.

Meanwhile, the Ju 88s of II./LG 1 were still trying to knock out the Oder crossings. On the night of 7 April 12 aircraft had attacked the bridges at Neu-Rathstock and Lebus-Northeast. The following night 13 machines targeted the spans at Göritz-North and Göritz-Central. The night after that they returned to Göritz-North and Göritz-South. The sum total of all their efforts was slight damage to several of the bridges and their approaches.

The next day, 10 April, the Eighth Air Force again struck at German airfields 'known or suspected of being used by jet enemy aircraft' and again they unwittingly dealt the *Mistel* force a heavy blow. The raid by 100+ B-24s on Rechlin-Lärz destroyed 18 *Mistel* composites on the ground. It is uncertain, however, to which exact unit these belonged as their loss was simply listed under *Fliegerführer* 200's combined casualty returns. 48 hours later a small formation of four *Misteln*, led by a Ju 88 pathfinder of I./KG 66, took off from Peenemünde to attack the railway bridge across the Oder at Küstrin. The results could not be observed, but all indications were that the mission had been unsuccessful.

It was on this same 12 April that the *Gefechtsverband* Helbig was withdrawn from the control of *Luftflotte* 6 and subordinated to the newly established (and extremely short-lived) *Luftwaffenkommando Nordost*. On paper this meant that Helbig's declining forces were now also responsible for destroying the bridges over the River Elbe and the Upper Danube as well. Such administrative niceties weighed little in the face of events on the ground, for on 16 April eight Soviet armies had stormed across the River Oder to begin the final assault on Berlin.

KG(J) 30 was to fly just two more missions in their attempts to delay the Red Army's advance. On 26 April seven *Misteln*, accompanied by a trio of Ju 188s, lifted off from Peenemünde to attack the six bridges still spanning the Oder at Küstrin. No hits were achieved and only two of the *Mistel* pilots made it back.

Then, on 30 April – the day Hauptmann Karl Peter's II./LG 1 was disbanded – the *Misteln* took to the air for the last time. Their objective was the Oder bridge at Tantow, south of Stettin. By the time they approached it, the tiny force of four composites had been reduced to three. With the target little more than six miles dead ahead, but hidden beneath a layer of low cloud, the leader of the group, Leutnant Dittmann, gave the signal to separate. Each pilot was to attack individually. Enemy anti-aircraft fire was ferocious. The lower component of Oberfeldwebel Braun's *Mistel* was soon a mass of flames, but he managed to release it and succeeded in returning to base. So too did Leutnant Dittmann, who reported on landing 'a column of smoke rising above the river'. The third pilot, Unteroffizier Seitz, disappeared without trace.

Eight days later the war in Europe was over.

A *Mistel* captured intact at war's end by the Red Army somewhere in eastern Germany. This particular composite is the S 1 version, which combined a Bf 109 fighter with a standard Ju 88A-4 bomber. Other variants (S 2, S 3, etc.) utilised an Fw 190 fighter as the upper component, coupled to a Ju 88G nightfighter below. Some Ju 88s – both A- and G-models – had hollow-charge warheads fitted in place of the normal crew cabin (see *Osprey Combat Aircraft 17*, page 82)

APPENDICES

REPRESENTATIVE Ju 88 BOMBER STRENGTHS
ON THE RUSSIAN FRONT 1941-44

A) 22 JUNE 1941 *BARBAROSSA*

Luftflotte 1 (Northern Sector)		Base	Est-Serv
II./KG 1	Hptm Otto Stams	Powunden	29-27
III./KG 1	Maj Walter Lehwess-Litzmann	Eichwalde	30-29
Stab KG 76	Oberst *Dr. Ing.* Ernst Bormann	Gerdauen	1-0
I./KG 76	Hptm von Sichart	Gerdauen	30-22
II./KG 76	Hptm Volprecht *Freiherr* Riedesel zu Eisenbach	Jürgenfelde	30-25
III./KG 76	Maj Franz von Benda	Schippenbeil	29-22
Stab/KG 77	Oberst Johann Raithel	Heiligenbeil	1-1
I./KG 77	(Hptm Joachim Poetter)	Jesau	30-23
II./KG 77	Hptm Dietrich Peltz	Wormditt	31-23
III./KG 77	Maj von Frankenberg	Heiligenbeil	29-20
KGr 806	Maj Hans Emig	Prowehren	30-18
Luftflotte 2 (Central Sector)			
Stab KG 3	Oberst Wolfgang von Chamier-Glisczinski	(Deblin)	2-2
I./KG 3	Maj Heinze	(Deblin)	41-32
II./KG 3	Hptm Kurd Peters	(Deblin)	38-32
Luftflotte 4 (Southern Sector)			
Stab KG 51	Maj Hans Bruno Schulz-Heyn	Krosno	2-2
I./KG 51	Hptm Heinrich Hahn	Krosno	22-22
II./KG 51	Hptm Max Stadelmeier	Krosno	36-29
III./KG 51	Maj Walter Marienfeld	Lezany	32-28
Stab KG 54	Obstlt Otto Höhne	Swidnik	1-1
I./KG 54	Hptm Richard Linke	Swidnik	34-31
II./KG 54	Maj Erhart Krafft von Dellmensingen	Swidnik	36-33
Luftflotte 5 (Arctic Front)			
I./KG 30	Maj Horst von Riesen	Banak	34-19
II./KG 30	Hptm Eberhard Roeger	Banak	31-22

Totals			**579-463**

B) 28 JUNE 1942 *BLAU*

Luftflotte 1 (Northern Sector)		Base	Est-Serv
II./KG 1	Maj Herbert Lorch	Dno	29-17
III./KG 1	Maj Hans Keppler	Dno	26-19
Luftwaffenkommando Ost (Central Sector)			
Stab KG 3	Oberst Heinich Conrady	Bryansk	2-1
I./KG 3	(Maj Günther Dörffel)	Rzhev	36-18
II./KG 3	Hptm Peter-Paul Breu	Bryansk	27-16
III./KG 3	(Maj Erich Rathmann)	(Bryansk)	29-20

Luftflotte 4 (Southern Sector)		Base	Est-Serv
Stab KG 51	Oberst Paul Koester	Zaporozhe	2-2
I./KG 54	Maj Hans-Joachim Ritter	Kharkov-West	32-26
II./KG 51	Hptm Rudolf Henne	Zaporozhe	33-19
III./KG 51	Maj Ernst *Freiherr* von Bibra	Kharkov-West	33-24
II./KG 54	Hptm Otto Köhnke	Kharkov	28-16
Stab KG 76	Oberst *Dr-Ing* Erst Bormann	Sarabuz	3-2
II./KG 76	Hptm Volprecht *Freiherr* Riedesel zu Eisenbach	Sarabuz	32-20
III./KG 76	?	Sarabuz	33-15
III./LG 1	Hptm Hermann Hogeback	(Crimea)	26-11
Luftflotte 5 (Arctic Front)			
I./KG 30	Hptm Konrad Kahl	Banak	36-28
II./KG 30	Hptm Erich Stoffregen	Banak	32-26
III./KG 30	Hptm Hajo Herrmann	Banak	36-32

Totals			**475-312**

C) 5 JULY 1943 *ZITADELLE*

Luftflotte 6 (Central Sector)		Base	Est-Serv
III./KG 1	Hptm Werner Kanther	Orel-West	29-17
Stab KG 51	Maj Hanns Heise	Bryansk	2-1
II./KG 51	Maj Herbert Voss	Bryansk	41-27
III./KG 51	Hptm Wilhelm Rath	Bryansk	22-15
Luftflotte 4 (Southern Sector)			
Stab KG 3	Oberst Walter Lehwess-Litzmann	Poltava	1-1
I./KG 3	(Hptm Heinz Laube)	Poltava	35-1
II./KG 3	(Hptm Fritz Rahe)	Poltava	37-27
Luftflotte 5 (Arctic Front)			
I./KG 30		?	
Banak		34-30	

Totals			**201-137**

D) 15 OCTOBER 1944

Luftflotte 6 (Central Sector)		Base	Est-Serv
14.(Eis)/KG 3	?	Graudenz	14-7

Totals			**14-7**

NOTE

Details in (brackets) are uncorroborated

COLOUR PLATES

1
Ju 88A-5 'V4+KS' of 8./KG 1, Eichwalde, East Prussia, June 1941
With all traces of the temporary black camouflage paint that had adorned its undersides during recent night operations over Great Britain now removed, and resplendent in freshly applied yellow eastern front markings, 8. *Staffel's* 'KS' is typical of the unit's machines during the opening rounds of *Barbarossa*. This may well be the 'V4+KS' (Wk-Nr. 8193) that was reported missing in action over the Lake Ilmen area on 16 July 1941, the aircraft having possibly fallen victim to a Soviet fighter.

2
Ju 88A-4 'V4+FR' of 7./KG 1, Pleskau-South, Northern Sector, May 1942
III./KG 1 was one of the later eastern front Ju 88 *Kampfgruppen* to convert from the A-5 to the improved A-4 variant, not being pulled out of the line for re-equipment until some ten months into the campaign. The *Gruppe's* new mounts did not remain pristine for long, however, as witness the copious amounts of spring mud already caking the rear fuselage of 7./KG 1's 'FR'. Note also the *Staffel's* unique, and subtle, identifying mark – a small white diamond centred at the top of the rudder hinge line.

3
Ju 88C-6 'V4+DT' of 9.(Eis)/KG 1, Dno, Northern Sector, February 1943
Looking, if anything, even grubbier and altogether more 'war weary' than the aircraft in the previous profile, 9. *Staffel's* hastily winter-camouflaged, train-busting C-6 displays all the evidence of its hard use against the extensive Soviet railway network south of Leningrad during the winter of 1942/43.

4
Ju 88A-4 '5K+BN' of 5./KG 3, Minsk, Central Sector, August 1941
One of the aircraft presumably involved in the night raids on Moscow during the late summer/early autumn of 1941, this machine has had liberal quantities of temporary black paint daubed on its undersides as well as over all national markings and unit codes – even the red spinner tip has been crudely obliterated. The only distinguishing marks it now carries are the miniscule 'last two' on the rear fuselage and a slightly larger individual letter 'B' at the base of the tailfin.

5
Ju 88A-4 '5K+HH' of 1./KG 3, Rzhev, Central Sector, summer 1942
Although unusual, the practice of fully outlining a bomber's fuselage code markings thinly in white – as depicted here on 1./KG 3's 'HH' – was not unique (indeed, some Do 17Zs of KG 77 had earlier displayed their codes in a similar manner). What is not known, however, is whether this practice was repeated at unit level, or whether such cases were quite simply the result of an individual groundcrew with clearly too much time on its hands!

6
Ju 88A-4 '5K+EK' of 2./KG 3, Kharkov-West, Southern Sector, January 1943
No need for fancy white outlining on this immaculately winter camouflaged A-4 of 2. *Staffel*. Such cleanliness in the depths of a Russian winter would seem to suggest that this is either a newly arrived replacement machine, or an aircraft that has been freshly repainted during a recent major overhaul.

7
Ju 88C-6 '5K+IP' of 6.(Eis)/KG 3, Poltava, Southern Sector, July 1943
A heavy-fighter 'train-buster' of 6. (Eisenbahn) *Staffel* shown in standard finish and markings as worn during Operation *Zitadelle*. This unit would later (January 1944) incorporate the C-6s of 9.(Eis)/KG 1 into its ranks to form 14.(Eis)/KG 3, which in turn became the very last Ju 88 'bomber' unit to remain operational over Russia in the summer of 1944.

8
Ju 88A-17 '1H+BH' of 1./KG 26, Bardufoss, northern Norway, December 1944
Wearing a tight meander or 'scribble' pattern camouflage on both upper and lower surfaces, this A-17 torpedo-bomber of 1./KG 26 is suitably attired for its part in the closing rounds of the long running campaign against the Allies' Russian convoys. Note the simplified (outline only) national markings and the reduced size of the *Geschwader* code '1H'.

9
Ju 88A-5 '4D+FP' of 6./KG 30, Banak, northern Norway, June 1941
The first Ju 88 *Kampfgruppe* to operate against Soviet forces in the Arctic theatre was II./KG 30. Initially, the only visible sign of the unit's move from the western side of *Luftflotte* 5's area of command to the eastern was the narrow yellow band encircling each machine's rear fuselage, as seen here on 6. *Staffel's* 'FP'. Note the glare shield on the windscreen-mounted MG 81 machine gun and the exhaust shroud – both indicative of recent night operations – plus the additional 20 mm cannon projecting through the nose glazing.

10
Ju 88A-4 '4D+CN' of 5./KG 30, Banak, northern Norway, April 1942
By the spring of 1942, with the Luftwaffe's battle against the Arctic convoys fully joined, the original

thin yellow band as worn by the A-5 in the previous profile had been replaced on II./KG 30's brand new A-4s (the unit had re-equipped late in 1941) by a full set of regulation eastern front markings.

11
Ju 88A-4 '9K+HR' of 7./KG 51, Balti, Rumania, September 1941
After nearly six weeks spent re-equipping at Wiener Neustadt, III./KG 51 took their factory fresh A-4s to Balti, in Rumania, in late August 1941 to commence operations along the southernmost flank of the Russian front. Note that unlike II./KG 30 above, which displayed its *Gruppe* identifying colour (red) on the tips of its spinners, III./KG 51 chose to sport its yellow III. *Gruppe* identifier in the form of a thin stripe around the front of its engine nacelles.

12
Ju 88C-6 '9K+MR' of 7.(Eis)/KG 51, Bagerovo, Crimea, spring 1943
Early in 1943 7./KG 51 was selected to become the *Geschwader's* 'train-busting' *Staffel*. Converted to C-6 cannon-armed heavy fighters and redesignated 7.(Eis)/KG 51, some of the unit's first missions were flown against the Soviet rail supply network deep in the Caucasus. Note the attempt to disguise the *Staffel's* new role by painting 'bomber'-style glazing on the machine's solid nose (and compare this somewhat crude effort with the much more professional paint job applied by groundcrews to the aircraft of 4.(Eis)/KG 76 illustrated on page 79).

13
Ju 88A-4 '9K+BP' of 6./KG 51, Zhitomir, Southern Sector, September 1943
Some of II./KG 51's machines were also cannon-armed, being fitted with a single 20 mm MG FF cannon in the ventral gondola. Primarily intended for anti-shipping operations, this powerful weapon was also used to good effect by Ju 88 crews against the enemy's armoured and soft-skinned vehicles. Note the recent overpainting of the hitherto standard scale *Geschwader* code ('9K') and its replacement by one of much smaller (officially one-fifth) size.

14
Ju 88A-5 'B3+AH' of 1./KG 54, Swidnik, Poland, June 1941
It has been suggested that the diagonal fuselage stripe seen on some KG 54 machines during the opening phases of *Barbarossa* (and earlier in the Battles of France and Britain) were used to identify unit or formation leaders. Whether true or not, the stripe on the aircraft depicted here certainly attracted the attention of one Soviet fighter pilot over Cherkassy on 23 July 1941, for he promptly rammed the bomber! Despite a mangled port wing, the pilot of 'AH' managed to pull off an emergency landing.

15
Ju 88A-4 'B3+CC' of *Stab* II./KG 54, Orsha-South, Central Sector, February 1942
Withdrawn from Russia back to the Reich late in

1941, and from there fully expecting to follow I./KG 54 down to the Mediterranean, the crews and aircraft of II./KG 54 were instead subjected to a crash programme of 'winterisation' before being rushed back to the eastern front in mid-January 1942. After some four weeks of intensive frontline operations against Soviet road and rail networks, 'CC's new coat of white paint is already showing distinct signs of wear and tear.

16
Ju 88S-3 '(Z6)+EL' of 3./KG 66, Tutow-South/Mecklenburg, Germany, spring 1945
Tasked not only with pathfinding duties for *Mistel* operations against the Oder bridges during the closing weeks of the war, but also with other, longer range missions of their own, some of I./KG 66's machines were equipped to carry no fewer than four underwing fuel tanks – two under the centre-sections and two outboard of the engines. Note the low-key 'scribble' camouflage overall and the simplified markings which consisted of outline-only national insignia and the 'last two' of the fuselage code now displayed much reduced in size alongside the tailfin swastika.

17
Ju 88A-5 'F1+PR' of 7./KG 76, Schippenbeil, East Prussia, June 1941
From the very end of the Russian campaign with the previous profile back to the very beginning with this one. The A-5 of 7./KG 76 depicted here carries a textbook set of markings as laid down by regulations for the launch of *Barbarossa*. Note also the thin vertical band around the fuselage aft of the wing root. This appeared on a number of KG 76's machines (including its earlier Do 17Zs), and presumably served a similar purpose to the diagonal stripes sported by aircraft of KG 54 (see profile 14).

18
Ju 88A-4 'F1+GT' of 9./KG 76, Smolensk, Central Sector, December 1941
Suitably garbed in a fresh coat of white camouflage paint, 9. *Staffel's* 'GT' was part of the KG 76 force that supported Army Group Centre's defensive battles in front of Moscow during the harsh winter of 1941/42. It was to be the *Geschwader's* first and last taste of a hellish Russian winter – 11 months hence the unit would be *en route* to the sunnier climes of the Mediterranean.

19
Ju 88A-5 '3Z+AH' of 1./KG 77, Heiligenbeil, East Prussia, June 1941
Another of the units gathered in East Prussia for the start of the Russian campaign in June 1941 was KG 77. Its aircraft wore the standard finish and markings of the period, the only touch of individuality being the positioning of the yellow fuselage band, which was centred on – and almost obscured by – the *Balkenkreuz* as shown here on 1. *Staffel's* 'AH'.

93

20

Ju 88A-4 '3Z+CL' of 3./KG 77, Orsha, Central Sector, February 1942

By late 1941 all three *Gruppen* of KG 77 had been returned to the Reich for re-equipment with the A-4 prior to being transferred to the Mediterranean theatre. In the event, I. *Gruppe's* flight south was to be delayed. Like II./KG 54 (see profile 15), it was instead sent back to the eastern front (central sector) early in 1942, where it would remain until July of that year.

21

Ju 88A-5 'S4+RH' of 1./KGr 506, Malmi, Finland, autumn 1941

Originating from a pre-war maritime unit (*Küstenfliegergruppe* 506), KGr 506 re-equipped with Ju 88 bombers in the late summer of 1941. It then saw service on the northern sector of the Russian front – based both in the Baltic States and in Finland – before being redesignated as III./KG 26 the following year. During their time in the east some of the *Gruppe's* machines, including 'S4+RH' seen here, appear to have bucked regulations by wearing their yellow theatre band *ahead* of the fuselage cross.

22

Ju 88A-5 'M7+HK' of 2./KGr 806, Prowehren, East Prussia, June 1941

Although also ostensibly formed as a maritime unit (*KüFlGr* 806) in the early months of the war, KGr 806 was equipped with bombers (He 111s) from the outset. It then converted to Ju 88s in time to participate in the Battle of Britain. During the opening rounds of *Barbarossa* it too operated over the Baltic Sea area, being based variously in East Prussia, Finland and the Baltic States, before transfer to the Mediterranean and redesignation as III./KG 54 in 1942. Note that 'HK' has found yet another location for the Russian front's yellow fuselage band.

23

Ju 88A-4 '(L1)+NP' of 6./LG 1, Pretzsch/Saxony, Germany, spring 1945

No yellow theatre band or *Geschwader* code on this anonymous machine, just low-visibility finish and markings, together with black undersides and exhaust flame dampers – all signs of nocturnal use. In fact, although since overshadowed by the numerous *Mistel* sorties being flown at the same time, II./LG 1's attacks on the Oder bridges in the spring of 1945 were among the last true Ju 88 bomber operations of the war against the Soviet Union.

24

Ju 88D-1 'G2+DH' of 1.(F)/124, Kirkenes, northern Norway, July 1942

Regrettably, a lack of space has prevented much mention being made in the main text of the Ju 88 reconnaissance *Staffeln* on the Russian front. However, these units played an important – at times vital – part in the air war in the east, and none more so than those stationed in northern Norway and Finland during the historic Arctic Convoy battles. The resident long-range reconnaissance *Staffel* in this area throughout the entire period from 1941 to 1945 was 1.(F)/124, whose 'DH' is depicted here.

25

Ju 88D-1 'F6+FN' of 4.(F)/122, Taganrog, Southern Sector, February 1943

Like their bomber counterparts, the reconnaissance Ju 88s were also given a coat of temporary white camouflage paint during the winter months. 'FN's' finish is looking decidedly the worse for wear, which is an indication, perhaps, of the many hours flying time the *Staffel* was putting in monitoring the movements of the Red Army in the immediate aftermath of the fall of Stalingrad.

26

Ju 88D 'K7+MK' of *Nachtaufklärungsstaffel* 2, Gomel, Central Sector, October 1943

Just prior to *Barbarossa*, each of the three main eastern front sectors was assigned a Do 17-equipped long-range night reconnaissance *Staffel* – Nos 1, 2 and 3 operating on the southern, central and northern sectors, respectively, with a fourth being added in August 1942 for service under the then newly established *Lw.Kdo.Don*. During the course of the war against the Soviet Union these nocturnal *Staffeln* were equipped with a miscellany of types, including the Ju 88 of *Nacht Aufkl.St.* 2 shown here.

27

Ju 88D '5Z+GA' of *Wekusta* 76, Debrecen, Hungary, August 1944

A similar system to that above ensured that each of the eastern front sectors also had its own meteorological *Staffel*, or *Wekusta* (*Wettererkuundungsstaffel* or Weather Observation Squadron). The situation regarding these units was made slightly more complex, however, by the inclusion of the Arctic front, by transfers to other theatres and by the temporary splitting of some *Staffeln* into two. In all, there were thus at least eight *Wekustas* serving in the east at one time or another. *Wekusta* 76, whose 'GA' is seen here, operated on the southern sector from 1941 until the end of 1944.

28

Ju 88A-4 'B1+47' of the *Ung.K.St.*, Zamosc, Poland, spring 1944

Brief mention should perhaps also be made here of the other Axis air forces that flew the Ju 88 on the eastern front. Hungary reportedly received 111 examples of the type – some 83 bombers (including a small number of C-6 heavy fighters) and 28 reconnaissance models. Although the machine depicted here is listed on *Luftflotte* 4's orders of battle simply as belonging to the *Ungarische Kampfstaffel* (Hungarian Bomber Squadron), its actual unit is believed to have been the Hungarian air force's 102/1 *Bombázoszázad* (102/1 Bomber Squadron).

29
Ju 88A-4 '127a' of *Grupul 5 bombardament*, Tecuci, Rumania, June 1944

Rumania was the second largest recipient of Ju 88s, taking delivery of 80+ bombers and 20 reconnaissance machines. *Grupul 5* formed part of the mixed-force *Corpul 1 Aerian Român*, which was subordinated *en bloc* to *Luftflotte* 4 and referred to in Luftwaffe records as the *Rum. I. Fliegerkorps* (with *Grupul 5 bombardament's* Germanic designation being *Rum.V. Kgr.*). Note the overpainted Luftwaffe markings and the 'a' suffix to the aircraft's individual number, the latter indicating that this was a replacement machine for an earlier '127' that had been either lost in combat or written off.

30
Ju 88A-4 JK-260/'4' of PLeLv 44, Onttola, Finland, June 1944

The third country to use the Ju 88 bomber against the Soviet Union was Finland, which purchased 24 A-4s from Germany in the spring of 1943. Originally delivered in standard Luftwaffe colours, a number of these machines were subsequently repainted in Finnish camouflage as seen here (the light blue-grey numeral on the fin indicating that this is aircraft No 4 of PLeLv (Bomber Squadron) 44's third flight). Unlike many of the Hungarian and Rumanian units (above), Finnish squadrons were not integrated into the Luftwaffe's command structure, but remained separate entities under the direct control of their own air force.

INDEX

References to illustrations are shown in **bold**. Plates are prefixed pl, and their corresponding captions can be found on the page in brackets.

OSPREY COMBAT AIRCRAFT •

Ju 88
KAMPFGESCHWADER
OF NORTH AFRICA AND THE
MEDITERRANEAN

SERIES EDITOR: TONY HOLMES

OSPREY COMBAT AIRCRAFT • 75

Ju 88

KAMPFGESCHWADER

OF NORTH AFRICA AND THE

MEDITERRANEAN

JOHN WEAL

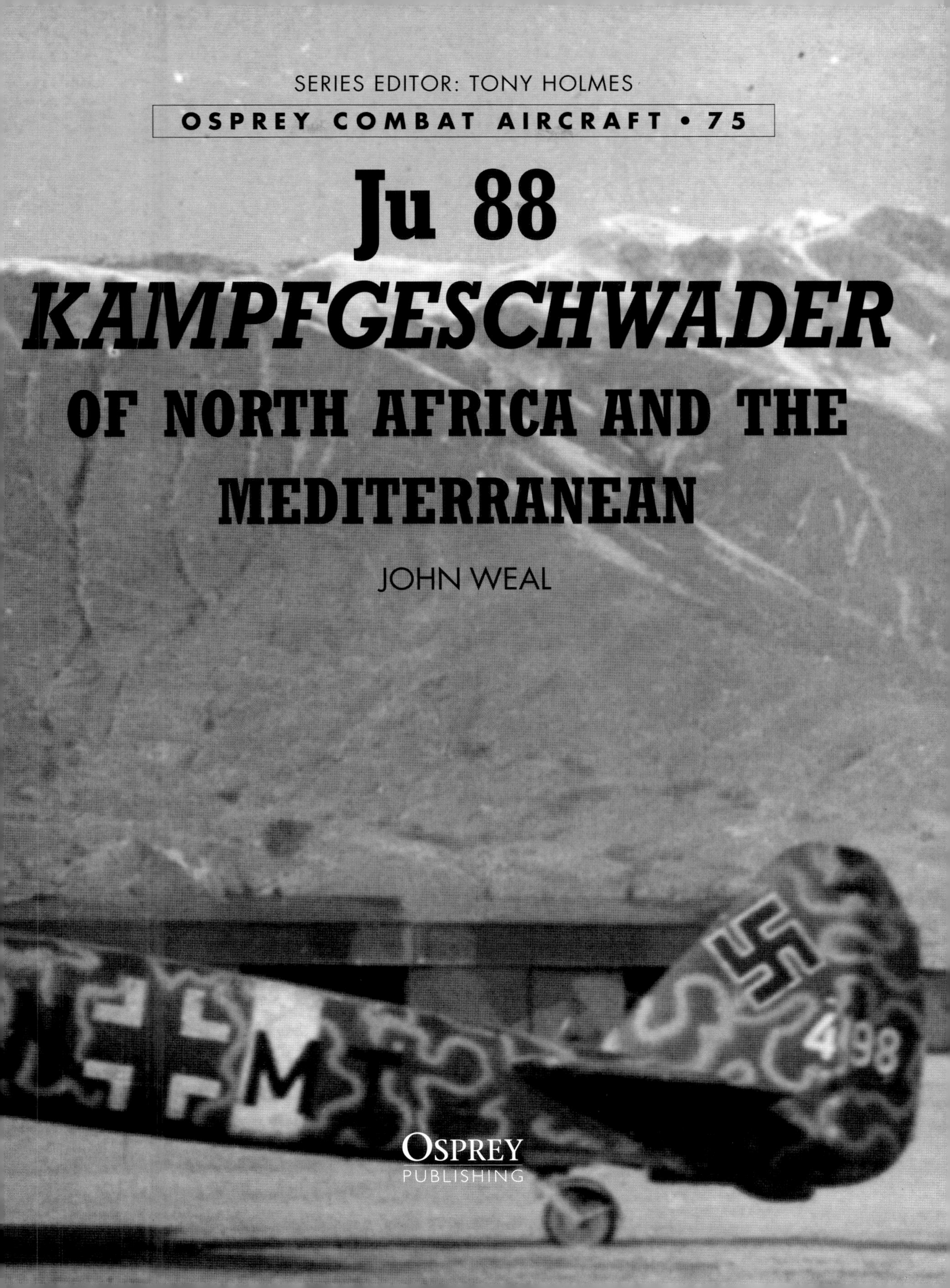

OSPREY
PUBLISHING

Front cover
The most famous Luftwaffe fighter pilot in North Africa was undoubtedly Hans-Joachim Marseille of *Jagdgeschwader* 27. His name is still familiar to enthusiasts today. But his counterpart in the bomber arm, one Joachim Helbig, is now all but forgotten. 'Jochen' Helbig, as he was universally known, was a somewhat unwilling recruit to the Luftwaffe when he was transferred from his first love, the artillery, to the fledgling air arm of the Third Reich in 1936. Despite this initial reluctance, however, he rose to prominence in his new role, beginning the war as an oberleutnant and observer with *Lehrgeschwader* (LG) 1 and subsequently rising to the rank of oberst and becoming *Geschwaderkommodore* of the unit.

And just as Marseille is associated with Bf 109s bearing the numeral 'Yellow 14', so Helbig, after being appointed *Staffelkapitän* of 4./LG 1 in the spring of 1940, always preferred to fly a Ju 88A coded 'L1+AM'. Even more remarkably, he apparently retained not just the same markings but the same aircraft too. According to some sources, Helbig's 'Anton-Marie' was the only Ju 88 in the Luftwaffe to complete over 1000 flying hours – some 750 of them on operations.

The partnership between man and machine that had lasted for over three years finally came to an end when 'L1+AM' fell victim to a US heavy bomber raid on Pordenone airfield in northern Italy. In Helbig's own words, 'She was only a machine, but to her pilot, her loyal crew and her inconsolable chief mechanic she had become a living, breathing something . . . and now she was taking her leave of us'.

Wiek Luijken's striking cover painting, reconstructing one of the many camouflage schemes 'Anton-Marie' wore during its long career, neatly encapsulates two of the aircraft's roles in the Mediterranean theatre as it takes time out from supporting the *Akrika Korps* in the Western Desert to attack an Allied convoy at sea (*Cover artwork by Wiek Luijken*)

First published in Great Britain in 2009 by Osprey Publishing
Midland House, West Way, Botley, Oxford, OX2 0PH
443 Park Avenue South, New York, NY, 10016, USA
E-mail: info@ospreypublishing.com

ISBN: 978 1 84603 318 6
E-book ISBN: 978 1 84603 888 4

Edited by Tony Holmes
Page design by Tony Truscott
Cover Artwork by Wiek Luijken
Aircraft Profiles by John Weal
Index by Michael Forder
Originated by PDQ Media, Bungay, UK
Printed in China through Bookbuilders

09 10 11 12 13   10 9 8 7 6 5 4 3 2 1

For a catalogue of all books published by Osprey please contact;

North America
Osprey Direct, C/o Random House Distribution Center,
400 Hahn Road, Westminster, MD 21157
E-mail; uscustomerservice@ospreypublishing.com

ACKNOWLEDGEMENTS
Osprey Direct, The Book Service Ltd, Distribution Centre,
Colchester Road, Frating Green, Colchester, Essex, CO7 7DW, UK
E-mail; customerservice@ospreypublishing.com

www.ospreypublishing.com

CONTENTS

BATTLE IS JOINED

irst flown in prototype form on 21 December 1936, Junkers' twin-engined Ju 88 was subsequently to evolve into what was arguably the most versatile machine to serve with the Luftwaffe in World War 2. And nowhere was that versatility more graphically demonstrated than in the Mediterranean theatre, where the Ju 88 – initially designed and classified as a *Schnellbomber*, or high-speed bomber – operated as a dive-bomber, medium-altitude level bomber, torpedo-bomber, heavy fighter, nightfighter, reconnaissance aircraft, convoy escort and maritime patrol fighter, courier aircraft and emergency transport.

The Luftwaffe's involvement in the air war in the Mediterranean came about as a direct result of Italy's declaring war on France and Great Britain on 10 June 1940. With the *Blitzkrieg* in the west by then at its height and France already on the point of collapse, the Italian *Duce,* Benito Mussolini, saw this as a golden opportunity to share in the spoils of victory with German co-dictator Adolf Hitler. Instead, Italian forces soon found themselves in dire trouble. At sea, the Royal Navy engaged Italian vessels, inflicting a succession of defeats and giving the lie to Mussolini's proud boast that the Mediterranean was *mare nostrum* – 'our sea'. In North Africa, the Italian army invaded Egypt, only to be driven back halfway across Libya and all but destroyed by British and Commonwealth troops.

Unable to ignore the growing instability on his southern flank, Hitler ordered that Luftwaffe units be sent to the area to restore the situation. The command selected to make the transfer was *General der Flieger* Hans Geisler's *X. Fliegerkorps*, then stationed in Norway. And to provide the *Korps* with the necessary striking power, two *Gruppen* each of Ju 87s and Ju 88s were added to its order of battle. For the Stukas, the move south would give them the chance to regain something of the fearsome reputation they had lost after being trounced by the RAF in the Battle of Britain. The Ju 88 had no need to prove anything. By late 1940 it had already firmly established itself as the best bomber in the Luftwaffe's armoury.

The two Ju 88 *Gruppen* involved in the initial transfer both came from the same parent *Geschwader, Lehrgeschwader* 1. One of only two such units established by the Luftwaffe (a third had been planned but never reached full strength), the *Lehrgeschwader* were unique in that they were created as operational training and evaluation wings, with each of their component *Gruppen* being equipped with a different type of aircraft. *Lehrgeschwader* 1, for example, which was first activated

The two most famous Luftwaffe units, one fighter and one bomber, that dominated much of the air war in North Africa and the Mediterranean were JG 26 and LG 1. Here, a representative from each *Geschwader* – a Bf 109F-4/trop of 6./JG 27 and a Ju 88A-4 of 12./LG 1 – stand cheek by jowl at Martuba, in Libya, during the spring of 1942

in 1936, ultimately comprised five *Gruppen* – two flying bombers, one flying fighters, another operating *Zerstörer* and the fifth equipped with dive-bombers. It was the task of these disparate *Gruppen* to develop and refine the combat tactics to be used by the many new aircraft entering Luftwaffe service in the run-up to World War 2.

One of LG 1's early arrivals in the Mediterranean theatre runs up its engines prior to take-off. A single heavy bomb is just visible beneath each wing centre-section. Note too the small fairing immediately behind the nose glazing (beneath the windscreen gun), indicating that this is a Ju 88A-6, which had presumably been fitted with a balloon-cable fender and cutter during the recent night Blitz over Britain

With the outbreak of hostilities in September 1939 their work was effectively done. By the time of the Battle of Britain, three of LG 1's *Gruppen* had therefore been re-equipped with Ju 88s, and this part of the unit was, to all intents and purposes, operating as a standard *Kampfgeschwader* (the two remaining *Gruppen* would later be redesignated and incorporated into the nightfighter and dive-bomber arms). And it was in late 1940, just as the night Blitz on Britain was intensifying, that II. and III./LG 1 were suddenly withdrawn from *Luftflotte* 3 in western France and ordered to the Mediterranean. Departing their bases at Orléans-Bricy and Châteaudun, respectively, they were to stage, via Lechfeld, in Germany, down the length of Italy to Catania, on the island of Sicily.

Although they did not know it at the time, their sojourn in the south was to be a lengthy one. In fact, LG 1 would not return to *Luftflotte* 3 in northwest Europe until recalled to combat the Allied invasion of Normandy in June 1944. In the intervening three-a-half years, LG 1 forged for itself a name as *the* Mediterranean *Kampfgeschwader*. It became that theatre's bomber equivalent of the famed *Jagdgeschwader* 27 '*Afrika*'. And just as JG 27 had its Hans-Joachim Marseille, so too did LG 1 produce one outstanding personality.

Staffelkapitän of 4./LG 1 at the time of the transfer to Sicily, and already a holder of the Knight's Cross in recognition of his operations over Poland, Norway, France and Great Britain, Hauptmann Joachim 'Jochen' Helbig would subsequently become *Geschwaderkommodore* of LG 1. He was also one of the few Luftwaffe bomber pilots whose name would be familiar to both friend and foe alike. Before it finally left the Mediterranean in mid-1944, the unit he commanded, while still officially *Lehrgeschwader* 1, was being more commonly referred to by both sides as the 'Helbig Flyers'.

Hauptmann Joachim Helbig (right) and his crew pictured in the cockpit of their trusty 'AM'. This photograph was taken sometime after 30 August 1941, when Oberfeldwebel Franz Schlund – seen at the rear – became the Luftwaffe's first wireless-operator/air gunner to be awarded the Knight's Cross

The British were fully aware of *X. Fliegerkorps*' initial migration southwards, the RAF's wireless interception service reporting the first four Ju 88s of LG 1 as having arrived at Catania, on the eastern coast of Sicily, by the evening of 26 December 1940. The Luftwaffe's

Sitting in the midday sun at Catania, 5./LG 1's 'DN' is checked over prior to departing on its next mission. Although the white aft fuselage band of the Mediterranean area is clearly in evidence, there is no corresponding white tip outboard of that small underwing individual aircraft letter 'D'. There is every likelihood that this is the 'L1+DN' that was lost in action on 21 March 1941 attacking Allied convoy AN-21, carrying Commonwealth troops from Alexandria to Greece

movements continued to be closely monitored in the weeks that followed, and by mid-January 1941, signals intelligence had not only established that 49 Ju 88s of *Stab*, II. and III./LG 1 were concentrated at Catania, they had even pinpointed a number of stragglers, beset by mechanical problems, strung out on fields down the leg of Italy, including one at Reggio nell' Emilia, two at Pisa, and another at Naples.

General der Flieger Geisler set up his *Korps* HQ in the Hotel Domenico at Taormina, a holiday resort some 30 miles up the coast from Catania.

Given its relatively limited numbers, the list of operational tasks that *X. Fliegerkorps* was expected to carry out was daunting, to say the least. Firstly, it was to close the central Mediterranean (i.e. the Sicilian Narrows) to the passage of Allied convoys between Gibraltar and Alexandria, thereby starving the island of Malta of essential supplies. Secondly, it was to disrupt the lines of supply of Gen Wavell's Desert Army by mining the Suez Canal (a job for the *Korps'* He 111s). Thirdly, it was to support Italian land forces in Libya in order to halt the further advance of British and Commonwealth troops, and thus retain hold of Tripoli, the intended port of disembarkation for Rommel's *Afrika Korps*. And fourthly, it was to secure the Axis convoy routes transporting supplies across the Mediterranean from Italy to North Africa.

INTO ACTION

Lehrgeschwader 1's operational debut in the Mediterranean was low-key and far from successful. On the afternoon of 10 January three Ju 88s were sent out against the Royal Navy carrier HMS *Illustrious*, which was limping towards Malta after being severely damaged by Ju 87s. But the trio was intercepted and driven off by Hurricanes, which forced them to jettison their bombs and turn tail for home. A second raid by several more III. *Gruppe* machines shortly afterwards proved equally fruitless.

Worse was to come. Two days later III./LG 1 were on the receiving end. After first taking the precaution of despatching a reconnaissance machine to overfly Catania – which was meant to persuade the Germans that their presence on the field had been detected from the air, and thus disguise the fact that their approach and arrival had, in reality, been closely monitored by radio intercepts – the RAF mounted a night raid by Malta-based Wellingtons. Five Axis aircraft were destroyed on the ground, including two of III. *Gruppe's* Ju 88s.

It was 15 January before the bulk of II./LG 1 reached Catania. That same evening 16 of their number took off again to attack *Illustrious*, which had by now reached the dubious safety of Malta's Grand Harbour. The Ju 88s bombed through cloud and registered no hits. At the same time the Wellingtons were back over Catania, where they destroyed four aircraft and inflicted the first casualties to be suffered by LG 1 in-theatre. One of the two killed was Leutnant Horst Nagel, a 6. *Staffel* pilot whose Ju 88 had been declared unserviceable and who was on temporary duty in

The Royal Navy carrier HMS *Illustrious* is hidden by fountains of water thrown up by near misses (right) close to its berth at the entrance to French Creek in Malta's Grand Harbour

It was not only in the skies over Malta that LG 1's machines were at risk. Here at Catania, one of the unit's Ju 88A-5s has been rammed by an Italian Savoia-Marchetti SM.79 bomber. The caption to the original print – on which Mount Etna may just be seen in the left background – reads simply 'A difference of opinion!'

the ops room. The *Geschwader* also reported eight wounded.

The following day witnessed *X. Fliegerkorps'* first major raid on Malta. The target was again *Illustrious*, and among the attacking force were 17 Ju 88s from II. and III./LG 1. Due to poor weather conditions, the Bf 110 escorts failed to make the rendezvous so the Ju 88s pressed on alone. Two of their bombs exploded in the water between the carrier's hull and the harbour wall at the entrance to French Creek against which it was moored, causing the vessel further damage.

A number of claims were made by the island's defending fighters and anti-aircraft gunners, but only one Ju 88 was in fact lost. This was 9. *Staffel's* 'L1+CT', which was engaged by a Fleet Air Arm Fulmar and went down into the sea, taking Oberleutnant Kurt Pichler and his crew with it. Three others crash-landed back at Catania due to combat damage, and a fourth, piloted by Oberleutnant Theodor Hagen, just reached Sicily before making an emergency landing on the beach of Pozzallo. In addition, the *Geschwader* was to lose two more Ju 88s before the day was out, written off on the ground when an Italian aircraft collided with them.

Forty-eight hours later, III. *Gruppe* reported another crew missing when Leutnant Horst Dunkel was forced to ditch 'L1+ER' after being attacked by Hurricanes during a raid on Malta's Hal Far airfield.

The next day, 19 January, the *Geschwader* turned its attention back to *Illustrious*. Although the island's defences claimed eight of the 30 attacking Junkers destroyed, only two machines – both from 8. *Staffel*, one being that of the *Staffelkapitän*, Hauptmann Wilhelm Dürbeck – failed to return. Dürbeck's 'L1+AS' is listed by one source as having fallen victim to a Hurricane, but Feldwebel Herbert Isachsen, the pilot of the aircraft following him down in the dive on the carrier, described after his return to Catania how he saw the *Staffelkapitän's* machine hit by flak and break apart in the air. A third Ju 88 chased out to sea with an engine on fire by a Hurricane was almost certainly the aircraft of III. *Gruppe's Stabskette* that was destroyed when it too forced-landed near Pozallo.

This stretch along the southeastern coast of Sicily, the nearest piece of friendly territory for any badly damaged machine struggling to make it back from Malta, was soon to acquire a reputation as something of an aircraft graveyard!

Bad weather over Sicily on 20 January kept the resident Luftwaffe units' activities to a minimum during the day, but did not prevent Malta's Wellingtons from again

Here, the pilot of Ju 88A-5 'White N' (from either 4. or 7./LG 1) has managed to pull off a successful belly landing back on Sicily after being attacked by RAF fighters over Malta – note the chewed-up fin and rudder . . .

bombing Catania after darkness had fallen. The next evening, therefore, the Ju 88s made the short hop across the Straits of Messina to Reggio di Calabria, on the toe of the Italian mainland, in order to escape further attack. These overnight deployments to Reggio would become a regular feature in the weeks ahead.

By 23 January *Illustrious* had been sufficiently patched up to allow it to slip undetected out of Malta. When a reconnaissance machine reported the vessel's absence, III./LG 1 despatched 11 Junkers to find it. Heavy cloud and frequent rain squalls out to sea hampered their efforts. Eight aircraft returned to Catania after an hour's fruitless search, having experienced strong interference with their radio and navigational equipment. But three Ju 88s of 8. *Staffel*, led by Leutnant Hermann Böhmer, remained unaccounted for.

It later transpired that all three had run out of fuel in thick cloud to the south of Italy. Although unsure of their position, Böhmer had given the order to bail out. Of the 12 crewmen, only Feldwebel Isachsen – the pilot who had witnessed the demise of his *Staffelkapitän* over Grand Harbour four days earlier – came down on land and survived to tell the tale. Five bodies were subsequently washed ashore along the coast of southern Italy, and a sixth was found weeks later on a beach in Albania, 150 miles away.

Illustrious and its four attendant destroyers were sighted twice by reconnaissance aircraft on 24 January, and 31 Ju 88s of II. and III./LG 1 were ordered off from Catania. It is not certain whether the bombers found the carrier on this occasion, let alone attacked it, but 9. *Staffel* did, somewhat inexplicably, report damaging two cruisers. Running low on fuel, some bombers put down at Benina, in Libya, where they stayed overnight. Others set course for the long, two-hour haul back to Sicily;

'The automatic flight control system was switched back on and the pilot took his feet off the pedals. As always during the homeward flight, the tension eased. We chatted, sucked sweets and chocolate, or stuffed biscuits into each others' mouths.'

. . . but not everyone was so lucky. In this fortunately rather blurred print, a crewman lies dead among the blazing wreckage of his unidentified Ju 88 'somewhere on Malta'

Two Junkers were damaged in crash landings upon their return to Catania. Some aircraft of LG 1 were clearly also in action over Malta on this same 24 January, with 4. *Staffel* reporting one of its machines missing after an attack on Hal Far airfield. 'L1+HM' was downed by the meteorological Gladiator that it chanced upon while approaching the target and, perhaps rather unwisely, fired at in passing, for the biplane promptly forsook its weather duties and chased the Ju 88 down into the dive and then out to sea 'yapping at its heels like a terrier.'

The following day *Illustrious* reached Alexandria. From there the vessel would make its way, via the Suez Canal, to the east coast of America, where it was to undergo major repairs. Although these would keep the carrier out of the war for a full year, the bombers of *X. Fliegerkorps* had thus failed to accomplish the first task they had been given in the Mediterranean – namely, to send the 23,000-ton carrier to the bottom.

But there were plenty of other objectives to keep the Ju 88s occupied in their new theatre of operations, not least the island of Malta itself, which sat foursquare astride the direct sea route between Italy and Tripoli, the seaport capital of Libya. The island fortress was rightly described at the time as an 'unsinkable aircraft carrier on Mussolini's doorstep'. Its neutralisation as an air and sea base was therefore a matter of prime importance if the lines of supply to Axis troops in North Africa were to be kept open. And Ju 88 crews would find themselves returning to it time and time again in the weeks and months to come.

Nor was it just the bombers that had to brave Malta's defences. A close watch needed to be kept on Allied shipping movements and other activities on and around the island. And very soon the Ju 88s of *X. Fliegerkorps'* sole long-range reconnaissance *Staffel*, 1.(F)/121, which were based alongside LG 1 at Catania, were also discovering just how dangerous the skies above Malta could be. One of the unit's earliest casualties was Leutnant Helmut Fund's '7A+DH', reported missing on 26 January after coming under attack from two of the island's Hurricanes.

During the closing week of January and the first half of February 1941 the two *Gruppen* of LG 1 continued to attack Malta. They usually timed their raids to come in around dusk, or later, in order to minimise the risk from enemy fighters. They nonetheless had six Ju 88s either damaged or written-off during this period, most of them in crash-landings at Catania.

It was at this juncture too that LG 1's Ju 88s began to venture further a field. At dawn on 9 February units of Force 'H' (the Royal Navy's Western Mediterranean Fleet) comprising the aircraft carrier *Ark Royal*, the battleship *Malaya* and battlecruiser *Renown*, accompanied by the cruiser *Sheffield* and ten destroyers, carried out a surprise air and sea bombardment of the Italian ports of Genoa, Spezia and Leghorn.

Although some 40 of LG 1's bombers had been over Malta only hours earlier, 21 machines, led by Hauptmann Gerhard Kollewe, the *Gruppenkommandeur* of II./LG 1, were ordered to find and attack the British vessels as they headed back to Gibraltar. They were reported to be somewhere in the 110-mile stretch of water between the northeastern tip of Corsica and the coast of southern France. But once again the weather intervened. Heavy clouds prevented Kollewe's crews from sighting the enemy, and all they got for their pains were some inaccurate bursts of fire from

The white bird emblem (variously described as a swan or a wild goose) visible on the nose of this early reconnaissance Ju 88D identifies it as a machine of 1.(F)/121. This is corroborated by the fuselage code, '7A+GH', although the total lack of white theatre markings may indicate that this photograph was taken prior to, or during *X. Fliegerkorps'* move from Norway to Sicily

nervous Italian anti-aircraft gunners as they passed close to the island of Sardinia, and an escort of suspicious *Regia Aeronautica* fighters, which shadowed them until they were safely out of range.

This foray to the northern reaches of the Mediterranean was something of a one-off, however. During the latter half of February the main focus of military activity in the area – and therefore of LG 1's operations – was to shift southwards to the shores of Africa. There, British forces had captured Benghazi from the Italians on 6 February and advanced towards El Agheila, on the Gulf of Sirte. Tripoli itself would soon be coming under threat. But on 11 February the first ships carrying troops of the *Afrika Korps* docked in the Libyan capital. On that same date aircraft of LG 1 were despatched on an armed reconnaissance sweep along the North African coast. They flew east as far as Mersa Matruh, in Egypt, but failed to spot any shipping.

On the following day, which was marked by General Rommel's arrival in Africa, 18 Ju 88s of II. and III./LG 1 attacked British troops and encampments along the coastal highway between Benghazi and El Agheila. They suffered a single loss when 6. *Staffel's* 'L1+IP' was downed by anti-aircraft fire southwest of Soluch. Although the pilot and air-gunner survived the crash-landing, the latter was killed by a marauding band of armed Arabs two nights later as the pair tried to reach the Italian lines.

Even as the 18 Ju 88s were searching for targets along Libya's Via Balbia, another six were escorting a troop convoy across the Mediterranean, and three more were raiding Malta. This division of labour was indicative of LG 1's priorities in the immediate weeks ahead. Malta would be temporarily relegated to third place while the *Geschwader's* Ju 88s first concentrated their efforts on shepherding convoys to Libya in order to build up the strength of the *Afrika Korps*, and then in supporting Rommel's troops in the field, or rather the desert, as they set out to push British and Commonwealth forces back from whence they came – to the Egyptian border and beyond.

ATTACKING BENGHAZI

The first major target of the North African campaign for LG 1 was the port of Benghazi. Captured by the British just a week earlier, the enemy were already using it to bring in supplies and reinforcements to strengthen their positions around El Agheila. The *Geschwader's* Ju 88s took off from Catania to bomb the harbour on a regular, almost daily basis. During one such raid by 15 machines of III. *Gruppe* early on the morning of 15 February, flak damaged one of the attackers. Rather than attempting to make it back to Sicily on just one engine, the pilot decided instead to crash-land in the desert outside Tripoli. It was a lucky escape for future Swords winner Oberleutnant Hermann Hogeback. Another crew were not so fortunate.

Intercepted and chased out to sea by a Hurricane, 7. *Staffel's* 'L1+LR'

Tucked in close together, a pair of 6./LG 1 machines – 'L1+DP' in the foreground and 'L1+CP' to the rear – climb hard away from Sicily as they set out on another mission

was forced to ditch. All four crewmen were picked up by a British vessel after spending more than eight hours in their dinghy, but one subsequently died of his wounds in a Benghazi hospital.

Despite losses such as these, not everyone was impressed by the strength of Benghazi's defences. After another early morning raid two days later, one *Geschwader* member noted somewhat facetiously in his logbook, 'The "Tommies" have been out shopping and bought themselves three searchlights'.

On 18 February, during a raid on a small convoy that had just put in to Benghazi harbour, the crews of III./LG 1 reported the presence there of two British cruisers. In fact, the ships were the anti-aircraft cruiser *Coventry* and the 7200-ton monitor *Terror*. The latter, a shallow-draught vessel mounting two enormous high-angled 15-inch guns and eight smaller 4-inch weapons, had kept pace with the advance of Gen Wavell's troops along the coast road out of Egypt, harassing the retreating Italians all the way with a succession of devastating inshore bombardments.

Having helped to drive Italian forces back over the Egyptian border, *Terror's* guns had then cut off their line of withdrawal by blasting away a 150-yard stretch of the escarpment leading up to the infamous Halfaya Pass (inevitably 'Hellfire Pass' to the British), which was the only major route up on to the Libyan plateau. They next poured nearly 600 tons of high-explosive shells into Bardia, the first Italian stronghold just 12 miles inside Libya, before adding their weight to the naval bombardment of Tobruk, a further 75 miles along the coast.

Mindful of the havoc *Terror* could wreak on the *Afrika Korps* as Rommel's troops prepared to launch their push back along the coastal highway to regain the territory lost in the recent Italian retreat, the order was given to sink the elderly monitor. Thus, on the afternoon of 19 February, while the bulk of III./LG 1 was attacking a convoy some 30 miles off Benghazi, five Ju 88s were despatched to dive-bomb *Terror*, still berthed in Benghazi harbour. Greeted by a ferocious barrage of anti-aircraft fire, and harried by a single Hurricane, none of the Ju 88s succeeded in hitting the vessel. They came closer during a morning raid three days later, however, when two near misses caused considerable damage to *Terror's* hull plates.

The monitor began to take on water, and when the vessel was subjected to yet another attack that same evening, this time by machines of II. *Gruppe*, it was decided that Benghazi was becoming too hot for the warship, and that it should retire east along the coast out of harm's way. But just under 24 hours later, at 1822 hrs on 23 February, *Terror* was caught off Derna by two Ju 88s of III./LG 1 engaged on an anti-shipping sweep. Two bombs exploded in the water close alongside level with her bridge. Her hull split open, it took on a heavy list and slowly sank beneath the waves. The World War 1 monitor would not be the last warship of the Royal Navy to fall victim to Ju 88s in the Mediterranean. Indeed, just 24 hours were to pass before the next one followed it to the bottom.

The sinking of *Terror* had removed at least one threat to the *Afrika Korps* as it began its drive eastwards. Rommel's troops had initially encountered British forces near El Agheila on 20 February, and the first armed clash between the two sides occurred four days later. For the next few weeks the Ju 88s of LG 1 would divide their time between shepherding convoys across the Mediterranean in order to ensure a steady flow of supplies to the troops in North Africa, and in providing direct support to those troops as they began to push the British back towards Egypt.

FIRST ATTACK ON TOBRUK

In the early hours of 23 February, three machines of II./LG 1 had lifted off from Catania to carry out their first bombing raid on Tobruk. Situated less than 90 miles from the Egyptian frontier, this small harbour town had been captured by British forces a month earlier, and its defences had since been significantly strengthened. They certainly consisted of more than the 'three searchlights' previously attributed to Benghazi, and the trio of Ju 88s were lucky to escape unscathed from the reception they were given.

The following evening, a larger force of 14 bombers also headed for Tobruk to attack shipping reported to be in the harbour there. When they arrived over the target area shortly before 1900 hrs, the Ju 88s spotted two Royal Navy destroyers just putting out to sea. Several of the crews opted to dive on the warships rather than on the merchantmen berthed in the harbour. One bomb pierced the side of HMS *Dainty* and penetrated deep into its oil bunkers before exploding. The 1375-ton destroyer was quickly engulfed in flames and soon went down.

On 25 February the Ju 88s of 7./KG 30 flew in to Gerbini – another field on the Catanian plain south of Mount Etna. This *Staffel* was led by Oberleutnant Hajo Herrmann who, although now better known as the originator of the *Wilde Sau* nightfighter force later employed in the defence of the Reich, had been a highly successful bomber pilot during the early war years. He was already wearing the Knight's Cross by the time of his arrival on Sicily.

The rest of III./KG 30 was scheduled to follow 7. *Staffel* down from Holland some five days later. Until it did so, Herrmann's unit was to be subordinated to the *Stab* of LG 1. Little time was lost in calling upon their services. The groundcrews, who had accompanied the *Staffel* to Sicily aboard two Ju 52/3m transports, had scarcely had time to wash the black distemper off the undersides of the bombers (a legacy of their recent participation in the night Blitz over Britain) when Oberst Friedrich-Karl Knust, the *Geschwaderkommodore* of LG 1, was on the line to Hajo Herrmann. *X. Fliegerkorps* had ordered that a major raid be mounted against Malta the following day, and every available bomber was to take part – Ju 87s, He 111s and the Ju 88s of II. and III./LG 1 and 7./KG 30.

The attack of 26 February 1941 was one of the heaviest raids Malta had experienced to date. And although the island's ainti-aircraft gunners were credited with a Ju 88 shot down into the sea, and a Hurricane pilot claimed another as a probable, it appears that none were in fact lost. The Ju 88s would continue to mount smaller-scale raids on Malta, and they would

Many of LG 1's early Mediterranean missions were flown in penny-packet numbers, but not always in such neat arrowhead formation as displayed here – especially if RAF or FAA fighters were about!

The next Ju 88 bomber unit to join LG 1 on Sicily was 7./KG 30. This is '4D+DR', one of the *Staffel's* A-5s, pictured at Gerbini taking a breather between operations, with Mount Etna again providing the backdrop

suffer losses in the process. In another attack on Luqa exactly a week later, for example, one of 4./LG 1's machines failed to return. However, for most crews the end of February and the beginning of March meant a resumption of their routine convoy escort duties, interspersed with missions in support of Rommel's troops in Libya.

On 28 February aircraft of III./LG 1 bombed Tobruk. Although RAF fighters rose to intercept them, all the Ju 88s returned safely to Sicily. Meanwhile, 7./KG 30 had been despatched against a small formation of enemy ships reported to be heading westwards along the African coast. After searching in vain for the vessels in poor visibility, Hajo Herrmann and his crews subsequently put down at Tripoli to refuel, before they too headed back to Sicily. One machine that detoured to carry out a reconnaissance of Benghazi *en route* failed to make it. Emerging from low cloud over the harbour area, Unteroffizier Peter Müller's '4D+HR' fell victim to an RAAF Hurricane. That same evening the Knight's Cross-wearing Major Arved Crüger, *Gruppenkommandeur* of III./KG 30, landed in Sicily with his 8. and 9. *Staffeln*.

For much of the first half of March 1941, the aircraft of LG 1 continued with maritime patrol and convoy escort activities. They also mounted several harassing attacks on Malta, both by day and by night. 13 March was typical. While III. *Gruppe* spent most of that day shepherding yet more supply convoys across the Mediterranean, II./LG 1 divided its strength by despatching machines on two separate bombing raids, both in the early hours of the morning. One group targeted Malta's Grand Harbour, while the other struck at El Adem airfield in the desert south of Tobruk. Now occupied by the British, El Adem had been the largest Italian airbase in Libya. As they left the target area crews reported seeing hangars and parked aircraft burning fiercely, although many of the latter may have been unserviceable machines abandoned and left scattered about the field by the fleeing Italians.

The Ju 88s did not return immediately to Sicily, but flew instead to an airfield near Tripoli where they were refuelled and bombed up again. Then they headed back to Tobruk, attacking troop positions near the town, before finally heading northwest for Catania and home, which they reached shortly before midday – an 11-hour shuttle mission carried out without loss.

By the end of March the German advance along the African coast was gaining momentum. In the face of inexplicably weak resistance, what had initially been launched as a reconnaissance in force soon developed into a full-blown offensive. Rommel's superiors in Berlin and Rome tried to rein him in, but the general was having none of it. He urged his troops on. They would retake Agedabia on 2 April and enter Benghazi just two days after that. Now he had his sights set on Tobruk. He was being ably supported throughout by the Ju 87 Stukas of *Fliegerführer Afrika*. But the Sicilian-based Ju 88s were conspicuous by their absence. The main focus of *their* attentions had abruptly switched to the eastern Mediterranean.

Just as their initial transfer from the Channel front to Sicily had been brought about by Mussolini's ill-judged declaration of war against the Allies in June 1940, so the Ju 88s' latest change of direction, away from North Africa and towards the eastern end of the Mediterranean, was also the result of another botched offensive by the Italian *Duce*.

MARITA TO MERKUR

U nlike Hitler's territorial acquisitions in the period prior to World War 2 – the annexation of Austria and the occupation of Czechoslovakia spring immediately to mind – Mussolini's armed seaborne invasion of Albania at dawn on 7 April 1939, is now all but forgotten. Eighteen months later, having built up his forces on the far side of the Adriatic, Mussolini launched an attack on Greece. Expecting an easy victory, the *Duce* had neglected to tell Hitler of his plans. And like so many Italian forays, this one quickly ran into trouble. The embattled Greeks accepted Britain's offer of assistance and the invaders were not simply stopped in their tracks, but chased back into Albania.

Having driven the British Army out of northwest continental Europe in the early summer of 1940, the *Führer* did not now want his enemy – in the early spring of 1941 – setting firm foot in the southeastern reaches of

The Balkans campaign resulted in LG 1 switching its attentions from Malta to the eastern Mediterranean. This was to become its main area of operations for very nearly the next three years

his domain. He therefore ordered measures to be taken to disrupt the flow of Allied shipping transporting men and materials from Egypt to their forward base at Souda Bay, on the island of Crete, and thence onwards to southern Greece.

It is more than a little ironic that while the Axis were pouring supplies southwards across the Mediterranean to build up their forces in North Africa, the British were despatching convoys *northwards* every three days in support of the Greeks. It was this further weakening of Gen Wavell's overstretched and overburdened Desert Army that was allowing the *Afrika Korps* to make such significant gains in its advance through Libya.

LG 1's Sicilian-based *Gruppen* were heavily involved in this two-way traffic. While III./LG 1 continued to devote much of its time to escorting Rommel's supply convoys, II./LG 1 was given the job of interrupting the flow of Allied shipping between Egypt and Crete.

On 18 March 1941, 17 of the *Gruppe's* Ju 88s were sent off on an armed reconnaissance of the sea areas around Crete. Having been given strict instructions not to violate Greek airspace, the crews failed to spot any enemy vessels. After putting down on the Italian island of Rhodes to refuel, they returned to Catania with nothing to report.

It was to be a different story three days later, however, when a small formation of Ju 88s led by Hauptmann Joachim Helbig (the *Kapitän* of 4.*Staffel*) sighted a convoy of merchant vessels, escorted by capital ships of the Royal Navy – including the aircraft carrier *Formidable* and cruiser *Bonventure* – off the Kithera Channel between Crete and Greece. Helbig called up the rest of II. *Gruppe*, which was ready and waiting at Catania.

In a late afternoon attack north of Crete, the bombers claimed two of the four merchantmen sunk and a third severely damaged. But it would appear that none of the ships actually went down. The 'large tanker' credited to *Gruppenkommandeur* Hauptmann Gerhard Kollewe was, in all probability, the 8271-ton Danish tanker *Marie Maersk*, which although badly damaged and on fire, managed to reach Greece – only to be bombed and sunk in Piraeus harbour on 12 April.

This operation of 21 March resulted in LG 1's first combat loss of the month when one of the machines that had initially sighted the convoy shortly after midday was engaged by a Fulmar from *Formidable*. In trying to escape from the fighter, 5. *Staffel's* 'L1+DN' ventured too close to the ships and was brought down by naval anti-aircraft fire.

Further anti-shipping strikes were flown over the next few days. On 22 March two vessels were hit off Gavdo Island to the south of Crete, one of which – the 8070-ton Norwegian tanker *Solheim* – was bombed again and sent to the bottom by II./LG 1 24 hours later. Eleven aircraft of II. *Gruppe* failed to locate several cruisers southwest of Crete on 24 March, but an attack on a convoy in the same area the following day resulted in a claim by a member of LG 1's *Geschwaderstab* for one merchantman sunk;

'My three SC bombs hit the water directly alongside the largest freighter in the convoy. As I withdrew, the ship exploded in a cloud of white smoke. I landed back at Catania at 1850 hrs. Shortly afterwards I was credited in writing with the sinking of an 8000-tonner.'

Despite this, the vessel in question, the 6992-ton *Baluchistan,* survived the three near misses – and for another 12 months after that, until finally falling victim to a U-boat off the coast of West Africa in March 1942.

Irritated by the fact that Luftwaffe bombers were shouldering the full burden of the eastern Mediterranean anti-convoy operations, Hitler pressurised Mussolini to add his weight, insisting that 'the Italians must *at least* do something to prevent British supplies from reaching Greece'. Rome decided that the honour should fall to the Italian navy. On the evening of 26 March a battleship, five cruisers and ten destroyers sailed from ports in southern Italy to carry out a sweep to the southeast of Crete.

But instead of intercepting their intended target – a convoy bound for Piraeus – the Italians were met by units of the main British fleet. This was a far superior force including three battleships and the carrier *Formidable*. The ensuing Battle of Cape Matapan – an engagement described by the Allies at the time as 'the most momentous naval victory since Trafalgar' – ended disastrously for the Italians. Lacking the benefit of radar, their ships suffered heavy losses during the night of 28/29 March. The battleship

Three unidentified crewmen pose somewhat self-consciously in front of the shipping scoreboard painted on the tailfin of their Ju 88. The individual in the centre does, however . . .

. . . manage to summon up a broad smile for the official war photographer, whose shot was later used on the front cover of the *Berliner Illustrierte Zeitung* of 15 May 1941. He is pointing proudly to a hit scored on a '35,000-ton' warship on 24 March, which ties in neatly with III./KG 30's claims for hits on a 'battleship and a patrol boat' north of Benghazi on that date. But what of that top silhouette recording a hit on a carrier (almost certainly HMS *Formidable*) dated 29 March . . .

. . . which also features prominently on the tail of this machine? This oft-seen photo, showing a fourth merchantman sunk being added to the crew's overall score, has in the past been attributed to LG 1 . . .

Vittorio Veneto was damaged, and three heavy cruisers and two destroyers were sunk.

After first sighting and reporting the lightly defended ten-ship convoy that the Italians had hoped to annihilate (but which escaped detection by reversing course under cover of darkness), the Ju 88s of LG 1 had played little further direct part in the Battle of Cape Matapan. They were, however, charged with protecting the surviving Italian warships throughout the daylight hours of 24 March as they made their way back to their home ports. This cost them one of their number, some sources suggesting that 6. *Staffel's* 'L1+EP' was despatched by a Fulmar over the Gulf of Taranto. However, several crews reported seeing a Ju 88 shot down by flak from one of the Italian vessels that it was supposed to be escorting.

In the wake of Matapan, with III./LG 1 still primarily employed in the essential, but generally uneventful, shepherding of seaborne supplies to North Africa, II. *Gruppe* resumed its campaign against the convoys plying between Egypt and Greece. On 2 April, eight machines led by Hauptmann Joachim Helbig discovered two empty convoys southbound off Gardo Island on their way back to Egypt. Two ships were sunk, one of them the 5324-ton freighter *Homefield*, and a third was damaged.

At about the same time, a formation of Ju 88s headed by *Gruppenkommandeur* Gerhard Kollewe found another convoy, this one fully laden, heading north towards Greece. The 6054-ton merchantman *Devis* was hit, but was able to continue on to Piraeus, only to suffer further damage there during a bombing raid on 6 April. Before the convoy reached the illusory safety of the Greek port, however, it would be subjected to a second attack by Hauptmann Kollewe and his crews. This was delivered some 24 hours later, at about 1900 hrs on 3 April, when the vessels were in the Antikithera Channel northwest of Crete.

Although the convoy's escort had been strengthened in the meantime by the addition of the anti-aircraft cruiser *Calcutta*, this did not prevent the Ju 88s from hitting the *Northern Prince* with four bombs – two of them direct hits amidships. It immediately caught fire and began giving off clouds of smoke. Ten minutes later the vessel was torn apart by a huge explosion, the towering smoke and flames being visible 40 miles away. The 10,917-ton vessel had been packed with munitions and explosives.

II./LG 1's anti-convoy operations from Catania to the sea areas around and beyond Crete often entailed flights lasting anything up to six hours. Yet despite all their efforts – and successes such as the sinking of the *Northern Prince* – supplies were still getting through to Greece on a regular basis, and the position of the Italian forces in Albania was worsening daily. And it was his ally's plight, combined with instability in Yugoslavia, where a pro-Axis government had just been toppled by a popular uprising, which prompted Hitler to take further action. With his

... but another shot clearly identifies it as 7./KG 30's '4D+MR'. It is obviously a different aircraft from that featured on the cover of the Berlin newspaper. But is it a replacement machine flown by the same crew? Almost two months have passed since the earlier photographs were taken. The top silhouette superimposed on the tail swastika of 'MR' records a hit on a battleship scored on 23 May – possibly HMS *Barham* retiring after bombarding Scarpanto – and the life-jacketed figure seen here looks suspiciously like the individual on the left of the original trio. Definitely one for the historians to get their teeth into!

Although of dubious quality, this wartime cutting showing 8./KG 51's '9K+DS' getting clearance for take-off is sufficiently clear to illustrate the obvious difference between the white aft fuselage band of the Mediterranean theatre and the yellow markings (applied here to the machine's engine nacelles and rudder) carried during the brief campaign in the Balkans. Note that the gefreiter in the foreground is waving a white flag with a green cross on it, signalling the pilot that he is clear to take-off, while holding the red one (which, when raised, instructed to crew to remain where they were) close to the ground beside his leg

planned invasion of the USSR only weeks away, he could not afford to have the Balkans in turmoil to the rear of his advance into Russia.

Hitler had long ago decided to occupy Greece should this become necessary in order to secure his position in the eastern Mediterranean. Now he added Yugoslavia to his target list, determined to eradicate this unexpected thorn in his side before embarking on the more difficult task of subjugating the Greeks and driving their British allies back into the sea. Hitler's fury at the Yugoslav people for overthrowing the recently installed Axis-friendly government may be gauged from the wording of his War Directive No 15, dated 27 March 1941, in which he states that he would destroy the country 'militarily and as a national entity'. Yugoslavia, he went on to say, was to be pulverised 'with merciless brutality in a lightning operation'.

There was already a small Luftwaffe presence – mainly single-engined fighters and tactical reconnaissance units – stationed in Rumania to the northeast of Yugoslavia. But much more striking power was required for the forthcoming campaign, and a rapid build-up of Luftwaffe strength in the area was set in motion.

Foremost among the bomber units transferred to southeast Europe were the three *Gruppen* of Major Hans Bruno Schulz-Heyn's Ju 88-equipped *Kampfgeschwader* 51 'Edelweiss'. From their fields south of Paris, the units' 78 Junkers staged at low-level across France and Germany down into Austria to take up residence on their new bases around Vienna – *Stab*, I. and II. *Gruppen* at Wiener Neustadt and III./KG 51 at Schwechat. Here, they formed the largest single component of *Luftflotte* 4, the air

fleet charged with the major aerial offensive against Yugoslavia from the north.

At about the same time a single Ju 88 *Gruppe* that had also been serving in France was attached to *VIII. Fliegerkorps*, the Luftwaffe's primary close-support command, whose Stukas and ground-attack aircraft were gathering in Bulgaria in preparation for an assault on Yugoslavia from the east. This unit was I./LG 1, the only component of the *Lehrgeschwader* that had continued to operate over Great Britain after the transfer of *Stab*, II. and III./LG 1 to Sicily in late 1940. But I. *Gruppe* had remained at Orléans-Bricy for barely another month before being ordered back to Germany, and from there – via Austria and Rumania – to Bulgaria, where it touched down at Plovdiv-Krumovo in the second week of March.

Finally, almost closing the ring of steel being drawn around Yugoslavia, II. and III./LG 1 were temporarily moved forward from Catania to Grottaglie, on the heel of Italy, from where they would make the short hop across the Adriatic to attack Yugoslavia from the southeast. The other occupants of Catania, Major Arved Crüger's III./KG 30, remained on Sicily to continue their sweeps of the eastern Mediterranean sea lanes.

ACTION IN YUGOSLAVIA

It was the Austrian-based bombers of *Luftflotte* 4 (three of the seven *Gruppen* involved being the Ju 88s of KG 51) that were to strike the first blow against Yugoslavia. Hitler's orders to the air fleet were clear;

'As soon as sufficient forces have been assembled and the weather permits, the Yugoslavian air force's ground organisations and Belgrade are to be destroyed by the Luftwaffe in continuous day and night attacks'.

An unidentified Ju 88A-5 of LG 1 ('BN' or 'BS'?), purportedly photographed during II. and III. *Gruppen's* two-day deployment to Grottaglie, in Italy (note the twin-engined *Regia Aeronautica* Caproni Ca.310 in the background). The bombers' short-lived involvement over Yugoslavia presumably did not warrant the application of yellow Balkan campaign markings

Another cutting from a wartime magazine, the original caption to this illustration describes it as 'The bombing of Fortress Belgrade', adding that 'the smoke and flames were visible from a distance of 70 kilometres away'

Like every *Blitzkrieg* that preceded it, the assault on Yugoslavia opened with pre-emptive strikes on the enemy's airfields. Here, they were evidently successful, although just how great a threat to the invaders these particular machines – they appear to be Rogozarski trainers – might have posed is open to question

The fuselage codes on this Ju 88A-5 taxiing out to take off appear to be 'L1+GN', which would indicate its being a machine of 5./LG 1. As it is clearly wearing Balkan campaign yellow markings on nacelles (and rudder), it not only gives the lie to the caption of the photograph on page 20, it is also a perfect illustration of the old adage so dear to many ex-members of the Luftwaffe – 'the only hard-and-fast rule in the wartime Luftwaffe was that there *were* no hard-and-fast rules!'

That time came at 0515 hrs on 6 April 1941 when, without any prior declaration of war, *Luftflotte* 4's bombers struck at Belgrade's governmental quarter and every major Yugoslav airfield. From 10,500 ft out of a cloudless blue sky, KG 51's Ju 88s unloaded their high-explosive bombs and incendiaries on the enemy capital, causing widespread devastation. During another raid later in the day, Hauptmann Heinrich Hahn's I. *Gruppe* came under fierce attack from Yugoslav fighters and three of their machines returned to base with battle damage.

At the same time, far to the south, I./LG 1 flew three missions to widely differing targets. The first of these operations saw it attacking defence positions in the mountains bordering Greece. Later that morning the Ju 88s struck at an army HQ in Skoplje, before bombing the munitions works in Krusevac in mid-afternoon. No aircraft were lost.

Meanwhile, the Italian-based elements of LG 1 had crossed the Adriatic to strike at airfields in central and southern Yugoslavia. *Stab* and III. *Gruppe* hit Sarajevo, while II./LG 1 headed for Podgorica. Hauptmann Nietsch's III./LG 1 then undertook a second operation, dividing their strength to attack barracks at Mostar and the seaplane base at Kotor. II. and III. *Gruppe* each reported aircraft damaged in crash-landings back at Grottaglie, and the remainder returned that same evening to Catania, their short-lived part in the Yugoslavian campaign over.

After the clear blue skies of 5 April, a band of persistent bad weather set in over the Vienna area for the next five days. This did not make KG 51's task of mounting 'continuous day and night attacks' any easier, but the crews kept up the pressure on the enemy. On 7 April it was I. *Gruppe* that again bore the brunt of determined Yugoslav resistance, losing one aircraft from each of its three component *Staffeln*, while II. and III./LG 1 reported a machine apiece written off in crash-landings.

Poor weather conditions also hampered operations in the south of the country on 7 April. I./LG 1 flew an early morning raid against road and rail targets around Veles, but a second attack on the enemy HQ on Skoplje planned for the afternoon had to be aborted. During the course of the day two of the *Gruppe's* Ju 88s were damaged in crash-landings upon returning to base. One of them was flown by future Knight's Cross winner and 'Wilde Sau' pilot Leutnant Iro Ilk. He tried to put down at the nearby civil airfield near Plovdiv, but unlike the wide expanse of neighbouring Krumovo airfield, this proved too small for a machine the size of a Ju 88.

8 April witnessed a re-run of the previous day for I./LG 1 – a morning raid on road junctions around Nis before the weather again closed in during the afternoon. Heavy snow in the Plovdiv-Krumovo areas on 11 and 12 April finally brought the *Gruppe's* operations to a total standstill. It also effectively ended I./LG 1's part in the war against Yugoslavia, for with the Yugoslav army already on the ropes, the *Gruppe's* activities were now being directed against Greece.

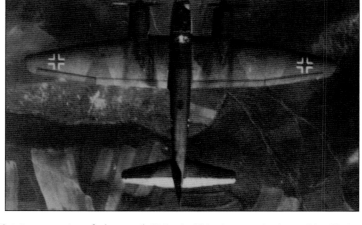

This photograph of an unidentified I./LG 1 aircraft, taken over Yugoslavia early in April 1941, muddies the waters even further: instead of yellow nacelles and rudder, it appears to have a yellow (some sources suggest white) nose and elevators!

While the campaign had cost I./LG 1 just two aircraft damaged, KG 51 continued to pay a price, albeit a small one, after an improvement in the weather in the Vienna region allowed the resumption of intensive bombing operations in the north. Details are sketchy (and conflicting), but in raids on such targets as Novi Sad, Banja Luka, Mostar and Dubrovnik, the *Geschwader* suffered the loss of several machines. These included II. *Gruppe's* '9K+LP', downed by a Yugoslav Hurricane near Banja Luka, and the aircraft of Hauptmann Hans Berlin, the *Kapitän* of 6. *Staffel*, who was killed together with his entire crew. Conversely, the rear gunner of another Ju 88 shot down an attacking Hurricane during the bombing of Mostar airfield.

On 13 April KG 51 participated in a series of heavy raids on the Sarajevo region. These were carried out on the personal orders of Hitler, who had apparently been informed that the Yugoslav government had sought refuge in several large hotels in the spa resort of Ilidza just to the west of the town. III. *Gruppe* alone flew 29 individual sorties against these targets. By this time the end in Yugoslavia was clearly in sight. On 14 April the army's commander-in-chief began negotiations for a general cease-fire. The following day KG 51 flew some of its final misions of the campaign when it dive-bombed shipping in Dubrovnik harbour. Forty-eight hours later Yugoslavia capitulated.

While *Stab*, II. and III./KG 51 remained at their bases around Vienna, I. *Gruppe* staged via Arad, in Rumania, down to Krumovo. Here it would operate alongside the Ju 88s of I./LG 1 against Greece for the best part of another month, before rejoining its parent unit in Austria in mid-May in

Another 'difference of opinion'. In this instance, 9./KG 51's '9K+LT' appears to be the guilty party, as both the Bf 110 and the Do 17 pictured on the right are swathed in tarpaulins, and were presumably stationary at the moment of impact

preparation for the move into Poland, its jumping-off point for the invasion of the USSR four weeks later. But this was not the last the Mediterranean theatre had seen of the 'Edelweiss' *Geschwader*. II./KG 51 would return briefly to Greece in the autumn of 1943.

ASSAULT ON GREECE

6 April 1941 had not only witnessed the start of the savage aerial bombardment of Belgrade, it also saw the launch of the ground and air onslaught on mainland Greece. But at least the Greeks received a declaration of war, even if it *was* delivered by Hitler's ambassador in Athens at 0530 hrs that morning, and deliberately timed to coincide with the first German troops crossing the Bulgarian border and beginning their drive on Salonika in Greece's northeastern province of Thessaloniki.

Until now the Luftwaffe had been concentrating its efforts on the supply convoys ferrying British troops up from Egypt. However, with the *Führer's* strict ban on violating Greek airspace a thing of the past, the war against the British and Greek Royal Air Forces could begin in earnest. But with all three *Gruppen* of LG 1 engaged over Yugoslavia on this opening day of the twin campaigns, it fell to the Ju 88 units still based in Sicily to score the first successes, and suffer the first casualties of Operation *Marita*, as the invasion of Greece had been code-named when plans were first drawn up back in December 1940.

The first loss sustained was one of the 14 Ju 88Ds of 2.(F)/123, a second long-range reconnaissance *Staffel* that had joined 1.(F)/122 at Catania in mid-March. Heading for the Athens area, Unteroffizier Fritz Dreyer's '4U+EK' was intercepted by an RAF Hurricane over the Gulf of Corinth and shot into the sea off Patras.

Indicative of the reconnaissance units' wide area of operations – and proof that the campaign in Greece was not being fought to the exclusion of other fronts – 'EK's' sister-ship, '4U+FK', was reported missing in very similar circumstances just 24 hours later, shot down by a Hurricane some 400 miles away! Caught over Tobruk harbour, Oberfeldwebel Werner Reinicke's Ju 88D crashed into the sea off Bardia.

And whereas the loss of the first Ju 88 over Greece may admittedly have been of little significance (except to the unfortunate Unteroffizier Dreyer and his crew), the Junkers' first success of the campaign was a devastating raid on Piraeus harbour. Serving as the destination for the vast majority of the supply convoys that had been bringing men and materials from Egypt since early February, Piraeus was packed with shipping on the evening of 6 April when 20 Ju 88s of III./KG 30 lifted off from Catania.

Most of the bombers were armed with just two aerial mines apiece, the intention being to block the narrow entrance to the harbour. But Hauptmann Hajo Herrmann had ordered that his 7. *Staffel* machines should each be loaded with two 250-kg bombs as well. At the end of the 465-mile flight to the target area, he did not want to see his mines drift down on their parachutes and simply disappear into the water. After all that effort, he was determined to attack the merchantmen berthed in the harbour – it was to prove a momentous decision.

The more heavily loaded aircraft of 7./KG 30 were flying the low position in the loose formation as the Ju 88s swooped down on Piraeus from the direction of Corinth at 2100 hrs. After releasing their mines as directed, Herrmann's crews made for the ships. At least three of the *Staffel's* bombs – Herrmann's among them – struck the 7529-ton *Clan Fraser*, a recently arrived ammunition ship packed with 350 tons of TNT, only 100 tons of which had been unloaded when the attack came in. As well as the three direct hits, it was surrounded by near misses, which destroyed buildings and stores on the quayside. The initial blast lifted the vessel out of the water and snapped its mooring lines. The shockwave from the explosion was felt by Herrmann and his crew as their '4D+AR' was thrown about 'like a leaf in a squall' 3300 ft above the harbour.

But worse was to follow. As the *Clan Fraser* drifted, its plates glowing from the fires raging inside her, the flames spread to other vessels in the harbour, including the 7100-ton *City of Roubaix*, which was also carrying munitions. Despite the danger, desperate efforts were made to get the situation under control. But the blazing ships could not be towed away for fear that they would hit a mine and block the harbour approach channel.

Suddenly, in the early hours of 7 April, the *Clan Fraser* erupted in a giant fireball. Minutes later the *City of Roubaix* went up as well. The resultant series of explosions, which destroyed nine other merchantmen and devastated the port of Piraeus, shattered windows in Athens seven miles away, and were reportedly heard over a distance of up to 150 miles.

In all, close on 100 vessels were lost, including some 60 small lighters and barges. Grievous as this was, the damage to the port of Piraeus itself was far more serious. In the explosions, described by one historian as 'of near nuclear proportions', it had been razed almost from end to end. Adm Sir Andrew Cunningham, C-in-C of the Mediterranean Fleet, called the raid on Piraeus a 'devastating blow'. At a single stroke it had destroyed the one port sufficiently and adequately equipped to serve as a base through which the British Army could be supplied.

Piraeus would be closed to all shipping for the next ten days. During this time incoming vessels had to be diverted to other ports such as nearby Salamis, or Volos far up on Greece's Aegean coast. And even after it had

This aerial shot of the Piraeus area, taken in late April 1941, gives little indication of the mayhem that occurred there earlier in the month during the night of 6-7 April, except, perhaps, for the dark streams of oil still leaking from the half-sunken ships

been partially reopened, such was the damage that it was no longer able to operate properly. The master of one vessel that put in to Salamis on 9 April and visited Piraeus two days later described the place as being 'in a state of chaos caused by the explosion of the *Clan Fraser*, which had been hit while discharging ammunition. The ship had disappeared and blown up the rest of the docks, and pieces of her were littered about the streets.'

The man responsible for much of this chaos and mayhem, Hauptmann Hajo Herrmann, had not escaped totally unscathed. At some stage during the raid the port engine of his Ju 88 had been damaged by anti-aircraft fire. And for safety's sake, rather than risk the long flight back to Catania, he headed eastwards and landed on Rhodes – only to run his aircraft off the end of the runway!

Adm Cunningham was undoubtedly right. The destruction of Piraeus *was* a disaster. But even if the port had been fully functional, it is unlikely that it would have altered the outcome of the brief but bloody campaign in Greece. The invaders were too powerful for the Greek and British Commonwealth troops opposing them, irrespective of how many last-minute reinforcements might have come through a still intact Piraeus.

In fact, in less than three weeks the British would be driven back down the length of Greece to some of the country's southernmost beaches, where they were rescued in a Dunkirk-like evacuation. This was not the end of their Grecian odyssey, however, for instead of being transported back to Egypt, they were delivered to the island of Crete, from where the survivors would undergo a second evacuation just over a month later.

TARGETING ALLIED SHIPS

Although the Mediterranean Ju 88s flew a number of sorties in support of the German army in the field in Greece (while at the same time also operating over Malta, North Africa and on convoy escort duties), most of the actions they were involved in during the Greek and Cretan campaigns were directed against Allied shipping. And during the combined ten days of the evacuations in which the two campaigns ended, they would exact a far greater toll of Allied warships and merchantmen than they had done during the entire ten weeks of anti-convoy missions flown before the ground fighting began.

The armed reconnaissance sweeps of the sea areas around Crete by aircraft of LG 1 on 8 and 10 April produced no sightings. But during a similar operation north of the island on the morning of 11 April machines of 9. *Staffel* found the Royal Navy's HMS *Calcutta*. This anti-aircraft vessel seemed to bear a charmed life. It had been attacked on numerous occasions while escorting convoys from Egypt during the previous weeks, and had been one of the three cruisers present in Piraeus harbour on the night of 6 April that had managed to put to sea before the second cataclysmic explosion of the *Clan Fraser*. Even now its luck held. Although bracketed by bombs to port and starboard the vessel sustained no hits.

In the evening of that same 11 April, eager to take advantage of the full moon, *X. Fliegerkorps* ordered a maximum effort by the Sicilian-based Ju 88s against any shipping still to be found in the Piraeus area (where 20 merchant vessels were anchored off the harbour, short of fuel). Some 45 bombers took off in two waves, 29 machines of LG 1 from Catania at 1800 hrs and 16 of III./KG 30 from Gerbini shortly after midnight. Four ships were sunk, including the damaged Danish tanker *Marie Maersk*. The last of the LG 1 aircraft to attack was that flown by Hauptmann Joachim Helbig, *Kapitän* of 4. *Staffel*. Recovering from the dive, his Ju 88 was coned by searchlights at an altitude of only some 1300 ft;

'I was a sitting duck for any nightfighter. And suddenly there one was, a twin-engined machine hurtling down at me from high on my right. At full throttle I pulled up hard to the left, and the fighter flashed past me. My radio-operator, Oberfeldwebel Franz Schlund, had him in his sights for just a split second. But that was enough. The enemy went down on fire and we saw him explode as he hit the ground.'

Helbig's opponent was almost certainly the Blenheim IF of No 30 Sqn reported lost that night.

Forty-eight hours later, elements of III./KG 30 were back over the Piraeus-Salamis areas, where they claimed a merchantman damaged, but lost two of their own number. 5./LG 1 also reported a crew missing on this 13 April when one of its Ju 88s was forced to ditch after attacking a convoy west of Crete.

By this stage I./LG 1 was also beginning to operate against Greek targets from its base at Krumovo, in Bulgaria. On 13 April 20 of its Ju 88s participated in a major raid on Volos Harbour. The port was severely damaged, and among the ships sunk was the 7140-ton *City of Karachi*, a vessel diverted to Volos after the destruction of Piraeus. But Hauptmann Hoffmann's *Gruppe* also had a price to pay for this success, for a machine from 1. *Staffel* was shot down by one of the RAF Hurricanes stationed at nearby Larissa. Later that same afternoon I./LG 1 attacked Australian and New Zealand troop positions around Servia.

Late in the evening of 14 April eight Ju 88s of Catania-based II./LG 1 again attacked Piraeus and the Gulf of Athens. Upon their return to Sicily they reported hits on two vessels. The damage inflicted was obviously greater than realised, for both the 7264-ton British steamer *Clan Cumming* and a smaller Turkish vessel went to the bottom. The following day, 24 of I./LG 1's aircraft returned to the Piraeus area. Among the seven vessels claimed sunk were the British merchantmen *Quiloa* (7765 tons) and *Goalpara* (5314 tons), both of which were subsequently beached and abandoned in Eleusis Bay. One crew failed to return from the raid, Unteroffizier Karl Stütz's 'L1+SK' last being seen four miles south of Athens, where it reportedly fell victim to yet another RAF Hurricane.

It would appear that I./LG 1 was accompanied on this occasion for the first time by aircraft of I./KG 51, which had just joined it in Bulgaria, for two badly-damaged 'Edelweiss' machines were written off in crash-landings back at Krumovo on this date. Two others put down with minor damage at Salonika, the major seaport in northeastern Greece that had been occupied by German troops six days earlier.

Heavy snow showers prevented operations out of Krumovo on 17 April (although the field was large, it was not equipped for bad-weather flying). Conditions improved sufficiently the following day to allow various

The duty NCO holds 2./LG 1's 'L1+BK' with a raised red flag while he checks that the runway is clear. This photograph was reportedly taken at Krumovo, in Bulgaria, and the low range of hills in the background certainly seems to support this – even the patches of snow on their flanks match the known weather conditions. But the machines are clearly Ju 88A-4s. Were this pair among the first of the improved series to be delivered to the *Geschwader*, the one in the rear not even wearing a white fuselage band yet?

Staffeln to carry out a number of missions in support of the ground fighting. These included bombing and strafing attacks on Allied positions around Larissa and Yanina. But when thick cloud descended over the mountains along the Greek-Bulgarian border, Major Kuno Hoffmann, the *Gruppenkommandeur* of I./LG 1, ordered his crews to divert to Salonika-Sedes rather than to attempt to make it back to base. This precaution was clearly necessary, as the *Kapitän* of 2./LG 1, Hauptmann Siegfried von Eichhorn, was badly injured when he crash-landed his machine due to severe icing-up.

By now British and Commonwealth forces were in full retreat. On 19 April the Germans occupied both Larissa and Trikkala. That afternoon, having returned to Krumovo, I./LG 1 mounted a heavy raid on Khalkis harbour, claiming four freighters sunk and two damaged. Twenty-four hours later it put in another attack on the shipping still clustered around Piraeus. Among the vessels sunk was the Greek hospital ship *Ellenis*. But this time the *Gruppe* did not escape scot-free. Unteroffizier Helmut Benke's 'L1+ZH' was downed by Hurricanes near Athens and a 2. *Staffel* machine, badly damaged and with the navigator dead on board, was lost when it was forced to ditch in shallow water six miles north of Karies.

It was on 20 April that II. and III./LG 1 resumed their activities in Cretan waters, flying operations to the north and southeast of the island respectively. The next day, II. *Gruppe* undertook a second armed reconnaissance mission, this time south of Crete, where it caught and sank the 6098-ton tanker *British Lord*. Also on 21 April, I./LG 1 flew a number of what were termed '*freie Jagd* sweeps against shipping' in the Khalkis area, which netted the crews involved at least three Greek vessels.

I./LG 1's anti-shipping operations were taking a heavy toll of Allied merchantmen, and none more so than those flown over southern Greece and Crete on 22 April. By the end of that day the *Gruppe* had claimed seven vessels probably sunk and a further twelve damaged. Among the known losses were six small Greek ships. Major Hoffmann's crews may, however, also have been responsible for sinking one, or both, of the Greek destroyers *Psara* and *Ydra*, each of 1389 tons, that were recorded as lost in action against German aircraft on this date.

I./LG 1 kept up the pressure throughout 23 and 24 April, flying numerous armed reconnaissance sweeps – mostly in *Ketten* of just three aircraft – over the same areas between southern Greece and Crete. On the second of these two dates in particular, Allied shipping losses hit an all-time high with no fewer than fourteen vessels being reported sunk. Again, most of the

An unidentified merchant vessel burns fiercely from a direct hit 'somewhere on the Greek coast'

casualties were Greek, but numbered among them were two British merchantmen, the 4665-ton *Santa Clara Valley* and the 2269-ton *Cavallo*, both of which were caught and bombed at Nauplia (the latter, although abandoned, did not actually sink until the following day).

German ground forces had been matching the Luftwaffe success for success. The British had by now been driven back to the southernmost reaches of Greece, and it was on the evening of 24 April that Operation *Demon*, the Royal Navy's hastily organised plans for evacuation from eight small southern Greek ports, was put into effect. All of Adm Cunningham's available light forces, from cruisers down to landing craft – some 35 ships in all – plus a dozen transports, were to take part. Over the course of the next five nights (lacking air cover, operations could only be carried out during the hours of darkness) they would succeed in lifting off just over 50,000 troops – about 80 percent of the number originally transported to Greece prior to, and during, the short-lived campaign.

Throughout that time it had been the Allied merchant navies that had borne the brunt of the Luftwaffe's attacks. But now, during the evacuation from Greece and subsequent operations around Crete, it would be the warships of the Royal Navy that began to feel the full fury of the German bombers and dive-bombers.

There were, however, a number of unarmed merchantmen still to be lost before the last troops left the soil of Greece. Late in the afternoon of 25 April, elements of I./LG 1 discovered a group of some half-dozen ships heading towards Greece as part of the preparations for the second night of the evacuations. A single bomb hit the 16,381-ton Dutch vessel *Pennland*. At first the ship tried to continue its journey, but it was soon forced to turn back towards Crete. Shortly afterwards the vessel was attacked again, two more bombs sending it to the bottom. *Pennland* was the largest merchantman lost during the Greek and Cretan campaigns.

On the morning of 26 April the Ju 88s flew one last mission in support of the ground fighting. Shortly after sunrise several machines from both I./LG 1 and I./KG 51 lifted off from Krumovo to attack the Allied troops holding out along the Corinth Canal. While the *Lehrgeschwader* crews carried out low-level passes, strafing and dropping light bombs, the Ju 88s from 1./KG 51 delivered their loads from high altitude. That afternoon much of I./LG 1 spent several hours searching in vain for a large convoy reported to be assembling north of Crete. The following day – which saw the first German troops enter Athens – I./LG 1 was back in the same area to the north of Crete where it caught and sank the 8672-ton Dutch freighter *Costa Rica*.

CRETE UNDER ATTACK

By 29 April, with the evacuation of British forces from Greece completed, the Luftwaffe's attentions were focussing entirely on Crete. I./LG 1 carried out an attack on shipping in Souda Bay on this date,

Merchantmen were often little more than sitting ducks. Fast and manoeuvrable warships in open water were a different proposition altogether, being much harder to hit, as witness this attack on the needle-like form of a Royal Navy destroyer heading into the glare of a sun-dappled patch of sea. The length of the vessel's wake and the puffs of smoke from its overworked boilers are vivid testimony to the speed at which the warship is travelling. It has evidently put the attacking Ju 88 off its aim, for what appears to be a full salvo of four 500-kg bombs has gone harmlessly into the water a good 250 yards off the vessel's port bow

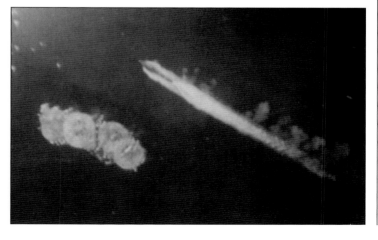

claiming damage to three vessels. This was to be its last operational mission of the campaign. Although personnel casualties had been relatively light, the past three weeks-plus of near continual flying had been costly in terms of material attrition. Down to just 17 serviceable machines at month's end, the *Gruppe* was taken off operations for a well-earned rest.

With Yugoslavia and Greece having been dealt with, Hitler now began to consider the question of Crete. He could hardly ignore the presence of an island base housing thousands of enemy troops just 62 miles off the southern extremities of his newly expanded *Festung Europa*. On 25 April the *Führer* therefore issued his War Directive No 28 for Operation *Merkur* ('Mercury'), the airborne invasion of Crete. However, his primary reason for the undertaking was, he declared in Paragraph 1 of the Directive, to secure the island 'as a base for air warfare against Great Britain in the Eastern Mediterranean'.

It would take several weeks to gather together the troops and transport aircraft required for the ambitious operation, and during that time an uneasy lull descended on the region. To fill the gap I./LG 1 was called back into action. On 3 May, despite having been stood down only days earlier, I./LG 1 took off on another six-hour mission to Souda Bay, the main anchorage on Crete's northern coast. It was accompanied by a handful of machines from I./KG 51. And although they would claim hits on the 7258-ton British merchantman *Araybank*, the raid cost the attackers two casualties. Both were aircraft of 1./KG 51 and both were reportedly brought down by Hurricanes, '9K+LH' crashing on the island and '9K+GH' going into the sea off Souda Bay.

The next day machines of the two units were back over Souda Bay again, the luckless *Araybank* receiving further damage that meant that it had to be run aground to prevent it sinking. The vessel was declared a total loss after being bombed for a third time on 16 May.

On 13 May I./KG 51 handed its remaining aircraft over to I./LG 1 and the personnel departed northwards by rail to rejoin their parent *Geschwaderstab*, re-equipping in readiness for the forthcoming invasion of the Soviet Union. Thus reinforced, I./LG 1 found itself heading back to Souda Bay the following day. In fact, it flew two missions against the anchorage on 14 May. With barely an hour on the ground at Krumovo in which to refuel and bomb-up, the crews were in the air from 0535 hrs until 1800 hrs. And at the end they had very little to show for it. The only confirmed sinking was that of the 6343-ton British steamship *Dalesman*. Fortune still smiled on *Calcutta,* however, as although the cruiser was targeted in both raids, not a hit was scored on it. On 15 May I./LG 1 left Krumovo and transferred down to Eleusis, near Athens, where it was joined by II. *Gruppe*, which flew in from Catania the following day.

On the afternoon of 18 May I./LG 1 was back over its familiar Souda Bay stamping ground. Compared to the previous long haul down from Krumovo, in Bulgaria, the northern coast of Crete was now but a stone's throw away, and the Ju 88s could thus carry a much greater bomb load. It was in Souda Bay, while executing temporary repairs, that the heavy cruiser HMS *York* had been attacked and severely damaged by an Italian explosive motorboat back on 26 March. To prevent it from becoming a total loss, the vessel had been towed into shallow water and grounded. Although subjected to numerous air attacks since, the cruiser's main

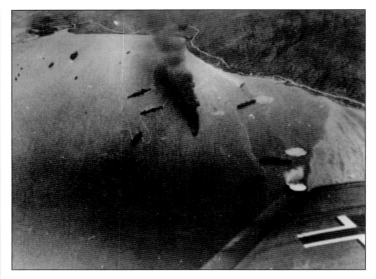

In enclosed waters naval and merchant vessels were equally vulnerable. This is Souda Bay on the northern coast of Crete, the island's main anchorage. It was the target of numerous raids by the Luftwaffe

armament of six 8-inch guns had remained intact, and it still posed a considerable threat to any invader.

During its raid of 18 May the crews of I./LG 1 greatly reduced this threat by knocking out the *York's* two forward turrets with their 1000-kg bombs. Whether they had been specifically ordered to target the cruiser on this occasion and with this particular purpose in mind is no longer clear. The results achieved were certainly opportune, however, for just 48 hours later the skies above Souda Bay reverberated to the sound of hundreds of aircraft engines. The airborne invasion of Crete had begun.

The 13-day battle for Crete is now remembered mainly for the enormous casualties inflicted upon the invading forces and the transport aircraft that ferried them and their supplies to the island. The Luftwaffe combat command covering the operation was *General der Flieger* von Richthofen's *VIII. Fliegerkorps*. The *Korps'* Stukas had gained fame – notoriety would perhaps be the better word – for their close-support of German ground troops in the Polish and French campaigns (and more recently, the Yugoslav and Greek). But Crete added a new dimension – the waters surrounding the island.

Von Richthofen's units now faced a twofold task. Not only were they expected to offer direct support to German forces on the ground, they were also charged with keeping the British Mediterranean Fleet away from the island while the fighting was going on and, more importantly, ensuring that there was no repetition of the successful seaborne evacuation from Greece. To enable it to carry out this latter commitment, the predominantly Ju 87-equipped *VIII. Fliegerkorps* was temporarily assigned several longer range *Kampfgruppen*. The only Ju 88 units among them were I. and II./LG 1, now based at Eleusis together with Oberst Friedrich-Karl Knust's *Geschwaderstab*.

Shortly after midday on 20 May – the opening day of *Merkur* – I./LG 1 raided Souda Bay again, registering two direct hits on a 6000-ton vessel (possibly the wreck of the 6200-ton *Dalesman*, already claimed sunk by the *Gruppe* six days earlier). That afternoon both I. and II./LG 1 were sent out to search for a force of 'six Royal Navy ships' reported by reconnaissance to be off the southeast coast of Crete. The enemy warships (the two cruisers and four destroyers of 'Force C') remained elusive, however, and after a long and fruitless search most crews unloaded their bombs on Souda Bay when *en route* back to Eleusis.

Next day, the two *Gruppen* could hardly fail to find the numerous warships converging on Crete from seemingly all directions. Early morning reconnaissance reported groups of enemy vessels to the southeast, north and west of the island. I./LG 1's first attack was directed against the latter, which was the main British Battle Squadron comprising the two battleships

Warspite and *Valiant* of 'Force A', plus a number of cruisers and destroyers. II./LG 1, meanwhile, had finally located 'Force C' off the eastern end of Crete

With little fear of Allied air intervention, aircraft shadowed and tracked the ships' movements throughout the day as one attack after the other went in against them. 21 May 1941 was to prove to be the beginning of one of the biggest air-sea engagements of the war to date, and by its end the two *Gruppen* of LG 1 alone had dropped 66 tons of

A view of Souda Bay from the ground, reportedly taken during I./LG 1's raid of 20 May. Columns of dense black smoke from two burning merchantmen darken the whole sky. In the centre of the photograph another merchant vessel has just been hit, while to the far left white smoke is pouring from the bow section of the unmistakable twin-funnelled shape of the listing and half-submerged cruiser *York* – perhaps from the attack two days earlier when I./LG 1 had claimed to have knocked out its two forward turrets

bombs. Collectively, they claimed five hits on battleships and six on cruisers, with considerable damage probably inflicted on three of the vessels. The reality fell far short of these optimistic claims. In fact, for the effort expended, the net result of the day's operations was abysmal – the cruiser *Ajax* slightly damaged by a near miss! The Luftwaffe's '*Wunderbomber*' had totally failed to live up to its reputation on this occasion. Indeed, the Royal Navy's only casualty – the destroyer *Juno* – had fallen victim to Ju 87s. But the Ju 88s were to redeem themselves 24 hours later.

22 May found the four groups of warships ('Forces A to D') still gathered in Cretan waters. Heartened by the Luftwaffe's relatively poor performance the previous day, the Royal Navy had remained on station, determined to frustrate the Axis attempts to follow up the airborne landings on Crete with an invasion by sea. One convoy of small craft crowded with German troops had already been repulsed with heavy losses during the night. Not long after dawn the strengthened 'Force C', now comprising four cruisers, plus destroyers, was caught to the north of Crete by aircraft of I./LG 1 and subjected to the first of a series of sustained attacks lasting nearly three-and-a-half hours in all. Some sources suggest that III./KG 30 was called in from Sicily to add its weight to the assault, which resulted in considerable damage to the cruisers *Naiad* and *Carlisle*.

In the meantime 'Force C' had encountered a second Axis convoy and forced it to turn back. But the warships were now dangerously exposed some 90 miles north of Crete, and the force commander ordered that the pursuit be abandoned and the formation withdraw to the southwest to join up with the main Battle Squadron.

In the afternoon I. and II./LG 1 resumed the attack on the combined British forces in the areas to the west and southwest of Crete. The two battleships of 'Force A' were damaged and the two cruisers of the detached 'Force B' sunk – *Gloucester* in the Kythera Channel and *Fiji* 85 miles to the south of it. The destroyer *Greyhound* also went down close to the *Gloucester*. Many other units, most notably the Ju 87s of *VIII. Fliegerkorps*, had played a major part in the day-long assault, but Oberst Knust, with his two *Gruppen* having flown 84 individual sorties, had no hesitation in claiming credit for all three sinkings in that evening's report to *Korps* HQ. Two of his Ju 88s had been lost to naval anti-aircraft fire, a third destroyed in a crash and two others damaged.

Irrespective of who had actually sent the three warships to the bottom, the Luftwaffe had achieved its object. Short of both fuel and anti-aircraft ammunition, the Royal Navy vessels were forced to retire to Alexandria some 420 miles away to the south. But another battle squadron, built around the aircraft carrier *Formidable* and comprising two battleships, two cruisers and nine destroyers, returned to the area during the night of 25/26 May to bombard the island of Scarpanto, east of Crete. Many Axis aircraft were based on the island, and it was

III./KG 30's '4D+LT' is refuelled and readied for another mission

hoped that if their operations could be disrupted, it would bring some desperately needed relief to the hard-pressed troops on Crete. Records would seem to indicate, however, that just one aircraft was destroyed on the ground and nine others damaged.

And, inevitably, the Royal Navy task force was quickly located by air reconnaissance the next morning as it was withdrawing. For nine hours the vessels were subjected to attack. I./LG 1 kept up a continual assault for six of those hours, sending its aircraft out in *Ketten* of threes commencing at 0940 hrs. In mid-afternoon I./LG 1 was relieved by the aircraft of II. *Gruppe*, which continued the aerial onslaught for a further three hours. Despite this all-out effort no ships were sunk, although the *Formidable*, battleship *Barham*, cruiser *Orion* and destroyer *Nubian* all suffered damage to varying degree (some of the worst being inflicted by the Ju 87s).

Throughout the day only two Ju 88s were lost, both being claimed by Fulmars launched by *Formidable*. One Junkers exploded in mid-air after coming under attack, while the other was forced to ditch, but not before the rear-gunner had hit the engine of the Fulmar on its tail. The two machines went into the water only some 200 yards apart, and both crews were quickly picked up by the destroyer *Hereward*.

27 May again found the machines of I. and II./LG 1 out hunting for units of the Royal Navy to the south and east of Crete. Among the vessels sighted was the fast minelayer *Abdiel,* hastening back to Alexandria after one of its many audacious night supply runs to Crete. The 2650-ton minelayer escaped unscathed, but the destroyer *Nizam* was hit and further damage was inflicted on the battleship *Barham*, which had one of its main turrets put out of action. During the afternoon, a formation of six Ju 88s had the misfortune to run into three RAF fighters – two Hurricanes and a Blenheim – flying north from Africa to attack the Ju 52/3m transports still pouring supplies into Crete. The three British machines each claimed a Junkers destroyed. In fact only one bomber went down.

It was to be the last Ju 88 loss of the campaign, for at about the same time as Leutnant Hans-Georg Freysoldt's 'L1+EW' disappeared beneath the waves south of Crete, the decision was being made to evacuate the island. Once again the Royal Navy was to come to the rescue of the beleaguered army. There were 32,000 troops to be taken off Crete and only four points of embarkation – the harbour of Heraklion on the north coast, and the tiny fishing villages of Sphakia, Tymbaki and Plaka Bay to south and east. The problem was that only at Heraklion, which was in imminent danger of capture, were there any port facilities. The other three locations would involve lifting men from open beaches.

Furthermore, because of Axis air superiority over Crete, the plan was to evacuate troops only between the hours of midnight and 0300 hrs. Naval ships would sorely need the few precious hours before and after these times to give them a chance to approach the beaches and then get away under the cover of darkness. Even so, it would be a risky venture.

The three cruisers and six destroyers of 'Force B' sailed from Alexandria for Heraklion at 0600 hrs on 28 May. During the afternoon, while negotiating the Kaso Strait to the east of Crete, the vessels were attacked by aircraft of II./LG 1, but apparently without any significant results (slight damage being reported to two ships). Meanwhile, I. *Gruppe* had raided Heraklion itself, claiming the sinking of the Greek freighter *Georgos*. At 0320 hrs on the morning of 29 May 'Force B' left Heraklion, having taken on board the port's entire garrison of some 4000 men. But it was already daylight when the ships turned south for the return run through the Kaso Strait to the open sea beyond.

For the next eight hours or more 'Force B' was subjected to near constant dive-bombing attack, the Ju 88s of II./LG 1 from Eleusis alternating with the Ju 87 *Gruppen* operating from nearby Scarpanto on the eastern side of the strait. The Stukas were credited with sinking the destroyer *Hereward*, but it was a crew from LG 1 that claimed a hit on the 5450-ton cruiser *Dido*, putting one of its forward turrets out of action. Although no bombers were lost in these operations, a lone reconnaissance Ju 88 of 2.(F)/123 that had been shadowing 'Force B' was shot down by RAF aircraft from North Africa.

Shortly before midnight on 29 May, 'Force D', comprising four cruisers, three destroyers and a fast naval transport, arrived off the tiny harbour of Sphakia on the south coast of Crete. When the vessels left some hours later, they took with them over 6000 troops. But the formation could not escape the patrolling Ju 88s of LG 1, which discovered the warships just after 0930 hrs on 30 May. Within minutes they had dive-bombed the ships, hitting the 6980-ton Australian cruiser HMAS *Perth*.

That same afternoon three machines of II./LG 1 also damaged the 1690-ton *Kelvin*, one of four destroyers heading north towards Sphakia

Aircraft 'L1+TH' of 1./LG 1 perches forlornly on a trestle as it awaits a replacement starboard wing and engine. This photograph was taken at Tanagra, in Greece – possibly the site of a repair and maintenance unit (note the sorry looking Bf 110 on the left). One source has suggested that the Ju 88 is in the process of being given a coat of overall desert tan camouflage paint. But refer back to the planview shot of the Ju 88 on page 22. This is exactly the area of forward fuselage covered by that machine's Balkan campaign markings

on another rescue mission. *Kelvin* was the second of this little group forced to turn back (the *Kandahar* having suffered a mechanical fault some three hours earlier). The remaining two destroyers got to Sphakia, took on board more than 1500 troops, and by 0230 hrs on 31 May were ready to run the gauntlet back to Alexandria. They both made it, but not without incident. At 0850 hrs the two warships were attacked by a dozen Ju 88s of II./LG 1. *Napier* was near-missed and damaged, but the vessel's anti-aircraft gunners claimed one of the attackers shot down. Three of the RAF aircraft sent to the destroyers' aid also claimed a bomber apiece. But only one Ju 88 was lost, having been written-off after a forced-landing at Heraklion on Crete due, reportedly, to anti-aircraft damage.

During the night of 31 May/1 June, 'Force D' made the last run to Sphakia. It returned to Alexandria with 4000 men, but another 12,000 or more had to be left behind on Crete. The Royal Navy had done its best, but Axis air power had simply proved too overwhelming. Even on this final trip, the Ju 88s of LG 1 were on the prowl. Machines of I. *Gruppe* sighted the force shortly after dawn, but were driven off by a trio of RAF Beaufighters. To provide the returning ships with additional support, the anti-aircraft cruisers *Calcutta* and *Coventry* had sailed from Alexandria to meet up with them. However, before making the rendezvous, they were themselves discovered by two machines of II./LG 1.

Diving out of the sun, the lead machine – piloted by Hauptmann Joachim Helbig – narrowly missed *Coventry*, but Leutnant Hans Sauer's bombs hit *Calcutta* with devastating effect. The gallant warship's luck had finally run out, and it sank within minutes with heavy loss of life. Landing back at Eleusis, the two crews claimed the sinking of a destroyer.

Calcutta was the Royal Navy's last loss of the campaign. Aircraft of LG 1 flew a series of overlapping patrols throughout the daylight hours of 1 June scouring the waters between Crete and Egypt, but not a single vessel was sighted. 'It was as if the sea had been swept clean', remarked one Ju 88 pilot.

The end of the Balkan and Cretan campaigns also marked the close of the most concentrated and successful period of operations the Ju 88 was to experience in the Mediterranean conflict. The Luftwaffe's *'Wunder-bomber'* would continue to provide a presence in the theatre for the next three years. Its numbers would even increase as other *Gruppen* came and went. *Lehrgeschwader* 1 remained the one constant throughout. But it, like all the other units that operated in this theatre, would find itself pushed gradually but inexorably on to the defensive.

There were still significant individual successes to be had in the months to come, but rarely again would the Ju 88 bask in the near undisputed mastery of the skies that it had enjoyed in the spring of 1941.

The tiny harbour and beach at Sphakia, where the last act of the evacuation of Crete was played out

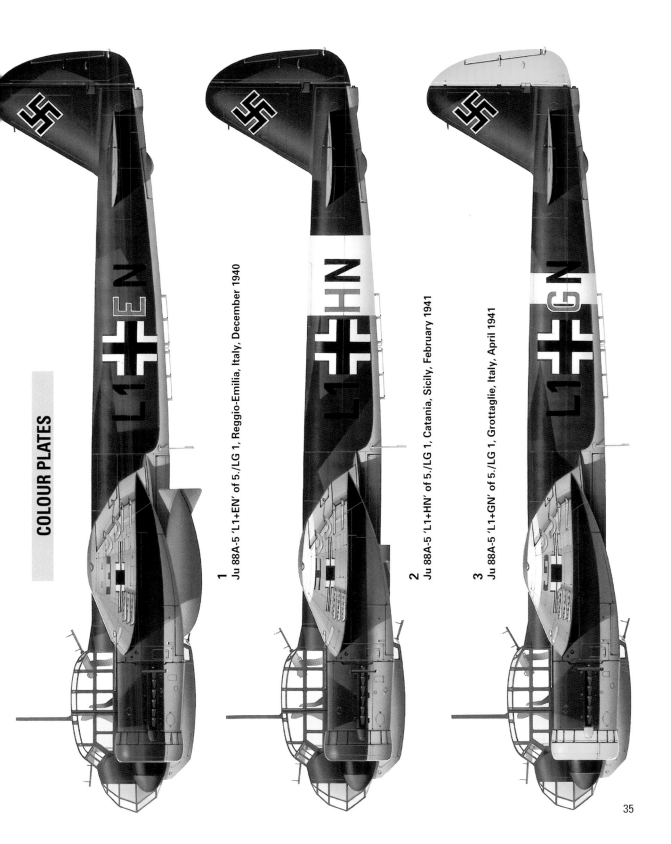

COLOUR PLATES

1
Ju 88A-5 'L1+EN' of 5./LG 1, Reggio-Emilia, Italy, December 1940

2
Ju 88A-5 'L1+HN' of 5./LG 1, Catania, Sicily, February 1941

3
Ju 88A-5 'L1+GN' of 5./LG 1, Grottaglie, Italy, April 1941

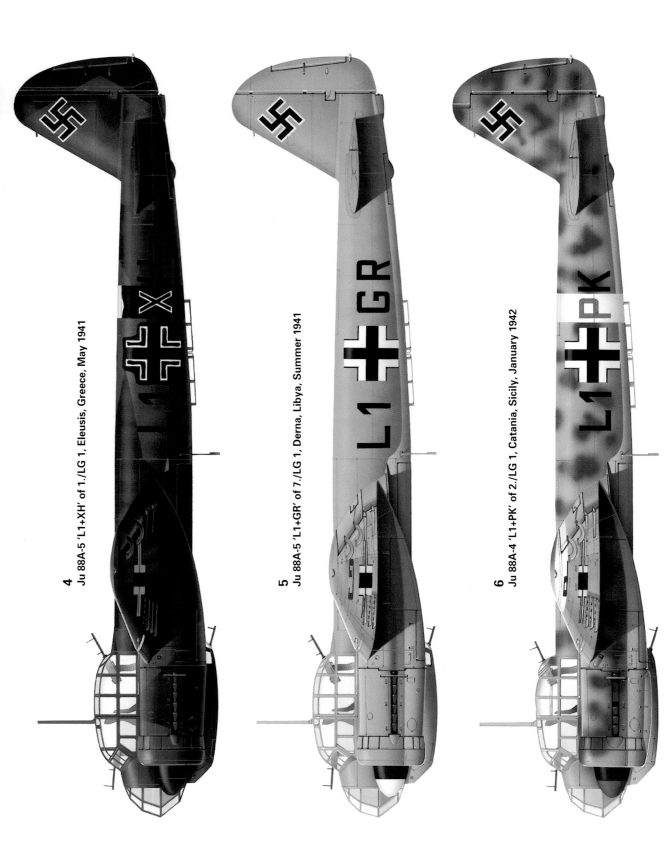

4
Ju 88A-5 'L1+XH' of 1./LG 1, Eleusis, Greece, May 1941

5
Ju 88A-5 'L1+GR' of 7./LG 1, Derna, Libya, Summer 1941

6
Ju 88A-4 'L1+PK' of 2./LG 1, Catania, Sicily, January 1942

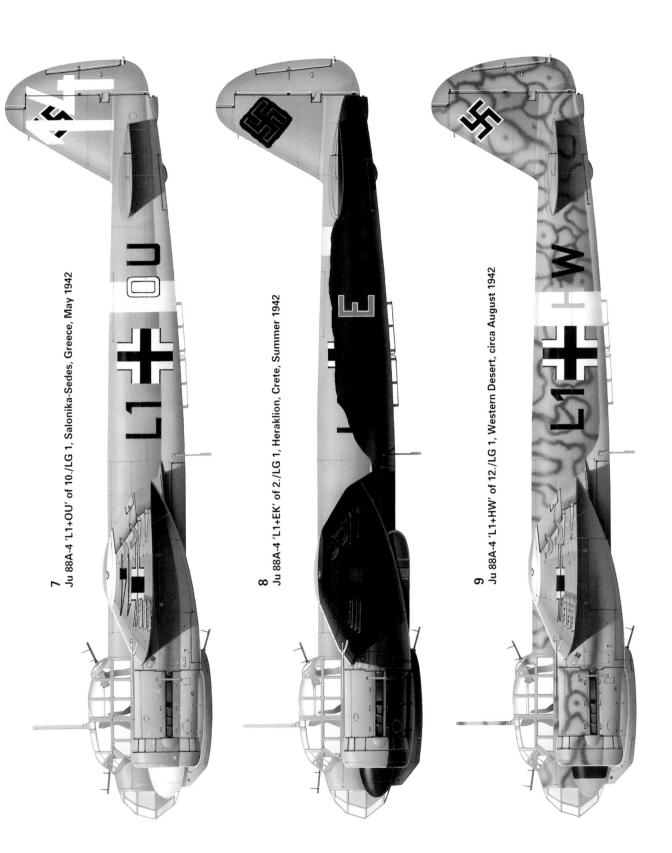

7
Ju 88A-4 'L1+OU' of 10./LG 1, Salonika-Sedes, Greece, May 1942

8
Ju 88A-4 'L1+EK' of 2./LG 1, Heraklion, Crete, Summer 1942

9
Ju 88A-4 'L1+HW' of 12./LG 1, Western Desert, circa August 1942

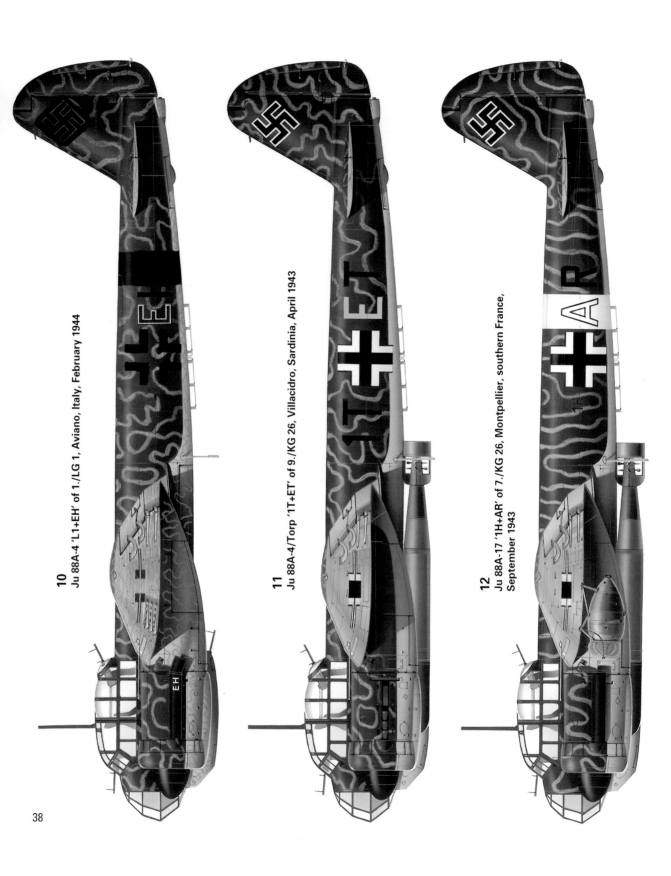

10
Ju 88A-4 'L1+EH' of 1./LG 1, Aviano, Italy, February 1944

11
Ju 88A-4/Torp 'T+ET' of 9./KG 26, Villacidro, Sardinia, April 1943

12
Ju 88A-17 '1H+AR' of 7./KG 26, Montpellier, southern France, September 1943

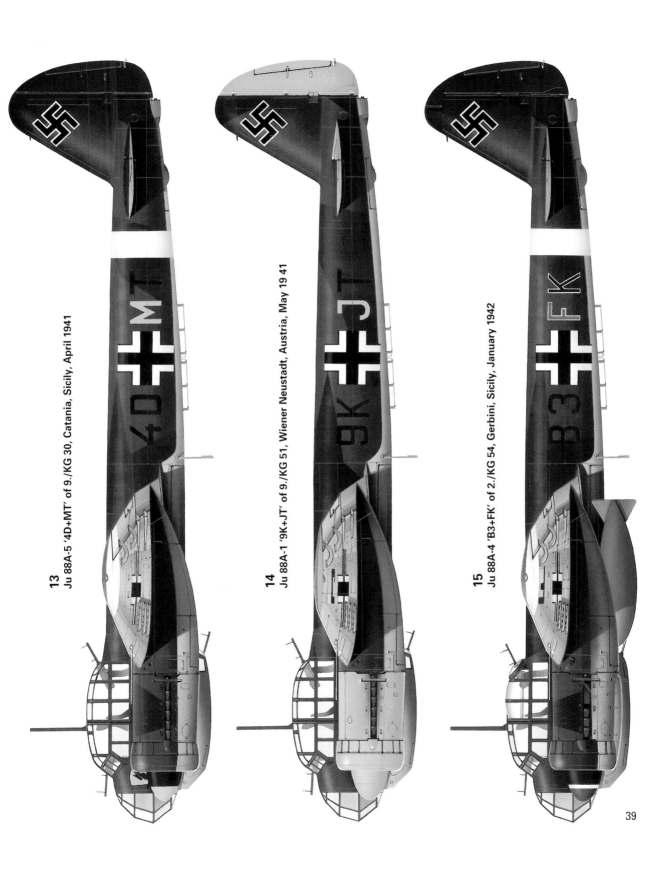

13
Ju 88A-5 '4D+MT' of 9./KG 30, Catania, Sicily, April 1941

14
Ju 88A-1 '9K+JT' of 9./KG 51, Wiener Neustadt, Austria, May 19 41

15
Ju 88A-4 'B3+FK' of 2./KG 54, Gerbini, Sicily, January 1942

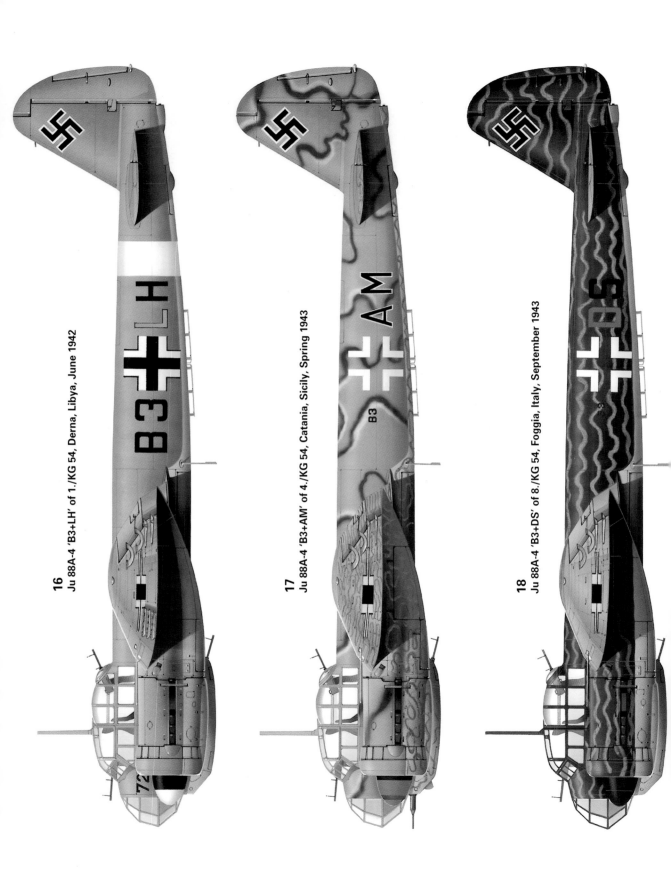

16
Ju 88A-4 'B3+LH' of 1./KG 54, Derna, Libya, June 1942

17
Ju 88A-4 'B3+AM' of 4./KG 54, Catania, Sicily, Spring 1943

18
Ju 88A-4 'B3+DS' of 8./KG 54, Foggia, Italy, September 1943

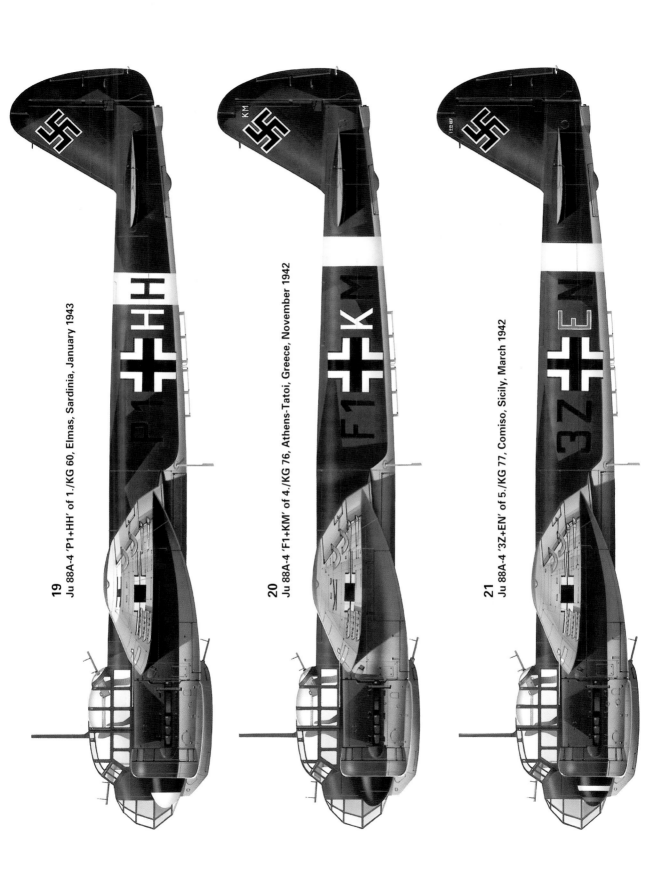

19
Ju 88A-4 'P1+HH' of 1./KG 60, Elmas, Sardinia, January 1943

20
Ju 88A-4 'F1+KM' of 4./KG 76, Athens-Tatoi, Greece, November 1942

21
Ju 88A-4 '3Z+EN' of 5./KG 77, Comiso, Sicily, March 1942

22
Ju 88A-5 '3Z+CT' of 9./KG 77, Libya, Summer 1942

23
Ju 88A-17 '3Z+DR' of 7./KG 77, Orange-Caritat, southern France,
April 1944

24
Ju 88A-4 '7T+BH' of 1./KGr 606, Catania, Sicily, Spring 1942

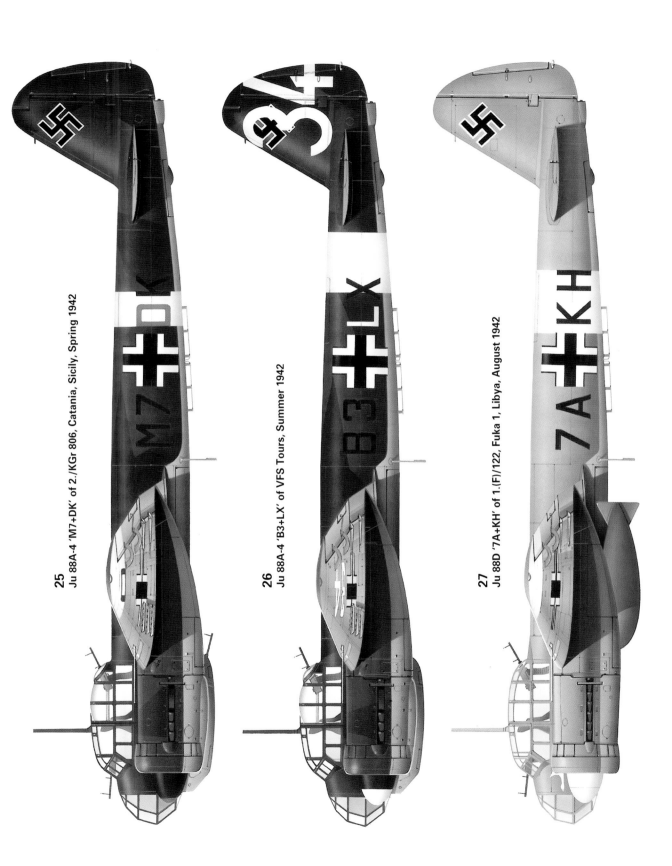

25
Ju 88A-4 'M7+DK' of 2./KGr 806, Catania, Sicily, Spring 1942

26
Ju 88A-4 'B3+LX' of VFS Tours, Summer 1942

27
Ju 88D '7A+KH' of 1.(F)/122, Fuka 1, Libya, August 1942

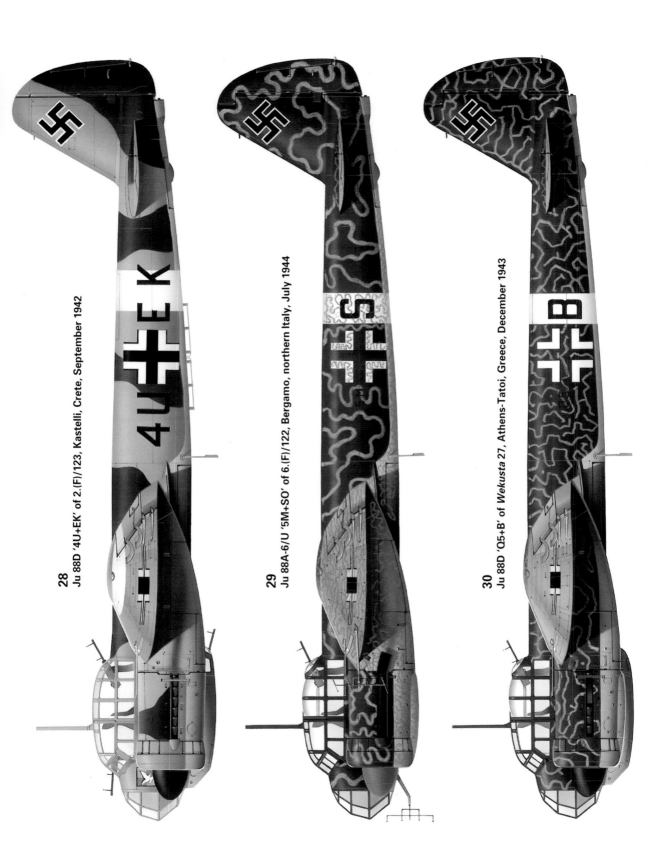

28
Ju 88D '4U+EK' of 2.(F)/123, Kastelli, Crete, September 1942

29
Ju 88A-6/U '5M+SO' of 6.(F)/122, Bergamo, northern Italy, July 1944

30
Ju 88D 'Q5+B' of *Wekusta* 27, Athens-Tatoi, Greece, December 1943

MALTA OR CAIRO?

While the world was following the events in Yugoslavia, Greece and Crete, it was still very much business as usual for the Ju 88 *Gruppen* based on Sicily. II./LG 1 (until its transfer to Eleusis) and III./KG 30 mounted sporadic raids on Malta and III./LG 1 was still engaged in the unremitting task of protecting Axis convoys ferrying men and materials across the Mediterranean to North Africa.

Here, developments were also taking place. With British forces in Libya weakened by the diversion of so many troops to Greece, Rommel's 'reconnaissance' eastwards along the coastal highway was by now in full swing. The harbour town of Tobruk had been bypassed and its garrison cut off by mid-April. And although Berlin was still urging caution on their firebrand general, recommending that he stop and consolidate along a line at Sollum on the Libyan-Egyptian border, Rommel was at least being given some additional air support. The nine machines of 8./LG 1 that transferred from Catania to Benghazi-Benina on 18 April were the first Ju 88s to be subordinated to the *Fliegerführer Afrika*, and thus the first to be directly engaged in the desert war.

The 20 Junkers that raided Tobruk the following day, however, were aircraft of III./KG 30 flying across from Sicily. Two machines of 8. *Staffel* failed to return from this operation, one of them being '4D+KS' flown by *Staffelkapitän* Hauptmann Alfred Neumann. On 21 April 8./LG 1, already down to just seven serviceable machines, moved forward from Benghazi to Derna, little more than 60 miles short of the Tobruk perimeter. Twenty-four hours later the unit lost one of those seven during an armed reconnaissance of Tobruk. References differ as to how the casualty came about, some records indicating that the Ju 88 fell foul of patrolling fighters (Fulmars of the Fleet Air Arm), while other sources suggest that it was brought down by an accurate burst of anti-aircraft fire.

The town's flak defences would play a vital role in the epic 240-day siege that the Tobruk garrison was about to endure. The gunners of the six anti-aircraft batteries waged a constant, almost personal, war against the Luftwaffe, and developed a love-hate relationship with their opponents in the process.

The Ju 88s were frequently sent over Tobruk in individual *Ketten* of threes. One particular target was the supply dumps, which seemed to be bombed every morning just as the ration trucks were drawing stores. Convinced that they were dealing with the same three aircraft every

In April 1941 8./LG 1 became the first Ju 88 unit to be based in North Africa. The small fairing behind the nose glazing reveals that this machine – 'L1+AS' – is another of LG 1's A-6s. It is presumably a replacement for the earlier 'AS' (a Ju 88A-5) in which *Staffelkapitän* Hauptmann Wilhelm Dürbeck was killed over Malta on 19 January (see text on page 9), but is it also the mount of the current *Staffelkapitän* and future Swords winner Oberleutnant Hermann Hogeback?

The rest of III./LG 1 joined 8. *Staffel* in Libya in early May. It was not long before the *Gruppe's* aircraft – like 7./LG 1's well wrapped-up 'L1+KR' seen here – began to sport camouflage finishes more suited to the unit's new desert environment

time, the gunners soon christened the trio 'Pip', 'Squeak' and 'Wilfred' after three popular cartoon strip characters of the day.

Similarly, whenever a pair of Ju 88s appeared overhead, they were always 'Mickey' and 'Minnie'. These two were accused of a particularly underhand trick – one would come roaring noisily out of the sun in a shallow dive while the other sneaked in from the opposite direction with its engines just ticking over. It was reckoned that this couple's activities lasted for the best part of two months before finally being brought to a halt when a direct hit took some three feet off the end of one of 'Mickey's' (or was it 'Minnie's'?) wings.

Lastly, any singleton – either a lone bomber carrying out a hit-and-run attack or a solitary reconnaissance snooper – was automatically called 'Jimmy'. On one occasion, 'Jimmy' hit an ammunition dump near the HQ of the 9th Australian Infantry Division, leaving an enormous cloud of smoke and thunderous explosions reverberating throughout the area for hours afterwards.

On 3 May the rest of III./LG 1 joined 8. *Staffel* in North Africa, but not before mounting at least one more raid on Malta. Flown in the early evening of 29 April, this had cost the *Gruppe* a single casualty when 9. *Staffel's* 'L1+BT' was shot down over Valetta, its entire crew bailing out to become prisoners of war. Later that same night the island had also been subjected to an attack in *Gruppe* strength by III./KG 30.

Starting on 4 May, III./LG 1 began a week of sustained bombing raids and armed reconnaissance sweeps in and around Tobruk. While III./LG 1 were thus engaged in the direct support of the desert war, the British were trying to run a convoy of five fast merchantmen, laden with tanks for the Army of the Nile, the length of the Mediterranean from west to east. This risky operation, code-named *Tiger*, was greatly helped by the poor weather conditions. Passing through the Straits of Gibraltar on 6 May, the ships did not come within range of Axis air attack until two days later. Even then, the combination of bad weather and a powerful naval escort prevented the vessels from suffering any appreciable damage. Only one of the five would be lost, and this after hitting a mine off Malta on 9 May.

Two days later still, on 11 May, nearly a dozen Ju 88s of III./LG 1 took off from Derna to attack the remaining ships, which were now reported to be north-northeast of Tobruk. Crews claimed no hits on the vessels and lost one of their number when a 7. *Staffel* machine was involved in a mid-air collision with a defending Fulmar in murky conditions.

III./LG 1 had more success the next day when it returned to Tobruk. Although the crews' primary objective was the town's pumping station, two direct hits were claimed on a small warship anchored in the harbour. This was the Royal Navy's 625-ton river gunboat *Ladybird*, recalled from the China station to take part in the earlier bombardment of Bardia. Just how many Ju 88s targeted the little vessel is no longer clear, but certainly fewer than the *Ladybird's* captain described at the time;

'Some 47 bombers swooped towards us. My chief gunner's mate saw the first aeroplane dropping out of the sunshine, and it laid a stick of bombs so near that the explosions flung the crew on the deck. Then there was a terrific screech, and there came another lot, one of which got us right aft, almost immediately putting the deck under water. Then another bomb got us in the engine room. The ship shivered from stem to stern and was obviously sinking.'

Ladybird went down in a matter of minutes, but a mixed force of British cruisers and destroyers encountered off the coast of Libya the following afternoon (13 May) did not offer such an easy target. Indeed, the *Gruppenstab* of III./LG 1 lost a machine to anti-aircraft fire from the cruiser *Ajax* when 'L1+AD' appeared to take a direct hit in the cockpit while in the middle of its dive.

Throughout the latter half of May 1941, while the fighting raged on and around Crete, III./LG 1 continued to support Rommel's desert advance. Hauptmann Nietsch's III./LG 1 crews also flew a number of convoy escort and maritime reconnaissance missions during this period. Their main target, however, remained the British and Commonwealth ground forces falling back on the Egyptian frontier. They attacked troops and vehicles in the Sollum and Fort Capuzzo areas, and attempted to block the Halfaya Pass. But it was to Tobruk that they returned time and time again. The battered but stubborn garrison was to be a thorn in Rommel's side for the next six months. Successive attempts to take Tobruk by direct land assault all ended in failure, and both the town and harbour would feature large in III./LG 1's activities in the weeks ahead.

Although based in Greece, 1.(F)/121 maintained a permanent presence of four aircraft (on a rotational basis) in North Africa throughout the latter half of 1941. This elaborately camouflaged example has barely made it back from Libya before belly-landing on a Cretan beach. One source states that this is the machine in which future reconnaissance Knight's Cross winner Oberleutnant Alfons Muggenthaler was flying as navigator/observer

FORCE REDEPLOYMENT

Following the successful conclusion of the Cretan campaign early in June, there was a wholesale redeployment of Luftwaffe units in the Mediterranean theatre. Clearly believing his enemy to be on the ropes – an assumption that was, at the time, not too far from the truth – Hitler ordered that pressure be kept up on the British. The OKL (Luftwaffe High Command) therefore transferred *X. Fliegerkorps en bloc* from Sicily to Greece and the Aegean in order to pursue 'operations against England (sic) in the eastern Mediterranean'. Already at Eleusis, I. and II./LG 1 were well placed to carry out such operations. And they were soon joined in Greece by those Ju 88 units still stationed on Sicily – III./KG 30 and the *Korps'* two strategic reconnaissance *Staffeln*, 1.(F)/121 and 2.(F)/123.

The bombers faced a formidable task. Not only were they to sweep the eastern Mediterranean for Allied naval and merchant ships, they were also to attack ports and coastal towns in the area, bomb military installations and RAF airfields in the Nile Delta region and mine strategic harbours and waterways, including the Suez Canal – a tall order for a force of just four *Kampfgruppen* (including the He 111s of II./KG 26) and one, moreover, that could field barely 50 serviceable machines from the outset.

Little time was lost in getting the offensive underway. I. and II./LG 1 flew their first operation (a raid on Alexandria) during the night of 7/8 June. Despite it being a maximum effort – all but two of the 33 serviceable aircraft despatched reportedly arriving over the target area – the bombing had little effect. And although no Ju 88s were lost, five suffered damage when landing back at either Eleusis or Rhodes-Gadurra.

In the months ahead it became not uncommon for crews of I. and II./LG 1 to put down on Italian-held Rhodes after a foray deep into the eastern Mediterranean. This was ostensibly to top up fuel tanks before the long overwater flight back to base in Greece (and later Crete). But there was another reason why the Ju 88s liked to drop in at Rhodes 'for safety's sake'. Provisions at their own recently-occupied airfields were not exactly abundant, and the long-established Italian airfield at Gadurra, on Rhodes, could nearly always be relied upon to come up with some additional delicacies that could either be consumed on the spot or taken back to base to augment and add variety to their own meagre mess tables.

The following night (8/9 June), II./LG 1 ventured further east still with a raid on Haifa, in Palestine, during which Hauptmann Joachim Helbig hit on an oil tank farm. Next afternoon the Ju 88s of I./LG 1 staged forwards to Rhodes with the intention of mounting a second night attack on Haifa. But this plan was abandoned when it was caught by a dusk RAF bombing raid on Gadurra. It thus fell to II. *Gruppe* to make the eight-hour round trip from Eleusis to Haifa alone. The 16 Ju 88s started a number of fires and one crew also reported a hit on the 5450-ton light cruiser *Phoebe* that was lying in the harbour. With I. *Gruppe* still licking its wounds on Rhodes, II./LG 1 returned to Haifa on 10/11 June for the third night in a row, bombing the harbour and mining its entrance.

Then, on the morning of 13 June, aerial reconnaissance sighted a group of Royal Navy ships – reported to be a cruiser and six destroyers – off the Palestinian coast. I. and II./LG 1 (the former having returned to Eleusis the day before) were despatched to attack the warships. They were the vessels

Straw-hatted groundcrew of II./LG 1 ride a bomb-train of 500-kg *Luftmine A* parachute mines out to the waiting aircraft at Heraklion

of the 15th Cruiser Squadron, which were patrolling close inshore as part of the naval force supporting the brief campaign currently being fought against the Vichy French in Syria. And the ships enjoyed aerial protection, courtesy of Tomahawks of the now Palestinian-based No 3 Sqn RAAF.

Unfortunately for the LG 1 crews, eight fighters arrived on the scene just as they commenced their dive on the warships. The Australians correctly identified the attackers as Ju 88s, but described them as 'wearing Italian markings' – perhaps the confusion arose from the Junkers' white aft fuselage bands? Be that as it may, the sudden appearance of the Tomahawks put the bombers off their aim. No ships were hit and two Ju 88s of II. *Gruppe* ('L1+DM' and 'L1+CN') were lost.

The two *Gruppen* had more success when they returned to the Syrian coast to attack the warships once again 48 hours later. Hits were claimed on four vessels, including the 1370-ton destroyers *Ilex* and *Isis*, both of which were badly damaged. The following day's OKW communiqué announced that a light cruiser had been sunk after suffering four direct hits and that a heavy cruiser had been badly damaged! This time the Royal Navy's aerial umbrella was being provided by Hurricanes of No 80 Sqn. Two aircraft of 5./LG 1 were forced to make emergency landings, with 'L1+EN' putting down to the north in neutral Turkey, where *Staffelkapitän* Oberleutnant Wilger Schacht and his crew were promptly interned.

While I. and II./LG 1 were employed in these strategic operations in the eastern Mediterranean, III. *Gruppe* had been engaged in the Luftwaffe's more customary tactical role flying in support of Rommel's troops in the Western Desert. During the past week their targets had included enemy positions at Sidi Barrani, Mersa, Fuka and, of course, Tobruk. But then on 14 June – the day Hauptmann Kuno Hoffmann, *Kommandeur* of I./LG 1, was awarded the Knight's Cross for his *Gruppe's* performance in the recent Balkan and Cretan campaigns – the British launched Operation *Battleaxe*, a limited counter-offensive aimed at the relief of Tobruk.

Although down to less than a dozen serviceable machines, III./LG 1 flew a constant round of missions during the daylight hours of 15 June against ground targets in the Sollum-Fort Capuzzo areas of the Egyptian-Libyan border, where Rommel's troops were offering fierce resistance. Three days later, on 18 June, I. and II./LG 1 were ordered down from Eleusis to add their weight to the aerial assault on the attacking British armour. But by then *Battleaxe* was already in serious trouble. There were reports of more than 150 British tanks having been knocked out, and the British themselves went so far as to admit that 'the land battle has swung very much in the enemy's favour'.

Within hours *Battleaxe* had been abandoned altogether. British and Commonwealth troops pulled back, and a period almost of stalemate settled over the Western Desert, at least on the ground, as both sides sought to build up their strength for the next major confrontation.

For the Eleusis-based I. and I./LG 1 it was quickly back to business as usual in the eastern Mediterranean. Their Ju 88s raided Alexandria during the night of 20/21 June and again 48 hours later. The two *Gruppen* visited Alexandria at least three more times. and Haifa once, before the month was out, all without loss.

In the meantime, crews from III. *Gruppe*, finding few targets of opportunity in their sweeps of Egypt's western frontier regions,

No such luxuries as bomb trolleys in the desert, apparently – but who needs them when eight men are all it takes to roll a 1000-kg bomb into position beneath this Ju 88A-6 of III./LG 1, perhaps in preparation for yet another raid on Tobruk. The original print of this photograph is dated 13 June 1941, just one day prior to Operation *Battleaxe*

more often than not rounded off their missions by unloading their bombs on long-suffering Tobruk during the flight back to base at Derna. They also regularly attacked the small coastal convoys that ran the gauntlet from Egypt to ferry supplies to the Tobruk garrison. One such operation on 29 June resulted in the loss of the 1100-ton destroyer *Waterhen* off Sollum. A near miss holed the vessel's engine-room, and although it was taken in tow, the warship sank.

The 758-ton tanker *Pass of Balmaha* was also claimed sunk on the 29th, but this is far from certain. Escorted by two sloops, the *Pass of Balmaha* had set out for Tobruk a week earlier. Surviving a heavy attack by Stukas on 24 June, it completed what was later described as 'probably the most important individual run ever made to Tobruk'. The 750 tons of fuel that she delivered averted a looming petrol crisis, and gave the garrison enough supplies for the next 70 days. This was particularly timely, as a bomb dropped during III./LG 1's raid on Tobruk on the afternoon of 9 July would put the town's bulk petrol pumping plant out of action for an entire month. It is perhaps possible that the *Pass of Balmaha* was then attacked and believed sunk during its return voyage, but any such belief was mistaken, for other reference sources – both English and German – list the ship as one of the two vessels torpedoed by the U-97 off Egypt on 17 October 1941.

The main burden of general supply during the Tobruk siege, however, fell upon the so-called 'destroyer-ferries', which transported men and materials into the garrison under cover of darkness. The crews of III./LG 1 found it difficult to deal with these. Thirty-four such 'Spud Runs', as they were known in the Royal Navy, would be made by the destroyers of the Tenth Flotilla during July – a figure that rose to 58 in August.

In the eastern Mediterranean, I. and II./LG 1 began July with a one-off attack on Famagusta harbour, in Cyprus, on the 4th. The following day at Eleusis, Hauptmann Gerhard Kollewe, the *Gruppenkommandeur* of II./LG 1, was presented with the Knight's Cross by *Geschwaderkommodore* Oberstleutnant Friedrich-Karl Knust. And just over 24 hours later still, the two *Gruppen* were back over familiar territory with a night raid on the Royal Navy's main base at Alexandria. Here they claimed the sinking of a small Greek freighter and damage to the carrier *Formidable*. The latter, incidentally, was undergoing repairs after being attacked by aircraft of III./KG 30 west of Crete on 29 June. This was one of the *Gruppe's* last major successes of its first tour in the Mediterranean.

By the beginning of July III./KG 30 had been reduced to just a single *Staffel* of seven serviceable machines, the other two *Staffeln* having already been withdrawn for re-equipment. By mid-month the *Gruppe* had retired from the theatre altogether and returned to the control of *Luftflotte* 3 in northwest Europe.

The departure of III./KG 30 meant that for the next four months or more *Lehrgeschwader* 1 would provide the sole Ju 88 bomber presence in the Mediterranean. And for much of that time the *Gruppen's* strict division of labour would remain as hitherto, with I. and II./LG 1 attacking strategic targets around the eastern Mediterranean rim and III./LG 1 supporting Rommel's forces in the desert.

During July, for example, the former bombed and mined Alexandria, the Suez Canal and the great Bitter Lake, carried out raids on Port Said,

Yet another 'AS'-coded machine, this one being '4D+AS' of 8./KG 30, pictured on a bright but breezy summer's day sometime around the end of June 1941 – shortly before the *Staffel* was withdrawn from the Mediterranean

This silhouette, clearly depicting a small twin-funnelled warship, together with the tonnage (1300) and date (11.7.41) recorded alongside, all point to the same thing – this must be the aircraft responsible for sinking the Royal Navy destroyer *Defender* off Sidi Barrani

Ismailia and Haifa, and attacked the airfield at Abu Sueir, where it was claimed – somewhat optimistically, perhaps – that over 100 aircraft were destroyed on the ground, three hangars were left blazing fiercely and the whole field was 'just one huge sea of flames'. But its greatest confirmed success of the month was achieved during the raid on shipping in Suez Bay on the night of 13/14 July when two bombs hit the 27,759-ton liner *Georgic*, now serving as a troop transport. Fire raged through the giant vessel, which was at first given up as a total loss.

III./LG 1 also had an anti-shipping success to report, albeit on a less gargantuan scale. Having already damaged the 1375-ton destroyer *Defender* north of Sollum in the early hours of 9 July, the *Gruppe* located the vessel again 48 hours later. Hit by another four bombs, the *Defender* was taken in tow by the destroyer *Vendetta*, but foundered off Sidi Barrani. But, as usual, it was Tobruk that received most of III./LG 1's attention in July, although other targets attacked during the month included a troop encampment near Mersa Matruh and the airfield at Fuka.

Given the intensity and frequency of the operations flown, it is incredible that the entire *Geschwader* suffered just one combat fatality throughout the whole of July. This was a 6. *Staffel* air gunner killed by anti-aircraft fire during the attack on British shipping off Haifa on the 8th. Three of the *Geschwader's* aircraft had been written off, however – one in an RAF bombing raid on Eleusis (also, coincidentally, on the 8th), another in a ditching and the third in an emergency landing.

In terms of operations flown, August was very much a continuation of July. But successes were becoming fewer and losses were starting to climb. The most serious material loss occurred on 17 August when three Ju 88s were destroyed at Eleusis, and another two severely damaged. The *Geschwader* reported these as being the result of yet another RAF raid, when in fact it appears that one of the aerial mines being loaded aboard the aircraft for that night's mission had been accidentally detonated.

The nearest the *Geschwader* came to a sinking in August was when III./LG 1 damaged the destroyer *Nizam* northwest of Mersa Matruh on the 21st. But two days later, when attacking a coastal convoy off Sidi Barrani, III. *Gruppe* lost an aircraft in a running fight with the ships' escorting Tomahawks. The month was to end on a happier note, however, when, on 30 August, Eleusis witnessed another Knight's Cross presentation by *Geschwaderkommodore* Oberstleutnant Knust. On this occasion the recipient was Oberfeldwebel Franz Schlund, a member of Hauptmann Joachim Helbig's crew. Having flown 200+ missions and successfully fought off 13 fighter attacks, Schlund was the first Luftwaffe wireless-operator/air gunner to be honoured with the Knight's Cross.

By mid-September 1941 it was becoming all too evident that Rommel was losing the Western Desert supply race – and losing it badly. It was clear that the earlier decision to transfer *X. Fliegerkorps* from Sicily to Greece and Crete had been not merely premature, but a major blunder.

Hauptmann Joachim Helbig, right, reports his 4. *Staffel* all present and correct to LG 1's *Geschwaderkommodore* Oberstleutnant Friedrich Karl Knust. The date is 30 August 1941, the place Eleusis airfield, Greece, and the occasion . . .

. . . the presentation of the Knight's Cross to Helbig's wireless-operator/air gunner, Oberfeldwebel Franz Schlund, seen here (centre) between Helbig and the *Geschwader's* standard bearer

The task of keeping Malta in check had been entrusted to the Italians, but this had proved too much for them alone. Malta's strength had been allowed to grow and now its air and sea forces were again wreaking havoc on the Axis supply convoys to North Africa. In an attempt to safeguard Rommel's vital seaborne supply line, *X. Fliegerkorps* was ordered to suspend its strategic operations in the eastern Mediterranean and divert all its energies instead to convoy escort and protection missions.

This, it was hoped, would help alleviate some of the immediate pressure being felt by Axis forces currently holding fast along the Libyan-Egyptian border region. But

Hauptmann Hermann Hogeback, the *Staffelkapitän* of 8./LG 1, was awarded the Knight's Cross in Africa on 8 September 1941. He is shown here (second from left) in early 1943 wearing the Oak Leaves as *Gruppenkommandeur* of III./KG 6 (the ex-III./LG 1). By war's end Oberstleutnant Hogeback had received the Swords and was *Geschwaderkommodore* of KG 6. But perhaps his greatest claim to fame is that by then his was the only bomber crew in the entire Luftwaffe with every member sporting the Knight's Cross!

An equally informal shot of Hauptmann 'Jochen' Helbig and his crew. They are, from left to right, Major Stefan (navigator/observer), Helbig (pilot), Oberfeldwebel Schlund (wireless-operator/air gunner) and Unteroffizier Czirpa (air gunner). Note the badge of II./LG 1 – the coat-of-arms of the city of Schwerin – on the machine in the background. Compare it with the stylised geese of III. *Gruppe* (the later III./KG 6) shown in the photo at bottom of page 52. Loss tables indicate that Wk-Nr. 4371 seen here was 'L1+KS', which was subsequently shot down by a Hurricane east of Derna on 27 December 1941 (see text on page 55)

it did nothing to address the root cause of the problem – the resurgence of Malta. This would require more drastic action. And drastic action was about to be taken.

With his armies in Russia slowly grinding to halt and beginning to dig in for the winter in front of Moscow, Hitler decreed that the HQ of the air fleet responsible for the central sector, *Luftflotte* 2 – together with one of its component *Fliegerkorps* – should be withdrawn from the eastern front and transferred lock, stock and barrel to Sicily to resume the air offensive against Malta. But the combat units involved in this large-scale move would need time to re-equip and recuperate from the rigours of the Russian front. And time was something Rommel did not have.

On 18 November Gen Auchinleck, the British C-in-C Middle East, launched his now considerable armoured strength in a wide sweeping movement through the desert around the southern flank of the German-held Halfaya Pass position. At first Rommel was unsure whether this was merely a reconnaissance or a major offensive. He was not left in uncertainty for long. Operation *Crusader* was a very different proposition indeed from the earlier ill-prepared and poorly executed *Battleaxe*. And all doubt was dispelled when the advancing troops linked up with the defenders of Tobruk, bringing to an end the historic eight-month siege.

Rommel began to retreat across Cyrenaica, mounting a series of counter-attacks, but totally unable to halt Auchinleck's progress. Benghazi was retaken on Christmas Eve 1941 and Rommel fell back on El Agheila. By year's end practically the whole of Cyrenaica was in British hands (although Bardia and Halfaya continued to hold out until January 1942). But Rommel's armies had not been completely destroyed. True, he had suffered a serious reversal, and over 30,000 of his men had been captured, but, crucially, the *Afrika Korps* remained in being – and immediately began preparing for a renewed counter-offensive of its own.

So much for the situation on the ground in North Africa during the last six weeks of 1941. But what of LG 1's activities during that same period? Heavy sand and rain storms in the Benghazi region on 17 November (the eve of *Crusader*) had kept III./LG 1 on the ground for much of the day. And then, indicative of the confusion in the German camp at the start of Auchinleck's offensive, a greater part of the next 48 hours was spent by the *Geschwader* out over the Mediterranean flying convoy-escort and anti-shipping patrols. It was not until 20 November that III. *Gruppe* intervened in the ground campaign by attacking troop movements along the Egyptian border. All aircraft returned safely, but a surprise raid by RAF fighters that same day destroyed three of III./LG 1's Ju 88s and damaged five more, three of which were written off. Despite – or perhaps because of – these losses, the bulk of I. and II./LG 1 flew in to Benina from Eleusis the following day.

On 22 November all three *Gruppen* operated in support of Rommel's troops. Two bombers were lost, 1. *Staffel's* 'L1+JH' being downed by anti-aircraft fire while attacking tanks and an unidentified Ju 88 of 4./LG 1 force-landing in the desert after being set upon by Hurricanes. It was the start of a costly period for the *Geschwader*. By year-end it had lost more than a dozen Ju 88s, with almost as many again damaged.

After just five days at Benina most of I. and II./LG 1's aircraft returned to Eleusis. Henceforth, the two *Gruppen* would operate primarily from their home base in Greece, attacking British lines of communication and supply routes to the rear of Auchinleck's advancing troops. A frequent target was the Egyptian coastal railway, particularly its western terminus – the railhead and large stores depots at Sidi Barrani. On occasion they would also deploy briefly to one or other of the Cyrenaican airfields still in Luftwaffe hands to offer more direct support to the embattled *Afrika*

Although based primarily in Greece, I./LG 1's Ju 88s flew numerous missions in support of the *Afrika Korps*. 2. *Staffel's* desert dappled 'L1+EK' (note 'last two' repeated on the rudder in white) is ideally garbed for such operations

Korps. Late in the afternoon of 29 November, for example, II./LG 1 flew in to Derna. The *Gruppe* would remain here for only a few hours before staging, via Benina, back to Eleusis. But it was long enough both for 4. *Staffel's* 'L1+CM' to be brought down by a nightfighter and for Hauptmann Joachim Helbig (who had been appointed *Kommandeur* of I. *Gruppe* on 5 November) to be slightly wounded in an RAF bombing raid on Benina.

It was at this time, too, that LG 1's establishment was increased to four *Gruppen*. Like nearly every other *Kampfgeschwader*, LG 1 had long had its own *Ergänzungsstaffeln*. These were the operational training squadrons that prepared newly qualified crews for frontline service with the unit. Back in September the first of LG 1's *Ergänzungsstaffeln* had been transferred from the homeland to Salonika, in Greece, where it was to gain operational experience by flying convoy escort missions in the Aegean.

On 23 November the three *Ergänzungsstaffeln* were amalgamated and redesignated officially to become IV./LG 1. Still based at Salonika, their primary task now was to conduct anti-submarine patrols in the Aegean area. This led to the possibly unique situation of there being two entirely separate *Gruppen* currently on the Luftwaffe's order of battle, each bearing the same designation. For in the far northern sector of the Russian front the original dive-bomber *Gruppe* of the pre-war *Lehrgeschwader* was still operating as IV.(St)/LG 1. Presumably it was felt that there was little fear of confusion

Having been given the green and white flag, 5./LG 1's 'L1+FN' roars down the runway – at Eleusis? – and is just about to lift off

given the geographical separation of the two units, one flying Ju 87s in the Arctic and the other flying Ju 88s in the Aegean. In the event, the matter was resolved two months later when the former was finally redesignated I./StG 5.

By 11 December I. and II./LG 1 were back in North Africa, at Derna and Tmimi respectively. Together with III. *Gruppe*, which was still operating out of Derna, raids were flown against Tobruk and attacks carried out on motorised columns near the desert fortress of Bir Hacheim. 1./LG 1 lost its second *Staffelkapitän* in just over four months when Oberleutnant Heinrich Paulus' 'L1+HH' was forced to land in the desert after being set upon by a mixed formation of Tomahawks and Hurricanes. Paulus and his crew were all taken into captivity.

By this stage Rommel was falling back on the Gazala Line to the west of Tobruk. The Luftwaffe's airfields in Cyrenaica were coming under increasing air attack, and as the fighting front approached they were abandoned one after the other, any unserviceable machines being blown up to prevent their falling into enemy hands. During the afternoon of 11 December all three *Gruppen* of LG 1 began withdrawing to Eleusis.

In the week that followed there was a brief resurgence in anti-shipping activity, with inconclusive attacks on Royal Navy warships on both the 14th and 17th. The latter date also witnessed the new IV. *Gruppe's* first operational loss when 'L1+KW' failed to return from an armed reconnaissance sweep of the sea to the west of Crete.

But still the *Geschwader* continued to offer what help it could to the hard-pressed *Afrika Korps*, sending one or more *Gruppen* across the Mediterranean to attack targets in the Western Desert every day until year's end. At least three Ju 88s fell victim to RAF fighters during this time, the last – 8. *Staffel's* 'L1+KS' – being claimed by the CO of the Hurricane-equipped No 229 Sqn between Gazala and Derna on 27 December. Three days later, the surviving desert veterans of III. *Gruppe* departed Eleusis for Salonika, where they passed their aircraft over to IV./LG 1 before entraining for Germany to rest and re-equip. Redesignated to become III./KG 6 in 1942, the *Gruppe* would return briefly to the Mediterranean in this new guise during the latter half of 1943.

By now the HQ of *Luftflotte* 2 had arrived in Sicily from Russia. The combat units of *II. Fliegerkorps* also began to assemble on the island in preparation for the renewal of the assault on Malta. The *Korps'* main striking power was concentrated in its five *Kampfgruppen*, all flying Ju 88s – I./KG 54 based at Gerbini, II. and III./KG 77 at Comiso and *Kampfgruppen* 606 and 806 at Catania, these last two being semi-autonomous bomber units created out of the *Küstenfliegergruppen* (coastal reconnaissance wings) of the early war years. Including *X. Fliegerkorps'* three Ju 88 *Gruppen* in Greece (I., II. and IV./LG 1), there were thus eight *Kampfgruppen* equipped with Ju 88s in the Mediterranean theatre at the beginning of 1942 (although none currently based in North Africa).

BACK TO MALTA

The opening of the second round of the air bombardment of Malta was another very low-key affair. It was almost as if the Luftwaffe had taken a leaf from their enemy's book. *II. Fliegerkorps'* operations, consisting of small formations of bombers – often as few as three or four per mission – strongly escorted by fighters, were very reminiscent of the 'Circus' tactics employed by the RAF when it began its 'lean into France' in the summer of 1941. Raids at this level, amounting to little more than harassing attacks, would continue to be flown against Malta until early March. There were, however, two fundamental differences from the earlier RAF operations over northwest Europe – a succession of such missions would be sent against Malta nearly every day, up to a maximum of some 40-50 individual bomber sorties, and the Luftwaffe also attacked the island by night.

Whether these raids achieved their desired effect is a moot point.

Some found Sicily a little harder to get used to. 'M7+DH' of 1./KGr 806 has nosed over in the soft soil, the result of a taxiing accident at Catania on 4 January 1942

They certainly took a small but steady toll of the Ju 88s ordered to fly them, both in terms of combat casualties and losses from other causes. Some of the earliest casualties were recorded even before 1941 was out – II./KG 77 and KGr.806 each lost a machine on 24 December. And by the end of January 1942 every one of the five Ju 88 *Gruppen* based on Sicily had suffered similarly.

The attrition continued throughout the following month. Among the crews lost was that of Oberleutnant Herbert Loerz, the *Staffelkapitän* of 7./KG 77, whose '3Z+DD' was shot into the sea north of Malta's Grand Harbour on 12 February. Ten days later *II. Fliegerkorps* was reinforced by the arrival at Catania of I./LG 1. This was to be the first of a number of deployments to Sicily by elements of LG 1 from their bases in Greece and Crete, presumably to add their Mediterranean expertise to specific missions or operations. On this initial occasion I. *Gruppe* carried out three raids on Malta before returning to Heraklion, on Crete, on 24 February.

The tempo of the attacks on Malta, its docks, and airfields gradually began to increase during the first half of March. This was reflected in the growing casualty returns of the Ju 88 *Gruppen*. Included among them was

another of KG 77's luckless *Staffel-kapitäne* – '3Z+LP', the machine piloted by Oberleutnant Gerhard Becker of 6./KG 77, was brought down by gunfire over Hal Far on 9 March. The previous afternoon I./LG 1 had flown back in to Catania for another three-day stint of Malta operations. The *Gruppe's* machines participated in a 40+ raid on Luqa and Hal Far airfields on 10 March when, for the first time, the Luftwaffe encountered RAF Spitfires in the skies above Malta.

On 16 March it was the turn of II./LG 1 to transfer from Crete to

As the evening clouds gather over Comiso, an unidentified machine of KG 77, all fuselage and tail markings blacked out, prepares for the coming night's raid on Malta. Note the Do 24 air-sea rescue flying-boat of the Taormina-based *Seenotstaffel* 6 overhead

Once arrived at Comiso, on Sicily, the crews of KG 77 quickly got down to business if those bombs in the foreground are anything to go by. The one on the left is a 2200-lb SC 1000 'Hermann', whilst that on the right a 3960-lb SC 1800 'Satan'. Both appear to be painted the standard light sky blue, and each has the yellow stripe between the tail fins denoting its SC category – i.e. *Sprengbombe-Cylindrisch* (thin-cased GP bomb)

Catania, where it would remain until the end of April. On the day of their arrival, Hauptmann Kollewe's crews were responsible for nine of the fifteen minor incursions logged by Malta's defenders between 0733 hrs and 1842 hrs on that date (the remaining six attacks being carried out by machines of KG 77). Twenty-four hours later, II./LG 1 was joined at Catania by I./LG 1, but again the latter's stay lasted just three days before it returned once more to Crete. Then, on 20 March, the Luftwaffe's assault on Malta underwent a dramatic change.

The day began in the usual manner, with penny-packets of Ju 88s (from II./LG 1 and II./KG 77) attacking various targets across the island. The only note out of the ordinary was provided by a pair of LG 1 machines that attacked the Royal Navy's submarine base at Manoel Island with rocket-assisted PC 1800 RS armour-piercing bombs – albeit to little effect. That evening, however, a massed raid of some 70 bombers drawn from all six Ju 88 *Kampfgruppen* currently based on Sicily was directed against Takali airfield. It was repeated the following day, when two of the attackers were shot down by the field's AA gunners – '7T+FH' of KGr.606 crashed in the middle of the runway and 5./KG 77's '3Z+FN' spun to earth minus a wing close to the perimeter.

This marked the start of a sustained blitz on Malta that would be kept up throughout almost all of April 'on the heaviest scale yet brought to bear by the Luftwaffe against any single objective for so long a period'. After the island had been sufficiently weakened by blockade and air bombardment, the German intention was to capture Malta by airborne invasion, just as Crete had been taken the previous year. This intention was never carried out. But so intense were the raids endured by the population of Malta during this spring of 1942 that HM King George VI was later moved to award the George Cross to the whole island in recognition of the gallantry under fire displayed by its inhabitants.

While it fell to the island's Hurricanes and Spitfires to counter the air raids, it was the job of the Royal Navy and Merchant Marine to beat the blockade. On 20 March a convoy of four ships – three large merchantmen and the naval supply vessel *Breconshire*, carrying between them nearly 30,000 tons of urgently-needed supplies – had sailed from Alexandria with a strong escort of warships. After beating off a succession of Axis air and sea attacks in the eastern Mediterranean, the convoy came within effective range of *II. Fliegerkorps'* units based on Sicily. The Ju 88s were the first to engage, among them the machines of II./LG 1 and *Stab* KG 77. The latter's attack, carried out late in the afternoon of 22 March, cost it dearly when '3Z+AA', piloted by Major Arved Crüger, ex-*Gruppenkommandeur* of III./KG 30 and KG 77's new *Geschwaderkommodore* of just nine days' standing, was shot into the sea by the ships' gunners.

The Norwegian *Talabot* under attack in Malta's Grand Harbour on 26 March

The following morning the slowest of the three merchantmen, the 7255-ton *Clan Campbell*, was sunk by Ju 88s (probably of II./LG 1) when 20 miles short of Malta. Not long afterwards the *Breconshire*, even closer to the island, was disabled by bomb-carrying Bf 109s of 10.(*Jabo*)/JG 53. After arriving in Grand Harbour, the two surviving freighters became a prime target for the Luftwaffe, whose crews were ordered to destroy them at their berths to prevent the unloading of their cargoes.

More attacks were carried out over the next three days, resulting in the loss of six Ju 88s to the island's defences, before a series of devastating raids on 26 March achieved the desired results. The 6758-ton Norwegian *Talabot* was hit several times, causing fires to break out in its ammunition holds. The vessel was scuttled to prevent the blaze from spreading. Three hours later, Oberleutnant Erwin Sy, *Staffelkapitän* of 4./LG 1, claimed a direct hit on a '6000-ton freighter'. This was in all likelihood the

Malta's airfields were also suffering. The original caption to this picture claims that these are bombs bursting on Luqa . . .

5415-ton *Pampas*, which also went down when a bomb penetrated its funnel and flooded the engine room. At the time of the attacks less than ten percent of the vessels' vital supplies had been unloaded.

Several other ships were sunk in these raids on Valetta's Grand Harbour, including the destroyer *Legion* and the submarine P 39. Meanwhile, the battered *Breconshire* – veteran of eight earlier Malta supply runs – had been towed into Marsaxlokk Bay on the island's southern coast, where, after being subjected to further attack, she finally capsized on 27 March.

II. Fliegerkorps' Gruppen continued their raids on Malta throughout April and into May. During this

... and this is a reconnaissance photo of the same target taken by a Ju 88 of 1.(F)/122 on the evening of 18 April 1942. The small white rings indicate fresh bomb craters that have appeared since the morning raid of 14 April. Photographic intelligence has also pinpointed and annotated five single-engined machines visible on the ground, plus five twin-engined aircraft, 15 wrecks and one still burning

6./KG 77's '3Z+AP' at rest between night raids over Malta. The machine's undersides have been painted black and the forward firing MG 81 machine-gun in the windscreen appears to have been fitted with a glare shield

period numerous warships were sunk or severely damaged in raids on Grand Harbour, including the submarines P 36 and *Pandora*, both of which were sent to the bottom on 1 April. Three weeks later the remaining boats of the Royal Navy's 10th Submarine Flotilla were ordered to leave Malta for Alexandria.

With the island's underwater teeth effectively drawn, the Ju 88s were now free to concentrate on the island's airfields in an attempt to neutralise the enemy's aerial striking power. Savage bombing attacks were mounted against Luqa, Takali and Hal Far almost daily. And these in turn led to lengthening casualty lists for each of the six *Kampfgruppen* involved, as crews were either brought down in combat over or near the island, or crash-landed damaged machines upon return to their Sicilian bases.

One of April's earliest losses was Oberleutnant Otto Bischoff, the *Staffelkapitän* of 4./KG 77, whose '3Z+LM' was downed by a Beaufighter on the night of 1 April. Having already distinguished himself during the night blitz on Britain and in Russia, Bischoff was awarded a posthumous Knight's Cross on 3 May. 3./KG 54's *Staffelkapitän*, Hauptmann Wilhelm Schmidt, was more fortunate when he was forced to ditch after being hit by anti-aircraft fire on 26 April. Although wounded, he was found and picked up by the German air-sea rescue service.

Forty-eight hours after Hauptmann Schmidt's 'B3+NL' sank beneath the waves east of Valetta, *II. Fliegerkorps* ordered a maximum effort to be mounted against 'all of Malta's remaining important military targets not yet destroyed'. Three separate raids – each comprising some 50-60+ bombers and dive-bombers, strongly escorted by fighters – were flown on 28 April. It was the last major attack the island was to suffer. The 'Ultra' intercepts that had first warned of the Ju 88s' arrival in the Mediterranean theatre nearly 18 months earlier, were now indicating that II. and III./KG 77 were preparing to leave Sicily for France. And with II./LG 1 about to return to Greece, to be followed by elements of I./KG 54 in mid-May, this left only two full *Gruppen* of Ju 88s – *Kampfgruppen* 606 and 806 – to maintain the pressure on Malta. This was to prove a difficult and expensive task.

It has been suggested that the turning point in the island's fortunes came on 10 May. On this date the island's defending fighters alone claimed 40 aircraft destroyed or damaged. Eleven of these claims were for Ju 88s, although in reality only four failed to return from the day's raids – two machines each from KGr 806 and I./KG 54. The former unit would continue to suffer regular attrition in the weeks ahead. Among the casualties were two of the *Gruppe's* three *Staffelkapitäne*, both

Aircraft of KGr 806 ('M7+BA' in the foreground) returning from another mission over Malta . . .

of whom fell to Spitfires. 1./KGr 806's Hauptmann Emil Braun was downed in an attack on Malta's airfields on 14 May, and Oberleutnant Kurt Kehrer of 2./KGr 806 was piloting one of the two aircraft shot into the sea in flames while attacking a convoy on 15 June.

MALTA RELIEF

Two reasons have been given for the easing of the heavy air raids on Malta. One is that many of the aircraft sent to the Mediterranean were needed back in Russia in readiness for the 1942 summer campaign on the eastern front. The other was that the renewed offensive by Rommel was making such tremendous gains in its advance on Egypt that the ultimate fall of Cairo, and subsequent Axis conquest of the Nile Delta, were now regarded very much as forgone conclusions. This in turn meant that an airborne invasion of Malta was no longer a necessity. For the second year in a row the bombing of Malta had been prematurely called off – or at least allowed to wither on the vine. The Axis powers would not be given the chance to make the same mistake a third time.

Rommel's resilience had indeed been remarkable. Launched back on 18 November 1941, Operation *Crusader* had carried British forces right across Cyrenaica to Benghazi and beyond. They had recaptured all the territory that they had taken from the Italians the year before, but had then lost to Rommel's first desert offensive. Now exactly the same thing was about to happen again. The moment Rommel sensed that his opponents were running out of momentum he immediately began preparations for a counterattack. The supply situation at Tripoli to his immediate rear had improved considerably. Now it was the British who were having to operate at the end of a long and vulnerable supply line.

The eastern Mediterranean *Gruppen* of LG 1 had been harassing the enemy's lengthening lines of communications throughout the recent German retreat, hitting not only at road and rail transport, but also the ports of Bardia and Tobruk, as well as the coastal supply convoys. It was towards the end of this period, on 16 January 1942, that Hauptmann Joachim Helbig, the *Kommandeur* of I./LG 1 was awarded the Oak Leaves to his Knight's Cross.

Two days later Rommel went onto the offensive, pushing forward from El Agheila to retake Agedabia on 23 January. The Ju 88s of LG 1 would continue to lend strategic support to the now advancing *Afrika Korps* by attacking land and sea targets to the enemy's rear. On 19 January a I. *Gruppe* machine had scored a direct hit on the 6655-ton Norwegian

. . . and one of the photographs they brought back. Although understandably somewhat out of focus – pilot Leutnant Kissling is only just beginning to climb away after the dive – the bomb bursts are clearly visible. Whether by accident or design, the aircraft's ordnance has struck the Custom House area of the Grand Harbour waterfront, almost exactly above the island's underground operations rooms and offices

freighter *Thermopylae.* This vessel had been part of a four-ship convoy making for Malta, but after developing an engine defect it had been detached and re-routed instead to Benghazi under strong naval escort. Badly damaged by the Ju 88's bombs and blazing fiercely, the ship – laden with munitions – had to be sunk.

The following evening 12 aircraft of I./LG 1 left Eleusis on a highly secret mission. Proving that the wireless intercept war was not all one-sided, Luftwaffe signals intelligence had learned that the HQ of the enemy's Desert Air Force was housed in a large villa on the outskirts of Barce. The mission was flown under strict radio silence. The exact results of the raid are not known, but at least one crew claimed hits on the building, for which each member received the Iron Cross, First Class!

On 29 January Rommel's troops retook Benghazi. The British had just got the port up and running again, but now they were forced to evacuate 'this very valuable advanced base' in a hurry, having been able to land only 6000 tons of supplies (nearly half of it petrol) during their brief five weeks' occupation. But Rommel did not stop there. By the end of the first week in February the *Afrika Korps* had advanced as far as the Gazala Line, less than 40 miles from Tobruk. This was a line of deep minefields, interspersed by defensive 'boxes' hastily set up by the retreating British. It stretched from El Gazala, on the coast road, some 35 miles down into the desert, where its southern end was anchored on the 'fortress' outpost of Bir Hacheim. And it was here that Rommel paused to gather strength.

Operation *Crusader* was now well and truly over. And for the next three months, in the words of one noted historian, there was 'a lull in desert air operations', while the eastern Mediterranean witnessed 'a certain amount of desultory harassing activity by Luftwaffe bomber forces based in Greece and Crete, directed mainly against the harbours of Port Said and Alexandria, and British supply depots and lines of communications in Egypt'.

To the crews of LG 1 actually flying the eight-hour missions across the eastern Mediterranean, their operations did not seem 'desultory' in the least. With the ground fighting stalled along the Gazala Line to the west of Tobruk, LG 1's three *Gruppen* – rarely mustering on average more than 40 serviceable machines between them – were hard pressed to carry out the many tasks they were being asked to perform. Nor, contrary to the somewhat dismissive quote above, were their objectives confined

An anonymous Ju 88A-4 (last two code letters are 'EN') already bombed up and now being refuelled 'somewhere in North Africa'. The prancing black horse badge on the door of the Opel Blitz fuel bowser ought to provide a clue as to the where and when, but so far this has defied positive identification

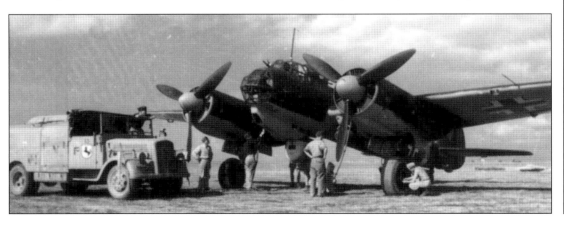

to Egypt. They also attacked targets close to the frontlines in Libya and continued to mount their anti-shipping sorties.

In the early hours of 12 February, for example, every available machine of I./LG 1 took off from Eleusis to attack Tobruk harbour. And it was on this same date that a three-ship convoy, protected by four Royal Navy cruisers and 16 destroyers, left Alexandria for Malta. Late the following day nine of the *Geschwader's* Ju 88s attacked the merchantmen, damaging one so badly that it had to be towed into Tobruk by two of the escorting destroyers. This was the 7255-ton *Clan Campbell*, which would be sunk during its next attempt to reach Malta, as already described above.

On the afternoon of 14 February five aircraft of I. *Gruppe* caught, dive-bombed and sank the *Clan Campbell's* 7262-ton sister-ship, the *Clan Chattan*. Finally, that same evening, 14 machines of II./LG 1 were despatched from Eleusis to attack the one remaining freighter. Already damaged and under tow, the 7798-ton *Rowallan Castle* suffered two further hits and had to be sunk shortly afterwards. Not a single merchantman of convoy MW 9 reached Malta.

Meanwhile, there was once again a Ju 88 presence in North Africa, albeit initially only a token one. During the last week of January 1942, Oberleutnant Rudolf Meier's 12./LG 1 had been detached from IV. *Gruppe* in Greece to provide direct support for the *Afrika Korps*. Operating at first from desert landing grounds astride Cyrenaica's border with Tripolitania, Meier's *Staffel* moved up to Benina after the recapture of Benghazi. 12/LG 1 would lose at least two of its aircraft to enemy fighters in the Tobruk area in the weeks ahead.

During the same period, from mid-February to mid-March, Hauptmann Joachim Helbig's I. *Gruppe* could perhaps be forgiven for feeling giddy, being transferred no fewer than seven times between Eleusis, Heraklion and Catania. This nomadic existence only came to an end when it was decided on 16 March to deploy II./LG 1 to Catania on a more permanent basis – or at least for the duration of the aerial bombardment of Malta. Before taking up residence on Catania, however, Hauptmann Kollewe's pilots had notched up another minor success by sinking two small British coastal vessels, the 2825-ton *Bintang* and the 1360-ton *Hanne* (the former claimed by the *Gruppe* to be an 8000 tonner!), off Bardia on 22 February. The attackers did not get away scot-free. They ran into a formation of Hurricanes on convoy patrol, which shot 6. *Staffel's* 'L1+LP' into the sea.

During the latter half of March and throughout April the Ju 88s of both I. *Gruppe* and 12. *Staffel* continued to strike at ground targets in North Africa. The latter – based at Benina and Berca, but also making use of Derna as a forward landing ground – operated primarily over Libyan territory immediately behind the Gazala Line. Objectives such as

On 28 April 1942 an aircraft coded 'L1+AA' was shot down over Alexandria. It is not known whether this was the actual machine in question (the Wk-Nr. is indecipherable on the original print), but what *is* on record is that the aircraft lost was not being flown by LG 1's *Geschwaderkommodore*, to whom it was officially assigned, but by an NCO crew of 2. *Staffel*. What was that again about the only hard-and-fast rule?

On the day following the loss of 'AA' in the eastern Mediterranean, 12./LG 1's 'L1+LW' was caught on camera as it beat up Benina airfield outside Benghazi after returning from another successful raid on Tobruk

Tobruk and the complex of fighter airfields around Gambut were attacked on a regular basis. Meanwhile, 'Jochen' Helbig's I. *Gruppe*, now based at Heraklion alongside the *Geschwaderstab* under new *Kommodore* Oberstleutnant Franz von Benda, concentrated mainly on targets in Egypt further to the enemy's rear. These included lines of communication, supply depots and airfields such as the RAF's bomber base at Qotafiya.

Neither unit suffered any combat casualties over the desert during these weeks, but I./LG 1 did lose two aircraft in raids on Alexandria. 2. *Staffel's* 'L1+KK' disappeared into the sea after being damaged by anti-aircraft fire over the target area on 16 April. And 12 days later, on the evening of 28th, 'L1+AA' was brought down by a nightfighter. Despite this aircraft's code letters, which identified it as the machine officially assigned to the *Geschwaderkommodore*, it too was being operated on this occasion by 2. *Staffel* and flown by an all-NCO crew, only one of whom survived to be taken into British captivity.

I./LG 1 more than made up for these losses when, on 11 May, they were despatched to attack four Royal Navy destroyers that had sailed from Alexandria to intercept an Axis supply convoy reported making for Benghazi. Fourteen of the *Gruppe's* aircraft caught the warships south of Crete and quickly sank the 1920-ton *Lively*. A follow-up attack by II./LG 1 (by now returned to Eleusis) later that same afternoon was unsuccessful. But a second mission mounted by Helbig's I. *Gruppe* at dusk claimed the two 1760-ton *Javelin* class sister-ships *Kipling* and *Jackal*, although the latter did not go down until the next day. Only the fourth vessel of the quartet, *Jervis*, escaped I./LG 1's onslaught, returning to Alexandria with 630 survivors from the other three on board.

DESERT OFFENSIVE

By this time, as described earlier in this chapter, the second air offensive against Malta had come to a close and Rommel was preparing to launch the next stage of his desert advance. His plan was to outflank the British and Commonwealth forces, destroy them from the rear and then march unopposed on Cairo. Underlining the importance attached to this ambitious undertaking – and at the same time demonstrating just how far the emphasis had swung away from Malta – HQ *Luftflotte* 2 was moved from Taormina, in Sicily, to North Africa shortly before Rommel began his attack on 26 May.

The only Ju 88s providing direct support at the start of the offensive were those of 12./LG 1. Commanded since 20 March by Oberleutnant Heinrich Boecker, this *Staffel* had now been amalgamated with the Ju 87s of StG 3 to form the *Gefechtsverband* 'Sigel'. But Rommel was also to benefit from the raids carried out by I. and II./LG 1 from Crete and Greece, most notably on such targets as Bir Hacheim and Tobruk. A newcomer to the North African arena at this point was I./KG 54, whose

Ju 88s were transferred from Eleusis on 1 June to divide their strength between Tympakion, on Crete, and Derna, in Libya. The unit's introduction to the desert war was not without incident. It lost one of the four machines sent to bomb Bir Hacheim on this date when 'B3+AH' failed to return. The desert fortress, stubbornly held by the Free French, would finally fall ten days later after being pounded into submission by an estimated 1400 individual sorties flown against it by the Luftwaffe.

Having broken through the British defences, the *Afrika Korps* advanced rapidly. And this time Rommel would not be diverted by the need to besiege Tobruk. Almost unbelievably, the town – which had held out for eight long months the previous year – would be taken on the run in just one day! Axis forces then crossed the border into Egypt, only to be brought to a halt at El Alamein at the beginning of July. Another operational stand-off ensued as both sides again sought to build up their supplies. But now, despite a doubling of the numbers of Ju 52/3m transport aircraft in the Mediterranean theatre from 150 to 300 before the month was out, it was Rommel who was very much at a disadvantage.

During this period the battle for supplies also dominated events in the central Mediterranean, where Malta, although no longer subjected to such intense air attacks, still found itself in a very precarious situation. The first two weeks of June saw six Ju 88s lost over, or close to, the island. All but one of these casualties were from the ranks of KGrs 606 and 806. The exception was KG 54's 'B3+AA', which was downed by a nightfighter late on 10 June. Although officially another *Geschwaderkommodore's* machine, 'AA' was being flown on this mission not by Oberstleutnant Walter Marienfeld himself, but by his Adjutant, Hauptmann Hans Humburg.

Three nights later, a number of coordinated commando raids were carried out on Luftwaffe airfields in Libya and on Crete. The North African raids achieved little, but a small raiding party that landed on Crete from the Greek submarine *Triton* was able to place delayed-action charges on some 20 aircraft at Heraklion. I./LG 1 reported that seven of its bombers were severely damaged, as were two Ju 88Ds of 2.(F)/124, a reconnaissance *Staffel* also currently based on the field.

These commando actions, designed to neutralise at least some of the Luftwaffe's striking power, were part and parcel of a much larger overall plan – to sail two supply

Rivulets of molten aluminium coagulate on the desert sand like the very life blood trickling from this mortally wounded Ju 88 of 6./LG 1 that was reportedly brought down by anti-aircraft fire from the Free French defenders of Bir Hacheim

1./KGr 606's '7T+FH' appears to be engaged here on routine convoy escort duty. The crew's obvious success in the more offensive anti-shipping role may be gauged from the impressive rudder scoreboard, which suggests this could be the machine flown by Leutnant Johannes Geismann. Also just visible on the nose of the aircraft is KGr 606's 'cockerel' badge, introduced by long-serving *Gruppenkommandeur* Oberstleutnant Joachim Hahn (*Hahn* being the German for cockerel), who was killed in action on 3 June 1942

convoys to Malta simultaneously from either end of the Mediterranean. The western force, code-named Operation *Harpoon* and consisting of five merchantmen and one tanker, was strongly escorted by units of the Royal Navy, including two carriers.

The vessels slipped through the Straits of Gibraltar into the western Mediterranean during the early hours of 12 June. The first opposition they faced came from Italian forces based on Sardinia. The first Luftwaffe machines to make contact with the convoy were the long-range reconnaissance Ju 88Ds of 1.(F)/122, operating out of Libya. They paid for their 'snooping' by losing two of their number, both, it is believed, to Sea Hurricanes launched from HMS *Eagle* – 'F6+HH' crashed in Algeria early on the afternoon of 13th, and 'F6+EH' came down in the sea the following morning.

By the evening of that same 14 June, the vessels were within range of the Luftwaffe's Malta-based bombers. Nine machines of KGr 606 dive-bombed the elderly carrier *Argus*, narrowly missing it. Two of the unit's Ju 88s also succumbed to Sea Hurricanes, '7T+IL' and '7T+HL' both failing to return from this mission.

The action peaked the next day. The first Ju 88s to attack were a small force from I./KG 54 that had been held back at Comiso when the bulk of the *Gruppe* transferred to Crete a fortnight earlier. Three bombs struck the 5600-ton *Chant*, an American merchantman, which slowly sank beneath the waves, while the 9308-ton US tanker *Kentucky* was disabled by a near miss. The I./KG 54 machines returned to the convoy shortly before noon. This time they damaged the 5601-ton British freighter *Burdwan*. Close on their heels came aircraft from KGr 606, who more than made up for their poor performance on the previous day by quickly sending both the *Burdwan* and the *Kentucky* to the bottom.

With another of the convoy's vessels having already been sunk by Italian torpedo-bombers, only two of the original six remained to make the final dash for Malta. This they succeeded in doing, despite one last attempt to stop them by about a dozen machines from KGr 806. Coming in at dusk, this attack was broken up by Malta-based Spitfires, who claimed two of the Ju 88s, including 'M7+FK' piloted by Oberleutnant Kurt Kehrer, the *Staffelkapitän* of 2./KGr.806

While *Harpoon* was battling its way towards Malta from the west, an even larger convoy – 11 vessels in all – had sailed from ports in the eastern Mediterranean. Officially convoy MW 11, the merchantmen – together with their cruiser and destroyer escort – were operating under the codename *Vigorous*. And the greatest perceived threat to *Vigorous* was the presence of the Luftwaffe's Ju 88s on Crete. By 14 June the ships were traversing 'Bomb Alley', the stretch of water between Crete and the North African coastline. They had been under near constant attack all day long, mainly from Ju 87s based in Libya. In the evening it was the turn of the Ju 88s.

In one three-hour period alone, the crews of I. and II./LG 1, together with elements of I./KG 54, flew no fewer than seven separate attacks, totalling close on 90 individual sorties in all. Despite this maximum effort (which resulted in the loss of five bombers, with as many again damaged or written-off in crash-landings back on Crete), only one merchantman was sunk – the 6104-ton British freighter *Bhutan*.

In this well-known shot of unfortunately less than perfect quality, the predatory shape of a KG 77 machine is silhouetted against Malta's Grand Harbour. Note the large merchant vessel at the mouth of Dockyard Creek just in front of the aircraft's port wing

This photograph of a KGr 806 formation over open water is as grainy as the one above, but it too is of interest for on the original print it is just possible to make out the markings of the aircraft at the top of the picture – 'M7+DH'. Is this perhaps the machine flown by Leutnant Karl-Erich Ritter, the first Luftwaffe bomber lost in the historic *Pedestal* convoy battle?

The intensity of the air attacks did have one other result, however. Although only halfway to Malta, the convoy's escorting warships were already running seriously low in anti-aircraft ammunition. And when, on top of that, an RAF reconnaissance Spitfire reported that heavy units of the Italian battle fleet had put to sea with the apparent intention of engaging the convoy, the decision was reluctantly taken to order the merchantmen to return to Alexandria. Between them, Operations *Harpoon/Vigorous* were to have delivered 115,000 tons of supplies to beleaguered Malta. In the event, only 15,000 tons reached the island. This was just enough to stave off an immediate crisis, but it was clear to both sides that another convoy would be needed, and needed soon.

Until that time the Ju 88s on Sicily were instructed to maintain as much pressure as possible on Malta. To help them do so, Oberstleutnant Hermann Schlüter's *Stab* KG 77, together with his II. and III. *Gruppen*, were transferred back from France at the end of June to rejoin *Kampfgruppen* 606 and 806 and I./KG 54 on Sicily. Throughout July these five *Gruppen* flew an almost unbroken succession of raids against Malta in strengths ranging from single aircraft to formations of two-dozen or more, mainly targeting the island's airfields. It cost them over 30 machines in all, plus many others damaged. Two-thirds of the casualties came from the ranks of KG 77. They included two *Staffelkapitäne* of the particularly unfortunate 7./KG 77, both of whom were brought down by Spitfires – Oberleutnant Erich Behr's '3Z+GR' failed to return from a raid on Luqa on 8 July and Oberleutnant Josef Zimmer's '3Z+JR' was shot into the sea on 27 July even before he could reach his target at Takali.

By this time the first vessels of what was to be the next Malta convoy were already beginning to converge on the River Clyde in Scotland. Only too aware of the Luftwaffe's current domination of the eastern Mediterranean, and not wishing to repeat the unhappy experience of *Vigorous*, Operation *Pedestal* was a less elaborate plan calling for one large convoy, heavily escorted by units of the Royal Navy, to sail through the Straits of Gibraltar and approach Malta from the west. It consisted of 13 fast, modern merchantmen, not one of them of less than 7000 tons, and a single tanker, which together were transporting over 85,000 tons of

supplies. Protection was to be provided by main covering and escorting forces composed of four carriers, two battleships, seven cruisers and no fewer than 26 destroyers.

The assemblage of an armada of this size could not escape detection for long and, to oppose it, Axis air strength on Sardinia and Sicily was increased to over 650 machines. Almost 150 of this total was made up of the seven Ju 88 *Kampfgruppen* now gathered on Sicily (the five resident *Gruppen* being temporarily reinforced by I. and II./LG 1 flying in from Greece and Crete). Thus the battle lines were drawn for the last great Malta convoy action of the Mediterranean war.

CONVOY ENGAGED

Pedestal slipped through the Straits of Gibraltar in the early hours of 10 August 1942. It did not suffer its first casualty until shortly after noon the following day, when the veteran carrier *Eagle*, which had been instrumental in the delivery of nearly 200 Spitfires to Malta over the previous five months, was torpedoed by U-73 some 85 miles north of Algiers.

The first air attack, mounted by Ju 88s, backed up by torpedo-carrying He 111s, came in just as night was falling. But neither this, nor a second assault by two-dozen machines of I. and II./LG 1 at mid-morning of the 12th, produced any results. The first did, however, see the loss of KGr 806's 'M7+DH', while the latter reportedly cost LG 1 seven machines (including one shot down in error by Italian fighters as it approached Sardinia after the mission to land and refuel).

A prolonged attack by some 70 Italian and German aircraft – over half of them Ju 88s of KGs 54 and 77 – south of Sardinia in the early afternoon fared slightly better. The battleships *Rodney* and *Nelson* were both shaken by near misses, while the 7516-ton freighter *Deucalion* was damaged. But one of 8./KG 77's machines, '3Z+ES' piloted by Oberleutnant Leopold Lagauer, failed to return.

Another Ju 88 went down during the last air attack on 12 August. Coming in at dusk, a force of 30 machines from KGs 54, 77 and KGr 806 – again backed by torpedo-carrying Heinkels – hit the convoy hard. Already damaged, the 12,688-ton *Empire Hope* took two direct hits from a Ju 88 that turned it into a blazing inferno. The Heinkels sank another of the merchantmen and delivered the *coup de grâce* to the *Deucalion*, while two more freighters were damaged. During the night of 12/13 August the remaining ships, by now widely scattered, rounded Cape Bon. In the early hours of the morning they were savaged by Italian MTBs, which immobilised the cruiser *Manchester*, sank four of the freighters and damaged a fifth.

But it fell to Ju 88s to claim the final *Pedestal* victim when, shortly after 0800 hrs on 13 August, bombers from 3./KGr 806, led by *Staffelkapitän* Oberleutnant Wolfgang Schulte, attacked the

Just two weeks after *Pedestal*, on 1 September 1942, KGr 806 was redesignated to become III./KG 54 (the first III./KG 54 having been disbanded back in July 1940 at the start of the Battle of Britain!). This photograph, from a British source, of 8. *Staffel's* 'B3+DS' abandoned in the desert, was clearly taken some time later during Rommel's retreat through Libya

12,843-ton merchantman *Waimarama* south of Pantellaria. The largest vessel in the convoy, the *Waimarama's* main cargo – like that of the *Empire Hope* sunk the evening before – consisted of cased petrol. Struck by four bombs, the vessel erupted in a huge ball of fire and went down in just a matter of seconds.

Three more Ju 88s would be brought down during the course of the next 24 hours. Others helped to finish off two of *Pedestal's* crippled stragglers. But to all intents and purposes, the action was over. Four of the original 13 merchantmen reached Malta, bringing with them some 32,000 tons of supplies.

Also in September 1942, KGr 606 was redesignated to become the new I./KG 77 (the original I./KG 77, which never served in the Mediterranean, had been renumbered I./KG 6 at the end of August). While retaining the 'cockerel' badge, the *Gruppe's* aircraft now wore the unit codes of their new parent *Geschwader*, as may be seen in this fine flying shot of '3Z+EH'. Note also what appears to be a 20 mm MG FF cannon projecting from the ventral gondola. This weapon was used for low-level attacks on shipping, which may also account for the disruptive spotted camouflage applied to the lower surfaces of the engine nacelles and forward fuselage

Last of all, the tanker *Ohio* – battered, grievously wounded, its decks almost awash – was later towed into Grand Harbour. The provisions unloaded from the four freighters allowed Malta to survive, while the aviation fuel pumped from the *Ohio* enabled the island to resume its air strikes against Rommel's supply convoys just as he was preparing to launch the desert offensive that was intended to drive the British out of Egypt for good.

After the intense air actions fought during the course of *Pedestal* in mid-month, the operations flown against Malta during the latter half of August were something of an anti-climax. Seven Ju 88s were lost for very little in return. September remained equally quiet, with all but one of the 20 KG 54 machines reported lost or damaged throughout the Mediterranean area that month being attributed to accidental or unknown causes. The the single exception was an aircraft destroyed in an RAF bombing raid on Heraklion.

The Ju 88 units on Sicily utilised this lull to gather strength and reorganize for one last blitz on Malta. The most obvious change was the incorporation of the two hitherto semi-autonomous *Kampfgruppen* into the ranks of the established *Kampfgeschwader*, with Hauptmann Rolf Siedschlag's KGr 606 being redesignated to become the new I./KG 77

Now flying '3Z+DB' (note the unusual treatment of the aircraft's individual letter) with the *Gruppenstab* of I./KG 77, Leutnant Johannes Geismann takes a souvenir snapshot of his scoreboard to date. In addition to his shipping successes – nine merchantmen sunk and one damaged – note the bar denoting a single aerial kill (claimed on 4 October 1942) beneath the miniature *Gruppe* badge at the top of the rudder. Awarded the Knight's Cross on 21 December 1942, Hauptmann Geismann would end the war flying nightfighters

Another of the erstwhile KGr 606's anti-shipping experts, Leutnant Karl Heinz Greve's scoreboard also features a single aerial kill in addition to the seven merchantmen sunk, and one carrier and one (minelaying) cruiser damaged. Greve won the Knight's Cross on 7 October 1942 and would also survive the war . . .

. . . unlike Hauptmann Heinrich Paepcke, the *Gruppenkommandeur* of II./KG 77 – pictured far right – who was killed in a mid-air collision with a Spitfire during a raid on Malta on 17 October 1942 (although whether in the distinctively camouflaged machine seen here is not known). Having been awarded the Knight's Cross on 5 September 1940, Hauptmann Paepcke would be honoured with posthumous Oak Leaves on 19 December 1942

and Major Richard Linke's KGr 806 filling the long-vacant III. *Gruppe* slot in KG 54.

By the beginning of October there were seven Ju 88 *Gruppen* poised on Sicily to renew the assault on Malta – KGs 54 and 77, both now at full three-*Gruppe* establishment, plus II./LG 1 brought back after briefly returning to Crete. In total, there were close on 200 machines all concentrated on the three airfields at Gerbini, Catania and Comiso.

FINAL MALTA BLITZ

The final all-out air offensive against Malta began on 11 October 1942, and lasted just one week. The island was no longer the soft target it had once been. Its rejuvenated defences took a heavy toll of the attacking Luftwaffe formations. Indeed, more than 30 Ju 88s were lost, either shot down or written off in crash-landings, during the week-long campaign. The most grievous losses occurred on the last day of all, 17 October, when the casualties included two highly-decorated *Gruppenkommandeure*.

Among the aircraft taking part in the morning raid on Malta on that date were seven Ju 88s of II./KG 77. Just off the coast to the southeast of Valetta, the leading machine, *Gruppenkommandeur* Major Heirich Paepcke's '3Z+AC', was involved in a head-on collision with a Spitfire. Both pilots were killed instantly (although, incredibly, the three other Luftwaffe crewmen were seen to bail out before the stricken bomber hit the water). Paepcke himself, who had won the Knight's Cross at the height of the Battle of Britain when Hajo Herrmann's predecessor as *Staffelkapitän* of 7./KG 30, had since distinguished himself at the head of II./KG 77 in the Mediterranean. His most recent success had been the sinking of a '12,000-ton transport during the Malta convoy battle of 12 August' – presumably a reference to the *Empire Hope*. Paepcke would be honoured with posthumous Oak Leaves on 19 December 1942.

A second raid shortly after midday by nearly 90 aircraft also included a formation of Ju 88s, this time eight machines of II./LG 1 led by *Gruppenkommandeur* Major Gerhard Kollewe in 'L1+YC'. Intercepted by Spitfires, the latter was shot into the sea off Valetta. Although the entire crew succeeded in bailing out, only the wireless-operator and gunner were picked up alive. Having been awarded the Knight's Cross on the eve of the invasion of Yugoslavia, Kollewe had then led his

Gruppe with great success in the Mediterranean, II./LG 1 being credited with sinking 148,000 tons of merchant shipping and two destroyers. He had been presented with the Oak Leaves just over two months earlier on 10 August 1942, the very day that *Pedestal* had entered the Straits of Gibraltar.

The deaths of these two leading Luftwaffe bomber pilots effectively wrote *finis* to the Axis air campaign against Malta. There would, of course, be further raids in the months ahead, but these would be mere pinpricks in comparison to the suffering endured by the island at the height of the major 1941 and 1942 offensives.

The desert's 'resident' long-range reconnaissance *Staffel* by mid-1942, 1.(F)/121 was of inestimable value to Rommel in the planning of his ground operations. But that ground could sometimes be treacherous, as witness the unit's 'sand-and-spinach' camouflaged '7A+BH' on its nose at Fuka I sometime in August 1942

Meanwhile, with Hitler having abandoned all plans to invade Malta from the air, every effort since had been directed towards building up Axis ground forces in North Africa in preparation for Rommel's drive on Cairo. During this period – July/August 1942 – those *Gruppen* of LG 1 based on Crete had continued to raid the eastern Mediterranean ports of Alexandra, Suez and Port Said, usually under cover of darkness, and had suffered over a dozen losses in the process. Rommel launched his last great offensive on 31 August. At first all went well, for he managed to turn the southern flank of the British front at El Alamein, but then instead of being able to advance on Cairo and Alexandria as planned, his forces suffered a crushing defeat at the Battle of Alam Halfa. In six days it was all over and he was forced back to his original positions.

Towards the end of August LG 1's *Gruppen* had been joined on Crete by elements of I./KG 54 and KG 77. And whereas the former were employed primarily on convoy protection duties, the other units provided the *Afrika Korps* with at least a measure of direct support during the Alam Halfa fighting. But after this, and for the next seven weeks, another lull was to descend over the Western Desert. With Rommel busy regrouping, the Ju 88s of LG 1 (together with those of KG 77) returned to their nocturnal harassment of the ports around the Nile Delta.

At this same time, however, the newly appointed commander of the British Eighth Army, a certain General Montgomery, was finalising the plans and preparations for his own El Alamein offensive. It would prove to be the turning point of the war in the west – 'The Stalingrad of the Desert', as one German historian later described it. Hitler's inability to decide whether to invade Malta or to capture Cairo had resulted in his forces' achieving neither objective. It was a fatal error.

When the Battle of El Alamein opened at 2200 hrs on 23 October to the thunder of 1000 Allied guns, it marked the beginning of the end of the war in the Mediterranean. And for the Ju 88 *Gruppen* in-theatre it heralded the start of almost 20 months of near constant retreats, growing losses and eventual withdrawal.

TWO-FRONT WAR IN AFRICA

For ten days the Battle of El Alamein hung in the balance. Axis forces at first resisted fiercely, and it was not until 3 November that the Eighth Army succeeded in breaking through Rommel's defences and advancing westwards. The veterans among the British ranks who had done it all twice before dubbed this latest offensive the 'Third Benghazi Stakes', but this time it would be different. The advance would not run out of steam just beyond Benghazi. It would continue onwards across the whole of Libya, into Tunisia, and only come to a halt with the surrender of all Axis troops in North Africa.

Rommel's long retreat was just four days old when, on 8 November 1942, Anglo-American forces stormed ashore in Morocco and Algeria. Suddenly, the whole emphasis of the air war switched to the western Mediterranean. The mass of shipping required for Operation *Torch* – the landings in Northwest Africa – had not escaped the notice of the Germans. Initially assuming that the large number of vessels converging on the Straits of Gibraltar were the makings of a vast convoy intended to reinforce Gen Montgomery's Eighth Army in Egypt, the Luftwaffe reacted with its customary speed.

Among the first, and most important, counter-measures taken – nearly a week before the actual landings occurred – was the order to transfer five anti-shipping *Kampfgruppen* down from northern Norway and Finland to the Mediterranean. Four of these units were equipped with Ju 88s, namely III./KG 26, II. and III./KG 30, and I./KG 60. The transfers themselves took anything from five to eight days. When they were completed the three latter *Gruppen* had joined KGs 54 and 77 on Sicily, while III./KG 26 had taken up residence at Grosseto, the Luftwaffe's torpedo school on the coast of Italy, 100 miles north of Rome.

Other Ju 88 *Gruppen* were sent to the Mediterranean theatre after the *Torch* landings had taken place. Evidently fearing a quick follow-up invasion of southern France, Hitler ordered his troops into previously unoccupied Vichy France on 11 November (the day Adm Darlan ordered the end of resistance in French North Africa).

Among the Luftwaffe units hastily moved from northwest Europe down into southern France were two

On 30 October 1942, at the height of the Battle of El Alamein, the crews of 1.(F)/121 took time out to celebrate the *Staffel's* 3000th operational mission. Although barely visible here, *Staffelkapitän* Hauptmann Erwin Fischer (second from the right) is already wearing the Knight's Cross, which was awarded to him on 12 April 1941. He would receive the Oak Leaves on 10 February 1943, thus becoming the first reconnaissance pilot to be so decorated. Second from left is Oberleutnant Alfons Muggenthaler, who would be awarded the Knight's Cross on 29 February 1944

Ju 88 *Ergänzungsgruppen*, IV./KG 76 transferring from Laon-Athies to Toulouse and IV./KG 77 from Bourges to Montpellier. Incidentally, another *Ergänzungsgruppe*, IV./KG 54, had been based at Grottaglie on the heel of Italy since March 1942, carrying out training and operational patrol duties.

Finally, in mid-November KG 76, which had been withdrawn from the Russian front some weeks earlier, was deployed to Athens-Tatoi and to Heraklion and Tymbakion, on Crete, to bolster LG 1's strength in the eastern Mediterranean (some of this *Geschwader's Staffeln* having been temporarily transferred to Sicily).

Just how far, and how rapidly, the Luftwaffe's fortunes in the eastern Mediterranean had declined may be gauged by Operation *Stoneage*. This was a four-ship convoy that departed Alexandria for Malta on 17 November. Nearly every attack by the Cretan-based Ju 88s was broken up by the convoys' excellent aerial cover, provided by RAF fighters flying in relays from their desert airfields. Although one unidentified Junkers managed to torpedo and damage the light cruiser *Arethusa*, all four of the merchantmen reached Malta unscathed in the early hours of the 20th.

Bringing with them an adequate supply of stores and aviation spirit, *Stoneage* marked, in the words of one official historian, 'the final and effective relief of Malta'. Henceforward, at least as far as the Luftwaffe was concerned, the once hotly contested eastern Mediterranean basin would become very much a backwater, for as the retreat of the *Afrika Korps* gathered pace, so the focus of operations – both on the ground and in the air – moved ever further westwards.

On Crete, a special battle group of Ju 88s – the *Einsatzgruppe Kreta1*, composed of elements from both LG 1 and KG 76 – was set up specifically to targets the Eighth Army's rear-area lines of communications and supply. Throughout the latter half of November and for much of December, machines of the *Einsatzgruppe* flew anti-shipping patrols and bombed coastal targets between Tobruk and Benghazi (Tobruk having been recaptured on 13 November and Benghazi exactly one week later). During this time a dozen or so Ju 88s were lost over Libya. Among the casualties were the *Gruppenkommandeur* of IV./LG 1, Major Erwin Schulz, whose machine was shot down over Derna on 21 November, and LG 1's *Kommodore*, Oberst Franz von Benda, who failed to return from what was described as 'a special mission to Tobruk' on 2 December.

But it was at the far western end of the Mediterranean – the scene of the *Torch* landings – where the fiercest air battles were now being fought. Eleven Ju 88s were reported missing in attacks on shipping in the Algiers area on the first two days of the invasion alone. A number of vessels were damaged in these raids, including the 9135-ton American troop transport USS *Leedstown*, which had its steering gear put out of action by an aerial torpedo on the afternoon of 8 November. After taking more torpedo and

Photographs of III./KG 26 aircraft taken in 1942 are notoriously difficult to identify. In January of that year the third III./KG 26 of the war was formed from I./KG 28 (*Geschwader* code '1T'), only to be redesignated I./KG 1 in July. It was immediately replaced by a fourth III./KG 26 (the ex-KGr 506), which for some reason continued to use the '1T' markings. So are these III./KG 26 machines ('1T+ZD' in the foreground and '1T+GR' in the background to the right) aircraft of the erstwhile I./KG 28 pictured in southern France in the first half of 1942, or machines of the previous KGr 506 based in Italy at the end of that year? The latter seems to be the more likely, the only clue being the 'ram's skull' badge, similar to that earlier associated with KGr 506, which can just be made out on the nose of the machine running up its engines in the centre background

Dawn on 12 November 1942 off Bougie and HMS *Karanja* is still blazing from the 'near miss' in her engine room

bomb hits, the vessel went down in the Bay of Algiers 24 hours later. The Royal Navy's 1300-ton sloop HMS *Ibis* was sent to the bottom north of Algiers the following day.

It was during the subsequent landings at Bougie, over 100 miles to the east of Algiers, on 11 November – where, by mischance, the assault force initially found itself devoid of effective fighter cover – that the Ju 88s scored their greatest successes. Three large troopships were sunk, the 15,225-ton *Cathay*, the 13,482-ton *Awatea* and the 9890-ton HMS *Karanja*. The captain of the latter vessel, taken over from the merchant marine a year earlier and now serving as an Infantry Landing Ship, was on the bridge when the ship was struck by at least two bombs in the early hours of 12 November. 'By God, those were close', he remarked to the officer standing beside him. Back came the classic reply, 'Yes, Sir. They are in the engine-room'.

Two days later, the 16,632-ton *Narkunda* was bombed and sunk in the Gulf of Bougie and the smaller 7479-ton *Glenfinlas* severely damaged while berthed in the harbour. By this time, however, Spitfires were operating out of nearby Djidjelli airfield (a No 242 Sqn machine had shot down 1./KG 54's 'B3+CK' during the raids of the 14th), and as the Allied fighter defences grew, so the Ju 88 units' casualty lists inevitably began to lengthen. For as well as continuing with their anti-shipping operations – for ever smaller returns, it might be added – and having to escort their own supply convoys across the Sicilian Narrows to Tunisia, the Ju 88 *Gruppen* were now conducting a sustained bombing offensive, both by day and by night, against the Allies' supply ports in northwest Africa.

Although the city and harbour of Algiers itself was to suffer numerous raids, it was the more easterly ports along the Algerian coast that received the most attention as the Ju 88s attempted to disrupt the Allied advance into Tunisia. Targets such as Bougie, Djidelli, Philippeville and Tabarka – the latter just across the Tunisian border – were all attacked regularly. But it was the port and airfield of Bône, soon to become the First Army's main forward base, which had to endure raids almost every night.

More than 30 Ju 88s were lost to direct enemy action during each of the three months from November 1942 to January 1943. This was the equivalent of one *Gruppe* per month, or an entire *Geschwader* in total. And to these figures must be added the countless other machines damaged, written-off in accidents and lost through other causes. Nor was the attrition purely material. Of even greater concern were the increasing numbers of experienced crews and unit leaders being lost. Major Kurt

Although KG 76's three *Gruppen* are known to have been based variously in Greece, Crete and Sicily, at least some elements of the *Geschwader* must have been deployed, however briefly, to North Africa, for this unfortunate machine appears to be in imminent danger of being swallowed up by what looks suspiciously like a desert sandstorm

Brand, *Gruppenkommandeur* of I./KG 60, was flying one of the two machines of this unit that failed to return from a mission on 28 November (possibly also victims of No 242 Sqn).

UNIT CHANGES

During the latter half of December several organisational changes took place. I./KG 54 and II. and III./KG 77 were all withdrawn from Sicily to rest and re-equip at Piacenza, in northern Italy. In their stead II./KG 76 flew in from Crete, thereby bringing to an end the short-lived *Einsatzgruppe Kreta*. II./KG 76 took up residence at Gerbini, close to Catania, where I./KG 76 had been based for the past three weeks busily flying convoy escort missions, carrying out anti-submarine patrols and transporting fuel to Tunisia. It is reported that the two I. *Gruppe* machines which collided in mid-air on 9 December were engaged in one such fuel delivery. Apart from LG 1, this left just III./KG 76 on Crete, where it would remain until transferred to Athens-Tatoi on 18 January 1943.

The new year started off well enough, with further heavy raids on Bône harbour resulting in the sinking of two merchantmen and extensive damage to three others. The only known Ju 88 loss during the first 48 hours of 1943 was 3./KG 77's '3Z+KL', shot down by P-38 Lightnings when it ventured deeper inland to attack the Americans' B-17 base at Biskra on 2 January. But it was not long before further casualties were suffered over both Algeria and Libya. A machine of I./LG 1 brought down north of Tobruk on 8 January was being flown by veteran NCO pilot Oberfeldwebel Herbert Isachsen, who survived the ditching to be awarded the Knight's Cross eight months later when in British captivity.

January's 'Hardest Day' was undoubtedly the 15th, when ten Ju 88s were reported missing, six of them from the ranks of I./KG 77 alone. But hardest hit in terms of unit leaders was KG 76, which had lost a *Gruppenkommandeur* and two of its *Staffelkapitäne* before the month was out. The former, III. *Gruppe's* Major Heinrich Schweickhardt, a recent Oak Leaves recipient, had failed to return to Crete after a

A tight formation of I./KG 77 aircraft wings its way across the Mediterranean. Note the coloured spinner rings

Above
The detritus of defeat. The see-saw nature of the fighting back and forth across the sands of Libya left numerous wrecked and abandoned aircraft in its wake. This dilapidated specimen ('7A+LH' of 1.(F)/121) has already had its tail swastika stripped by souvenir hunters . . .

Right
. . . while this Ju 88 (almost certainly another machine of 1.(F)/121, despite the absence of the *Staffel* emblem on the nose) is in even worse condition, having been cannibalised for spare parts . . .

mission on 9 January. 1./KG 76 suffered the loss of Oberleutnant Günter Haussmann nine days later, while 2./KG 76's Oberleutnant Fritz Köhler and his crew were shot down over Algiers in the early hours of 30 January.

By this time the Eighth Army's offensive, launched at El Alamein three months earlier, had taken it clear across Libya, and advance units had already crossed the border into southern Tunisia. Despite being attacked on two fronts, there was still fight left in the *Afrika Korps*. Rommel's forces even managed to

Above
. . . whereas 1./LG 1's 'L1+NH', being inspected by members of an unidentified Hurricane squadron at Gazala Landing Strip 3, appears to be intact (note the 'last two' again repeated in white on the rudder) . . .

Right
. . . and no, this is *not* the Russian steppe, but another desert landing ground. The hammer-and-sickle flag fluttering behind the sad remains of 'L1+EK' is the unofficial standard of an RAF fighter unit (possibly No 134 Sqn, which had spent two months stationed at Vaenga, in the Soviet Union, in late 1941)

stage a brief, but bloody, counter-offensive against US troops at Kasserine during the latter half of February. The month saw a slight reduction in overall Ju 88 losses, but the casualties did include another *Gruppenkommandeur* from the luckless KG 76, Major Richard Meyer of II. *Gruppe* being brought down by P-38s on 22 February.

The end of the war in North Africa was now in sight, and this fact was reflected in the dispositions of the Mediterranean Ju 88 units as of early March 1943, which clearly showed where the final battles were expected to be fought. Of the seven *Kampfgruppen* then operational in theatre, only one – II./LG 1 – was still based on Crete. Two, II./KG 30 and III./KG 77, were operating out of Sicily, targeting mainly the Eighth Army in southern Tunisia and its lines and ports of supply in Libya. And the remaining four (III./KG 26, I. and II./KG 54 and II./KG 76) were in Sardinia, from where they were ideally situated to mount raids along the Algerian and northern Tunisian coasts and against Anglo-American forces closing in on Tunis from the west.

The two *Gruppen* based in Sicily bore the brunt of the Ju 88 combat losses in March, with their casualties accounting for more than half of the month's total. The entry in the Luftwaffe's official Order of Battle for 10 March 1943, which lists just two(!) of II./KG 30's 45 machines as being serviceable, is almost certainly a misprint. The same source also shows that III./KG 77 – recently returned to Sicily after its period of rest and re-equipment at Piacenza – had 27 serviceable aircraft (out of 43) on that date. But 16 of that number would be lost during the latter half of the month, including three (together with a machine of II./KG 30) that were brought down during a raid mounted by the two *Gruppen* along the Libyan coast on 19 March, which resulted in the bombing and sinking of the 7174-ton *Ocean Voyager* in Tripoli harbour.

During this period it is reported that several Ju 88 *Kampfgruppen* also deployed small detachments to southern Tunisia, these including II./KG 30, whose aircraft operated briefly out of Gafsa, and I./KG 54, which was based on the coast at Sfax. These so-called *Kommandos* were presumably

In March 1943 IV./LG 1 ended its long-term occupation of Salonika-Sedes in northern Greece and returned to Wiener Neustadt – although 'L1+GV' is not going anywhere until that missing starboard elevator is replaced! Note the scribble-camouflaged machine in the background to the right

Despite the wartime censor's attempt to obliterate the unit badge, the machine seen here gunning its engines prior to take-off is identifiable as 4./LG 1's 'L1+JM'. The location is either Greece or Crete, and the very fact that the aircraft is sporting a badge may date the photograph back to 1942

By 1943, Mediterranean Ju 88s were being subjected to ever-increasing attacks on the ground from Allied aircraft. One advantage of desert airfields was that the loose sand absorbed much of the blast from bombs. Although this near-miss right alongside 'L1+AH' has covered its uppersurfaces in a thick layer of sand, the only significant damage appears to be to the trailing edge of the Ju 88's starboard wing. Out on the runway a working party hastily fills in the crater left by the next (or previous?) bomb in the stick

At first glance 'L1+GH', also from 1./LG 1, may seem undamaged. But closer inspection reveals that the machine is absolutely riddled with small bullet holes, almost certainly from the machine guns of a strafing RAF fighter. Note also the oil leaking down over the protective cover of the starboard main wheel

intended to provide direct tactical support to the embattled *Afrika Korps*, but it was all too little, too late. On 28 March Montgomery's Eighth Army breached the defences of the Mareth Line and began driving north towards Tunis.

With Axis forces falling back on Tunis under intense pressure from two fronts – west and south – and with the Luftwaffe doing all it could to relieve that pressure, as well as to keep the troops supplied with fuel and ammunition, it is little wonder that Ju 88 losses to enemy action escalated to well over 50 during April.

Nor was it just those units based on Sardinia and Sicily that were now feeling the weight of Allied air superiority. *Gruppen* in Italy that were ostensibly still undergoing retraining and re-equipment were thrown into the fray and suffered the inevitable consequences. Elements of II./LG 1 were also moved forward from Crete to Sicily to play their part in the final act of the African drama, only to lose two crews over Tunisia (although another of the *Gruppe's* Ju 88s based on Sicily was credited with sinking the submarine HMS *Sahib* off the northeastern tip of the island on 24 April). But one of April's last casualties was yet another of KG 76's unfortunate *Gruppenkommandeure* when Hauptmann Anton Stadler, who had taken over II./KG 76 after the loss of Major Richard Meyer on 22 February, himself failed to return from a night raid on Philippeville on 28 April.

Some half-dozen further Ju 88 losses would be reported before the last Axis troops in Tunisia surrendered on 13 May and the war in Africa was finally over. It would be an exaggeration to claim that the 200+ combat losses suffered since the *Torch* landings had broken the back of the Ju 88 *Kampfgruppen* in the Mediterranean, but they *were* another nail in the coffin. Prior to *Torch*, the Luftwaffe's '*Wunderbomber'* had been a mainstay of the *Blitzkrieg* in the Balkans, had played a major role in the bombing

of Malta and had been the scourge of the Royal and Merchant Navies over almost the whole length and breadth of the Mediterranean. But after the loss of Tunisia the Ju 88 *Kampfgruppen* became just another part of the gradual but general retreat northwards.

As Allied air power in the area grew from a position of numerical superiority to one of near total supremacy, so the Ju 88 bombers faced their final test. A test that in little more than a year would see their numbers in theatre fall from a peak of very nearly 300 machines to exactly nil!

THE 'SOFT UNDERBELLY'

With all of North Africa now in their hands, the next logical step for the Allies to take would be to mount a cross-Mediterranean invasion somewhere along the 'soft underbelly' of Europe. The question for Axis leaders was where exactly would the enemy strike? Despite some elaborate subterfuges and deceptions by the Allies in an effort to persuade Hitler that landings might take place on Sardinia, in southern France or even the Aegean, the consensus of opinion in the Axis camp was that the likeliest route for the Allies to take into southern Europe would be through Italy, using Sicily as a first stepping stone.

Thus the island that had been the home of the Mediterranean Ju 88s ever since the first machines of LG 1 touched down there in December 1940 was now itself in the frontline. This fact was underscored by the heavy pounding that Sicily's airfields were given by Allied bombers from Malta and North Africa as part of the pre-invasion softening-up process.

With Sicily rapidly becoming untenable, the early summer of 1943 witnessed yet further reorganisation of the Ju 88 *Kampfgruppen* in the Mediterranean. In the immediate aftermath of the Tunisian campaign, I. and II./KG 54 both returned to the Reich for re-equipment, leaving just III./KG 54 to transfer from Catania to Grottaglie in Italy. I. and III./KG 77 likewise disappeared from the order of battle, which meant that only II./KG 77 remained in Italy, based first at Foggia, before then moving to Rome-Ciampino.

To replace the four departed *Gruppen*, elements of two *Kampfgeschwader* new to the Mediterranean theatre were transferred in to Italy – I. and II./KG 1 from the Russian Front and I. and III./KG 6 from northwest Europe. III./KG 6, incidentally, was the original III./LG 1 of the 1941 desert war in Libya.

There were three other Ju 88 *Gruppen* in Italy – III./KG 30 at Viterbo and I. and II./KG 76 at Foggia and Grosseto respectively (although the latter two also deployed detachments temporarily to both Sardinia and southern France). Finally, Montpellier, in the south of France, was also the base of III./KG 26, while I./LG 1 still retained a small presence on Crete.

Nine of the eleven Ju 88 *Gruppen* currently in the Mediterranean were

As the war moved to the northern shores of the Mediterranean so the Allied air attacks grew heavier. This is the scene of devastation after a bombing raid on Grottaglie, in Italy, with the remains of a Ju 88 of KG 54 in the foreground and evidence of a bygone age, the hangar door of the field's huge airship hangar, still standing background right

With no *Gruppe* letters visible, it is impossible to be certain whether these are machines of II./KG 77 in Italy or aircraft of either I. or III. *Gruppe* undergoing retraining back in the Reich. The neatness of the line-up, apparent disregard of attack from the air and general air of unconcern would seem to suggest the latter

thus concentrated in southern and central Italy, where they were well within striking range of Sicily in readiness for the expected invasion. Yet when it came – before daybreak on 10 July – there was little they could do against the overwhelming might of the Allies' sea and air forces.

One history of Operation *Husky*, as the invasion of Sicily was code-named, states that well over 2000 ships and landing craft were involved. The Allies feared losses of 15 percent during the operation but, incredibly, only 12 vessels of any size fell victim to enemy action. Two of the casualties were US Liberty ships. The 7181-ton *Timothy Pickering*, laden with drums of aviation fuel, bombs, TNT and other explosives, suffered a direct hit and two near misses from three 250-kg bombs. Its back broken, the vessel went down in the Gulf of Noto south of Syracuse.

Two bombing attacks were made on shipping off the Gela landing beaches on Sicily's southern coast during the afternoon of 10 July, which resulted in the destruction of a single LST. But a strike by 'some 30 Ju 88s' in the same area 24 hours later caught the 7176-ton *Robert Rowan*. Its cargo of ammunition began to explode and the vessel was 'abandoned forthwith'. The identity of the attackers is not certain, although machines from both I./KG 6 and III./KG 54 were in the region at the time (neither formation, however, was anywhere near the 30 strong as reported above). Each *Gruppe* suffered the loss of two aircraft, with a third from III./KG 54 crash-landing damaged back at Grottaglie. II./KG 77 also lost two of its number to Spitfires south of Syracuse on 11 July.

The Ju 88s were finding it impossible to penetrate the strong fighter umbrellas that the Allies had established above the main invasion beaches. An attempt to mount a sneak raid on shipping off Augusta shortly after dawn on 13 July by a small formation of II./KG 1 machines was broken up by Spitfires. Two crews failed to make it back to the *Gruppe's* base at San Pancrazio, on the heel of Italy. A raid by II./KG 76 under cover of darkness on 14th against vessels anchored off Syracuse fared even worse. The six aircraft it lost providing ample proof, if proof were needed, that the invaders' defences were as efficient by night as they were by day.

But a rare success was achieved by some 12 machines of III./KG 26 (together with Do 217s of III./KG 100), which took off from their bases in southern France to raid Palermo harbour, on Sicily's northern coast, during the early hours of 1 August. Considerable damage was done to the dock area and the small 2708-ton British coastal freighter *Uskside* was sunk and two US Navy minesweepers damaged.

By this stage of the Sicilian campaign 40 Allied squadrons were on the island, operating either from captured Axis airfields or newly constructed airstrips. A number of these were targeted by small groups of Ju 88s, which also continued to raid Sicily's ports and harbour by night. But the outcome of the 38-day campaign was never in any doubt. Early on the morning of 17 August, the last German troops left the island and slipped across the narrow Straits of Messina to the Italian mainland. That same night, in what can only be seen as a gesture of defiance, two waves of Ju 88s – about 60 machines in all – bombed the Tunisian port of Bizerta.

The Ju 88s' last link with Sicily had been severed. The only remaining evidence of their 32-month tenure of the island were the abandoned wrecks of 80 aircraft that the Allies found littering airfields of the Catanian Plain and beyond. Now the Germans were facing the same problem that had confronted them after the loss of Tunisia – where would the Allies strike next? This time the answer had to be Italy, but where?

INVASION OF ITALY

On 3 September, little more than a fortnight after the final evacuation of Sicily, units of the Eighth Army followed the retreating Germans across the Straits of Messina to land at Reggio di Calabria, on the very toe of Italy. The British had thus set foot back on mainland Europe on the fourth anniversary to the day of their declaring war on Germany. It may have been symbolic, but it was hardly a full-scale invasion.

Realising this, and rightly anticipating that the major Allied effort would be made higher up the boot of Italy, *Luftflotte* 2 HQ replied in kind and limited its counter-measures at Reggio to fighter-bomber activity. The command's Ju 88 strike force, concentrated in the Foggia area, was ordered to disrupt the Allies' build-up of strength by undertaking longer-range missions to the North African supply ports. Algiers had already been raided late in August, 35 aircraft attacked a coastal convoy on the night of 2/3 September and 80 bombed Bizerta four nights later.

Then, early on the morning of 8 September, a Luftwaffe reconnaissance aircraft reported 'large gatherings' of enemy shipping off the coast of Italy to the south of Naples. Despite heavy Allied bombing of the Foggia airfield complex during the day, the Ju 88 *Kampfgruppen* managed to mount close on 150 sorties against the vessels after dark. These were their first missions in response to Operation *Avalanche*, the Allied landings at Salerno on 9 September. For much of the remainder of the month most crews made the 136-mile round trip from Foggia to attack shipping in the Gulf of Salerno at least once, and sometimes twice, a night in what has been described elsewhere as 'a level of operations greater than anything attained since those against Malta in March 1942'.

But, unsurprisingly, ships anchored offshore in the darkness proved much harder to hit than a 95-square mile island, and the Ju 88 units had little to show for their nightly endeavours other than a steady trickle of losses. In fact, their relegation to the hours of darkness was a tacit admission that the one-time *'Wunderbomber'* was now rapidly losing a lot of its gloss. The Luftwaffe had discovered that the single-engined fighter-bomber was more effective against a heavily defended mass of shipping. It was faster, smaller, more manoeuvrable and thus far less vulnerable. Furthermore, new technology in the form of radio-controlled and glider bombs was being introduced and employed by other *Kampfgruppen.*

But there was to be one last campaign in the Mediterranean where the Ju 88 was able, however briefly, to put its traditional dive-bombing abilities to good use. On 8 September – the eve of the Salerno landings – Italy had capitulated. Overnight, Germany's Axis partner had become her possible enemy. In Italy itself the situation was rapidly resolved by the Wehrmacht's taking over all the key military installations. Elsewhere, the position was less straightforward. At the entrance to the Aegean Sea, the Dodecanese – easternmost of all the Aegean island groups and close to the coast of Turkey – had long been under Italian rule. On Rhodes, the largest of the 12 islands, the German garrison managed to wrest control from a numerically superior Italian force. But on 19 September the Allies carried out landings on several of the smaller islands of the group.

The Germans reacted vigorously to this tiny, but potentially dangerous, enemy presence on their southeastern flank. Forces were despatched to the area to recapture the Dodecanese. Several Luftwaffe units were already in the region, including *Stab*/LG 1 (under new *Geschwaderkommodore* Oberst Joachim Helbig) together with parts of I./LG 1 on Crete. Other Mediterranean veterans – two *Jagdgruppen* and two *Stukagruppen* – were now deployed to Greece, with forward elements later being based on Rhodes. And to add longer-range striking power to these primarily tactical support units, two additional Ju 88 *Kampfgruppen* were also despatched to Greece, II./KG 6 direct from a period of working up in France and II./KG 51 straight from operations on the eastern front.

After the small force of Spitfires that had been flown in to Cos was forced to retire, the only air cover that could be provided for the Allied troops on the islands came from long-range RAF fighters based in Cyprus (augmented for a short period by USAAF P-38s operating out of Libya). This was not always effective, and the Germans quickly established local air superiority – something they had not enjoyed in the Mediterranean theatre for a long while.

6./KG 51's '9K+BP' returns from a mission over the Dodecanese in October 1943. The unit had arrived in the Aegean directly rom ground-strafing operations on the southern sector of the Russian front, so the fixed forward-firing 20 mm MG FF cannon projecting from the machine's ventral gondola was now presumably being employed against Allied shipping

The Ju 88 *Gruppen* made full use of their new-found freedom, flying a succession of almost unopposed bombing raids against Allied positions on the various islands, concentrating principally on Cos and Leros. During the course of these they accounted for two of the six Allied destroyers lost in the Dodecanese when they sank the Royal Navy's 1370-ton *Intrepid* and Greece's 1420-ton *Queen Olga* in Leros harbour on 26 September. Five days later, also at Leros, they damaged the 1092-ton Italian destroyer *Euro* so severely that it was declared a total

81

loss. Ironically, the *Euro* had been sunk once before – in shallow water in Tobruk harbour by *British* aircraft – before being refloated and towed to Taranto for repair!

In addition to the above successes, the Ju 88 crews participated in a number of joint operations with the Stukas of StG 3, which resulted in the sinking or damaging of many other vessels, including warships (from cruisers down to landing craft) and the small merchantmen that were trying to get supplies through to the isolated British forces holding the islands. The latter's efforts were in vain, as Cos was captured by the Germans on 3 October. Leros held out until 16 November, after which all British troops were evacuated from the other islands.

Although the German garrisons on most of the 12 Dodecanese islands remained isolated and cut off until the end of the war, they were not forgotten. Here, in December 1943, a reconnaissance Ju 88D of 2.(F)/123 probably at Tatoi, in Greece, is being prepared for a mission of a different kind – to deliver the load of Christmas trees seen on the roof of the Kübelwagen to one of the outlying islands

Ten of the twelve Dodecanese islands would remain in German hands until the very end of the war, but the Luftwaffe units that had been brought in to help take them departed again almost immediately after they had been secured. For II./KG 6 this meant a return to France to rejoin its parent *Geschwaderstab*, while II./KG 51 resumed its interrupted operations on the southern sector of the Russian front.

Meanwhile, in Italy, the US Fifth Army had broken out of its Salerno beachhead and advanced northwards, entering Naples on 1 October. With the Americans now pushing hard up the west coast of Italy and the British driving up the eastern side of the country, further withdrawals and reorganisation of the Ju 88 *Kampfgruppen* in Italy became necessary. Before September was out, I. and III./KG 6 had been transferred back to France. At the same time the remnants of I. and II./KG 1, which had suffered heavy losses over Sicily and Salerno, handed their remaining Ju 88s to KGs 54 and 76 and retired to northern Italy, prior to returning to the Reich and conversion onto the He 177. III./KG 30 was also pulled out of Italy, as was III./KG 54, who, after passing its aircraft over to the incoming II./KG 54, likewise withdrew by rail to Germany for refit.

This left just the 'veteran' I. and II./KG 76 to make the move from Foggia – taken by the advancing Eighth Army on 27 September – to fields in the far north of Italy, which they shared with I. and II./KG 30 and I. and II./KG 54. These four latter *Gruppen* had returned to Italy after lengthy periods of retraining, and the young and inexperienced crews who made up the bulk of their numbers were ill prepared for the difficult operational conditions and worsening weather they now faced.

The Allies were not only pressing forward along a continuous front in mainland Italy, they had also captured Sardinia and Corsica, forcing German troops to evacuate the two islands on 19 September and 4 October, respectively. In their first operation, a raid on Ajaccio harbour on Corsica's west coast on 12 October, the tyro crews of I. and II./KG 54 were fortunate to return to base without loss after having to fly through low cloud and violent thunderstorms.

The following day the new Italian government headed by Marshal Bodoglio officially declared war on Germany. It was not this new adversary, however, but a combination of the deteriorating winter weather, poor serviceability returns and the inexperience of many of the crews that led to a marked decline in Ju 88 activity during October and November. This was not lost on Allied military intelligence, which sniffily remarked upon the 'low scale of (the enemy's) long-range bomber effort', further noting that the Ju 88 units were flying 'one sortie every two weeks per serviceable aircraft'.

Although this assessment was somewhat wide of the mark, it cannot be denied that the Mediterranean Ju 88s were no longer the force they had once been. By this stage of the campaign in Italy their primary target was the port of Naples. Despite being badly damaged by Allied bombing during the months of German occupation, heroic attempts were being made to put Naples back into service again, and it was soon to become one of the theatre's major supply ports.

Even so, the Ju 88s managed to raid Naples on only six occasions between 2 October (the day after its loss) and 26 November. Each of these six missions involved a maximum effort of up to 100 aircraft or more. But sometimes less than a third of that number actually reached their objective. On the second of these raids, for example, on 23 October, only 15 to 20 aircraft out of the 90 involved were reported over the target area. The attacks were costly too, and not only in terms of novice crews. Among the casualties on 23 October was the *Gruppenkommandeur* of II./KG 54, Hauptmann Horst Bressel, who had been decorated with the German Cross in Gold exactly two months earlier.

On their next visit to Naples, during the night of 1/2 November, several Ju 88s launched LT 350 circling torpedoes into the harbour basin. But neither during this, nor any of the three other raids before the end of the month, was any appreciable damage done to shipping in the port.

After another mission to Corsica on 24 November, flown by 119 aircraft against the harbour town of Bastia, on the island's northeastern

Pictured under a lowering sky, these aircraft of LG 1 are reportedly returning to Greece after a raid on southern Italy late in October 1943. By this time the *Geschwader's* days in the eastern Mediterranean were already numbered

A crew from II./KG 54 relax in the sun between operations at Bergamo, in northern Italy, in November 1943

coast, the Ju 88s returned one last time to Naples on the 26th. Then, six days later – and against all expectations – they carried out what was, with the possible exception of Piraeus, arguably the single most successful and devastating raid of the entire Mediterranean war!

Late in the afternoon of 2 December 1943, aircraft from all six *Gruppen* (105 machines in all) took off from their bases in northern Italy. Crossing out over the coast between Ravenna and Rimini, they flew at low level down the Adriatic. Their target was the east coast port of Bari, where reconnaissance had reported the presence of over 30 Allied merchant ships. Turning to approach the target from seaward as dusk was falling, the Ju 88s began climbing hard. In the van was a small force of pathfinders, scattering strips of *Düppel* (the Luftwaffe's equivalent of 'Window') to confuse Allied radar and dropping flares. The latter were hardly necessary, as the harbour was already ablaze with light to facilitate unloading. This complacency – or was it a calculated risk? – could hardly have occurred at a worse time.

At about 1930 hrs the first bombs and LT 350 torpedoes were released. Accounts differ as to how many aircraft actually carried out the attack – German records specify an exact 88, while one Allied estimate put the number at 'only 30'. However many they were, the havoc they wrought was enormous. Two ammunition ships were hit almost at once. The resultant explosion devastated a large part of the dockside and much of the surrounding area. The bulk fuel pipe was severed and fuel spread across the surface of the harbour. Ignited by burning aviation spirit escaping from the damaged Italian tanker *Cassala*, it quickly engulfed many of the other ships that had so far escaped the bombs.

One reference source lists 15 vessels totally destroyed (others give higher figures – anything up to 19) plus seven severely damaged. A further horror was added to the carnage already caused when it was discovered that one of the four US Liberty ships sunk, the 7177-ton *John Harvey*, had been carrying 100 tons of mustard gas bombs in its holds. In addition to the 1000+ men who perished in the raid, over 600 unwittingly inhaled the deadly gas – 83 of them would die in the weeks ahead. Although there were four USAAF Beaufighter nightfighters in the area, only two Ju 88s reportedly failed to return from the raid, the cause of their loss uncertain.

The most destructive raid during the early days of the Ju 88 in the Mediterranean had undoubtedly been that on Piraeus harbour in Greece, which had resulted in tremendous damage to shipping and port installations alike. Now it seemed as if the Ju 88 was ending its days in the area in similar dramatic and explosive fashion. For in less than a month after the attack on Bari, all six *Gruppen* that had taken part in the raid had been withdrawn from Italy. By the end of December 1943 the only Ju 88 bombers on *Luftflotte* 2's strength were the five serviceable machines of the *Geschwaderstab* KG 76. But the story was not quite over yet.

ANZIO

In the early hours of 22 January 1944 the Allies made another amphibious landing on the west coast of Italy, this time at Anzio, behind the German frontlines and only some 30 miles south of Rome. Not expecting an operation such as this to be staged in mid-winter, the Germans were taken totally by surprise. But the Luftwaffe's response was prompt and energetic. Eight *Kampfgruppen*, all but one equipped with Ju 88s, were quickly despatched to northern Italy. Four – I. and II./KG 30 and I. and II./KG 76 – were hastily recalled after having only left the area only weeks earlier. To these were added III./KG 30 and I. and III./LG 1, the latter two flying in from Greece and Crete, thereby finally bringing to a close LG 1's long association with the eastern Mediterranean. This III./LG 1 was, of course, a 'new' unit formed from I./KG 55 in August 1943.

Initially, the Ju 88 crews were directed against Allied supply shipping in an attempt to disrupt the build-up of the enemy's beachhead. But, as at Salerno, it was soon accepted that the torpedo and glider bomb-equipped units were better suited to this task. Thereafter, the Ju 88 *Kampfgruppen* were restricted more and more to small-scale night harassment raids mainly against ground targets. But even these proved costly and rather ineffective. No doubt deciding that they could be better employed elsewhere, KG 30's three *Gruppen* were withdrawn from Italy in the first half of February. This left a force of about 50 serviceable machines out of the 140 that had been rushed back into northern Italy three weeks before. The serviceability returns for the four remaining *Gruppen* (I./KG 76 having been replaced by III./KG 76 in March) would hover around this same level for the final three months of their service in the Mediterranean.

Towards the close of this period they scored some minor successes in night raids on Allied lines of communications in the Cassino area and on airfields both in central Italy and on Corsica. About half their number even attacked Naples one last time in the early hours of 14 May. But these were little more than pinpricks in what was, as far as the Luftwaffe was concerned, now a secondary theatre of war. The end came with the

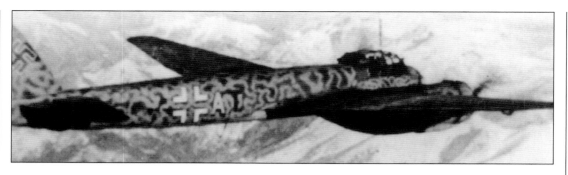

invasion of Normandy on 6 June 1944, which resulted in all four *Gruppen* finally leaving Italy for good.

Yet there was still one other small force that had been keeping alive the anti-shipping traditions of the Mediterranean Ju 88s for the past six months and more – the torpedo-bombers of III./KG 26, based at Montpellier, in southern France, under the command of recent Knight's Cross winner Hauptmann Klaus Nocken. Having operated out of Sardinia under *Luftflotte* 2 for the first five months of 1943, KG 26's two Mediterranean *Gruppen* (I./KG 26 was equipped with He 111s) had then transferred to France, where they were placed under the control of *Luftflotte* 3 at year-end.

From its new base III./KG 26 were ideally situated to engage the many Allied convoys passing through the Straits of Gibraltar into the western Mediterranean. One such operation involving the two *Gruppen* of KG 26 had taken place shortly before sunset on 6 November 1943 when they attacked convoy KMF-25A some ten miles off the Algerian coast. Approaching in two waves, the 36 torpedo-bombers scored hits on one of the convoy escorts and two of the troopships. The 1700-ton destroyer USS *Beatty*, its keel damaged, broke in two and sank several hours later. The two transports, the 19,355-ton *Marnix van St Aldegonde* and the 9135-ton *Santa Elena*, remained afloat until the following day, allowing all personnel – including the 100 nurses aboard the *Santa Elena* – to be transferred to other vessels.

Other successes quickly followed. Only five days later, on 11 November, 17 aircraft of III./KG 26 (together with the Heinkels of I. *Gruppe* and the glider bomb-carrying Dorniers of II./KG 100) were in action against convoy KMS-31 northeast of Oran. Three merchantmen were sunk – the 5151-ton *Birchbank*, the 8587-ton *Indian Prince* and the French 7217-ton *Carlier*. A second French vessel, the 4763-ton tanker *Nivôse*, was also torpedoed and sank after colliding with another ship. As on the previous mission, two of the *Gruppe's* Ju 88s failed to return.

After a relatively quiet December, KG 26's torpedo-bombers returned to the fray on 10 January 1944 when 30 of their number attacked convoy KMS-37 north of Oran. Again for the loss of two Ju 88s, the 7178-ton freighter *Ocean Hunter* was sunk and the 7176-ton Liberty ship *Daniel Webster* severely damaged. Although the crew managed to beach it, the latter vessel was subsequently declared a total loss.

On 23 January 1944, 24 hours after the Allied landings at Anzio, the Ju 88s of III./KG 26 were despatched to attack shipping in that area. Details of the four-hour mission are sketchy, but at least six of the *Gruppe's*

'F1+AT' of III./KG 76 is clearly flying over the Alps, but is it heading north or south? One source maintains that it is returning to northwest Europe to take part in January 1944's 'Little Blitz' on Britain (which is unlikely), while another claims that the bomber is *en route* from Hörsching, in Austria, to replace I. *Gruppe* in northern Italy

Although this aircraft of 5./KG 77 is clearly sporting a white aft fuselage band, the red and white stripes on the nose of the torpedo indicate that it is a practice weapon. This photograph was therefore probably taken at Barth, on Germany's Baltic coast (and could this machine be among the line-up pictured on page 79? Note the similar spinner rings

This, however, is the real thing. The torpedo being loaded here is a 'live one', and the background terrain suggests southern climes. III./KG 26 at Montpellier, perhaps?

machines were reported lost on this date. Among those missing were two of the unit's three *Staffelkapitäne*, Hauptleute Heinrich Deubel and Josef Wiszborn of 8. and 9./KG 26, respectively.

1 February saw the two *Gruppen* of KG 26 back off the Algerian coast, some 40 aircraft attacking convoy UGS-30 north of Oran and sinking the 7176-ton freighter *Edward Bates*. Intercepted by Sardinian-based Beaufighters, three Ju 88s were shot down.

For much of the remainder of February, III./KG 26's machines were engaged in individual sorties against shipping off Anzio. These were usually timed for either dawn or dusk. But then, in order to save the crews the long overwater approach flight, a forward base was set up for them at Piacenza, in northern Italy. From here they flew just two missions before the supply of torpedoes ran out, after which they were ordered to carry out raids on the beachhead itself using fragmentation bombs — something for which the aircraft were not equipped (for dive-bombing they lacked the

necessary bombsights, and for high-level bombing there was no oxygen equipment) and for which the specialist torpedo crews had not been trained! It was with no little relief that they returned to Montpellier in late February to resume their anti-convoy operations.

But March turned out to be a barren month. The Ju 88s again fell foul of Beaufighters from Sardinia before they could reach a convoy of troopships off Algiers on the 8th. And two other attempted attacks along the Algerian coast under the cover of darkness against convoys KMS-44 on 19 March and KMS-45 ten days later both proved abortive (and costly, with four crews lost).

At the end of March, I. *Gruppe*, down to just 12 Heinkel crews, was withdrawn to re-equip and retrain on Ju 88s. Its place in the south of France was taken by I. and III./KG 77, who flew in from the Reich, where they themselves had just completed training as torpedo-bomber units.

Before dawn on 1 April some 20 Ju 88s attacked convoy UGS-36 west of Algiers, sinking the 7191-ton Liberty ship *Jared Ingersoll* but losing at least three machines (all from III./KG 26) in the process. Another 20 aircraft (a mixed force of Ju 88s and Do 217s) were despatched against the next convoy – the 66-vessel UGS-37 – during the night of 11/12 April. Their only success was a single torpedo hit, which damaged the 1400-ton destroyer-escort USS *Holder*. The warship was towed to Algiers before making its own way back to New York Navy Yard, where the damage was judged to be too severe to warrant repair and the ship decommissioned.

On the evening of 20 April approximately 50 aircraft from all three torpedo *Gruppen* (plus some Do 217s of III./KG 100) again took off from their bases in southern France. This time their target was the even larger convoy UGS-38, consisting of nearly 90 merchantmen. While still 100 miles off the Algerian coast, part of the attacking force chanced upon a smaller convoy bound from Corsica and sank the 4678-ton French freighter *El Biar*. The remainder found UGS-38 steaming east off Cape Bengut. Making full use of the gathering dusk, the Ju 88s approached from ahead in three low-level waves, torpedoing and sinking the 1630-ton destroyer USS *Lansdale* (which, somewhat ironically, had been specially equipped to detect and jam radio-controlled glider bombs), as well as the 7900-ton British merchantman *Royal Star* and the 7177-ton US Liberty ship *Paul Hamilton*. Two other freighters were damaged, and at least three warships of the strong escorting force reported near misses from one or more torpedoes.

This was to be the last major success achieved by the torpedo-

Carrying two torpedoes, 9./KG 77's '3Z+UT' flies low over the Mediterranean as it sets out from Istres and heads for the Algerian coast on 20 April 1944

Another 'hot' start as a fully loaded Ju 88A-17 torpedo-bomber warms up its engines prior to firing the two rocket-assisted take-off packs just visible underwing. Note also the bulged fairing to the left of the nose glazing, which housed the equipment for adjusting the torpedoes' steering gear in the air

Adorned simply with its four-letter *Stammkennzeichen* fusleage code 'PN+MT' and a 'last three' (498) on the vertical tail surfaces, this FuG 200 Hohentwiel radar-equipped Ju 88A-6/U anti-shipping machine is pictured at Aviano, in northern Italy. The backdrop is no longer provided by Sicily's Mount Etna, but by the face of the Alps. The Ju 88 *Kampfgruppen* in the Mediterranean have finally run out of room to manoeuvre. There is nowhere else to go now but over those peaks back into the Reich

bombers. A similar mission against UGS-40 in the same area by 60+ Ju 88s on the evening of 11 May was again intercepted by RAF Beaufighters from Sardinia. Although the Ju 88 crews claimed one destroyer and seven merchantmen sunk, not a single vessel was in fact lost, while a staggering 19 aircraft – very nearly a third of the attacking force – were reported missing.

Then, late on 30 May, during an attack on UGS-42 northeast of Algiers, a torpedo struck and sank the 2873-ton British freighter *Nordeflinge*. This small steamship, on charter to the British Admiralty, was, in all probability, the very last vessel to be claimed by the Luftwaffe's Ju 88s during their three-and-a-half year Mediterranean war.

And that war was, to all intents and purposes, now effectively over. It was exactly one week after the luckless *Nordeflinge* went down that Allied forces landed in Normandy. But unlike the Ju 88 *Kampfgruppen* in northern Italy, the torpedo-bombers deployed along the French Mediterranean coast were not immediately rushed northwards. After D-Day, however, their missions did take them in that direction when they were ordered to fly the 550 miles to the Channel coast to attack shipping off the Normandy beaches. Even with a refuelling stop on the return flight, these lengthy operations put a great strain on men and machines alike.

In July KG 77 was disbanded, and when, on 15 August, the Allies invaded southern France, the remaining torpedo-bombers of KG 26 were near powerless to oppose them. As Allied troops then began to move inland, the time had finally come for III./KG 26 (and the recently arrived II./KG 26) to retire back into the Reich.

For the remaining nine months of the war the only Ju 88 presence in the Mediterranean area was provided by the reconnaissance units in Italy. And by the end even their numbers had shrunk to less than 12 serviceable machines huddled at the foot of the Alps in the far north of the country – a mere shadow of the force that had once bestrode the entire theatre.

APPENDICES

REPRESENTATIVE Ju 88 BOMBER (AND RECONNAISSANCE) STRENGTHS IN THE MEDITERRANEAN THEATRE 1941-44

A) 22 APRIL 1941

X. Fliegerkorps

	Base	Est-Serv
1.(F)/121	Catania	15-9
2.(F)/123	Catania	14-7
Stab LG 1	Catania	1-1
II./LG 1	Catania	26-20
III./LG 1 (exc. 8. *Staffel*)	Catania	40-11
III./KG 30	Catania	27-24

Fliegerführer Afrika

	Base	Est-Serv
8./LG 1	Benghazi-Benina	9-4

Totals — **Bombers 103-60**
Reconnaissance 29-16

B) 20 SEPTEMBER 1942

Luftflotte 2

	Base	Est-Serv
Oberbefehlshaber-Süd		
Stab AufklGr.(F) 122	Trapani	3-1
2.(F)/122	Trapani	11-8

II. Fliegerkorps (Sicily)

	Base	Est-Serv
1.(F)/122*	Catania	17-6
Stab KG 54	Catania	2-1
I./KG 54	Gerbini	32-14
II./KG 54	Gerbini	26-15
III./KG 54	Catania	31-9
Stab KG 77	Comino	2-2
I./KG 77	Catania/Comino	33-14

X. Fliegerkorps (Greece and Crete)

	Base	Est-Serv
2.(F)/123**	Kastelli	15-7
Stab LG 1	Heraklion	2-2
I./ LG 1	Heraklion	31-16
II./ LG 1	Heraklion	30-19
II./KG 77	Tympakion	28-13
III.KG 77	Tympakion	28-12

Totals — **Bombers 259-122**
Reconnaissance 56-27

*Also equipped with Bf 109
**Also equipped with Ju 86

C) 10 MARCH 1943

Luftflotte 2

	Base	Est-Serv
II. Fliegerkorps (Sicily and Sardinia)		
Stab AufklGr (F)/122	Sardinia	2-2
1.(F)/122	Sardinia	19-5
2.(F)/122	Sardinia	20-2
III./KG 26	Villacidro	22-12
Stab KG 30	Comiso	1-1
II./KG 30	Comiso	45-21
Stab KG 54	Catania	1-1
I./KG 54	Elmas	31-19
II./KG 54	Catania	25-10
Stab KG 76	Catania	2-2
II./KG 76	Gerbini	17-12
Stab KG 77*	Piacenza	1-1
I./KG 77*	Piacenza	12-9
III./KG 77	Sicily	43-27

X. Fliegerkorps (Greece and Crete)

	Base	Est-Serv
2.(F)/123	Crete	20-7
Stab LG 1	Heraklion	1-1
II./ LG 1	Heraklion	30-24

Fliegerführer Afrika

	Base	Est-Serv
1.(F)/121	Tunis	4-4

Totals — **Bombers 231-140**

*Re-equipping in northern Italy

D) 25 APRIL 1944

Luftflotte 2 (Italy)

	Base	Serv
2.(F)/122*	Perugia	2
1.(F)/123	Perugia	3
Stab LG 1	Ghedi	1
I./LG 1	Ghedi	14
III./LG 1	Villa Franca	21
Stab KG 76	Ronchi	0
5./KG 76	Aviano	5
III./KG 76	Villa Orba	16

Lw.Kdo.Südost (Greece)

Komm.Gen.d.dtsch.LW in Griechenland

	Base	Serv
Stab FAGr 4	Tatoi	1
3.(F)/33	Tatoi	4
2.(F)/123**	Tatoi	8

Luftflotte 3 (southern France)

	Base	Serv
1.(F)/33***	St Martin	3
III./KG 26	Montpellier	10
4. and 6./KG 76	Istres	3
Stab KG 77	Salon	0
I./KG 77	Orange-Caritat	11
III./KG 77	Orange-Caritat	15

Totals — **Bombers 96**

* Also equipped with Me 410
** Also equipped with Bf 109 and Ju 188
*** Also equipped with Ju 188

COLOUR PLATES

1
Ju 88A-5 'L1+EN' of 5./LG 1, Reggio-Emilia, Italy, December 1940
Depicted during II./LG 1's initial transfer from Orléans-Bricy, in France, to Catania, on Sicily, 5. *Staffel's* 'EN' wears standard northwest European finish and is carrying two 900-litre (198 Imp gal) long-range tanks under the inboard wing sections to help it cover the lengthy final stages down the leg of Italy. Note the lack of any white recognition markings.

2
Ju 88A-5 'L1+HN' of 5./LG 1, Catania, Sicily, February 1941
It was only upon arrival at Catania that LG 1's machines were given Mediterranean theatre markings of white underwing tips and aft fuselage bands. RLM guidelines were not always adhered to, however, and many of the unit's Ju 88s – including 'HN', seen here – sported extra wide fuselage bands upon which both the individual aircraft letter ('Red H') and *Staffel* code letter ('N') were displayed. This machine is carrying two 1000-kg bombs such as were commonly used in raids on Malta.

3
Ju 88A-5 'L1+GN' of 5./LG 1, Grottaglie, Italy, April 1941
Some doubt still exists as to the colour of the Balkans theatre markings applied to a number of LG 1 aircraft during the brief Yugoslav and Greek campaigns. Were their rudders and engine cowlings/nacelles painted yellow as per official instructions, or white as some sources maintain? Photographic sources (see photo on page 21) would seem to suggest the former, as shown in this profile.

4
Ju 88A-5 'L1+XH' of 1./LG 1, Eleusis, Greece, May 1941
By the time of the invasion of Crete and LG 1's operations against Allied shipping around the island, all high-visibility markings had been removed. The accent now was on toning down the prominent white Mediterranean theatre markings by hastily overpainting them with washable black distemper.

5
Ju 88A-5 'L1+GR' of 7./LG 1, Derna, Libya, Summer 1941
8. *Staffel* was the first element of LG 1 to be transferred to Libya (in April 1941), where it came under the direct control of the local *Fliegerführer Afrika*. It was followed a month later by the rest of III. *Gruppe*. As befitted their new theatre of war, III./LG 1's machines were given a coat of overall desert tan camouflage. Note, however, that 7. *Staffel's* 'GR' has not yet had its white aft fuselage band applied.

6
Ju 88A-4 'L1+PK' of 2./LG 1, Catania, Sicily, January 1942
The overall tan finish given to many LG 1 machines was soon being broken up by disruptive patches of green, which made the scheme better suited to the barren – but not necessarily desert – regions over which the *Geschwader* operated during its frequent deployments around the Mediterranean theatre from Sicily to North Africa, Greece and Crete. However, as camouflage, it seems particularly *unsuitable* to the unit's numerous overwater missions!

7
Ju 88A-4 'L1+OU' of 10./LG 1, Salonika-Sedes, Greece, May 1942
The IV. *Gruppe* (usually 10., 11. and 12 *Staffeln*) of a *Kampfgeschwader* performed the function of an operational training unit for its parent *Stab*, and was normally based either in the Reich or in a rear area of German-occupied territory. IV./LG 1 was formed in January 1942 by redesignating the *Ergänzungsgruppe* LG 1, which had transferred from Wiener Neustadt to Salonika-Sedes some weeks earlier. In Greece, the unit not only continued with its training activities (hence the aircraft's large identification numeral on the vertical tail surfaces), but also – despite the uncompromising desert tan finish of its machines – carried out routine anti-submarine patrols over the Aegean Sea.

8
Ju 88A-4 'L1+EK' of 2./LG 1, Heraklion, Crete, Summer 1942
From their base on Crete, aircraft of I./LG 1 regularly flew south across the Mediterranean in the summer of 1942 to support Rommel's latest desert offensive. Among the targets they attacked by night was the harbour of Tobruk, hence the copious amounts of temporary black distemper covering the undersides and almost obscuring the identity of this machine (which is almost certainly 'EK' of 2. *Staffel*). Note the 500-kg *Luftmine A* parachute mine just visible under the inboard wing section.

9
Ju 88A-4 'L1+HW' of 12./LG 1, Western Desert, circa August 1942
Although several sources list Salonika as IV./LG 1's sole base throughout its entire 15-month service in the Mediterranean (from formation in January 1942 until its return to Wiener Neustadt in March 1943), other records indicate that the *Gruppe's* 12.

Staffel operated over the Western Desert (based at Derna and Berka) for several months in mid-1942. 'HW' was probably one machine to be so deployed – why otherwise the elaborate 'scribble' camouflage over the basic desert tan finish?

10
Ju 88A-4 'L1+EH' of 1./LG 1, Aviano, Italy, February 1944
When LG 1 finally left the Aegean area in January 1944, its aircraft were at last wearing he *Wellenmuster* ('wave-pattern') camouflage scheme specifically devised and introduced for anti-shipping operations. Ironically, however, shortly after arriving in northern Italy the unit was restricted to flying missions against Allied ground forces and their lines of communications under cover of darkness, which explains the overpainting of the national insignia and aft fuselage band. Note also the exhaust shroud and *Geschwader* code 'L1' that has now been reduced to one-fifth of its earlier size.

11
Ju 88A-4/Torp '1T+ET' of 9./KG 26, Villacidro, Sardinia, April 1943
The history of III./KG 26 between 1940 and 1942 was particularly complex, even by Luftwaffe standards. Suffice it to say that during this period no fewer than three different *Gruppen* bearing the designation III./KG 26 were formed. And when a fourth, and final, III./KG 26 was brought into being in July 1942 (by redesignating KGr 506), its aircraft – for some unknown reason – initially wore the '1T' unit code of KG 28. The *Wellenmuster*-camouflaged Do17 depicted here, based on Sardinia for anti-shipping operations in the western Mediterranean, is still sporting the '1T' code a full nine months after the *Gruppe's* activation . . .

12
Ju 88A-17 '1H+AR' of 7./KG 26, Montpellier, southern France, September 1943
. . . but by the time they transferred to southern France, III./KG 26's torpedo-bombers were carrying the official wartime '1H' code of their parent *Geschwaderstab*.

13
Ju 88A-5 '4D+MT' of 9./KG 30, Catania, Sicily, April 1941
During III./KG 30's first foray to the Mediterranean – to take part in the Spring 1941 air offensive against Malta – its aircraft wore standard two-tone green European finish embellished simply with white underwing tips and narrow aft fuselage band theatre markings.

14
Ju 88A-1 '9K+JT' of 9./KG 51, Wiener Neustadt, Austria, May 19 41
In contrast to KG 30 above, KG 51's initial participation on the southern front only took

it as far as Wiener Neustadt, which was to be its main base throughout the Yugoslav and Greek campaigns of April-May 1941. As such, the *Geschwader's* machines carried no white Mediterranean theatre makings, but wore instead the bright yellow nacelles and rudders that identified Luftwaffe aircraft operating over the Balkans.

15
Ju 88A-4 'B3+FK' of 2./KG 54, Gerbini, Sicily, January 1942
Withdrawn from the southern sector of the Russian front in November 1941 to take part in the renewed assault on Malta in early 1942, I./KG 54's aircraft initially wore standard European finish, to which were added the usual Mediterranean markings. Of interest here are the multi-coloured spinners favoured by KG 54 – the narrow white ring for I. *Gruppe* and the red tip indicating 2. *Staffel*. Note also the 900-litre (198 Imp gal) underwing tanks, used either for ferry purposes or for overwater missions longer than the 125-mile round trip to Malta.

16
Ju 88A-4 'B3+LH' of 1./KG 54, Derna, Libya, June 1942
After transferring from Sicily to Tympakion, on Crete, many of I./KG 54's aircraft used Derna, in Libya, as a forward landing ground during their support of Rommel's second offensive. Wearing full desert rig, 1. *Staffel's* 'LH' was clearly one of them. Note, however, that although the Ju 88 carried the correct *Staffel* identity letter 'H', the bomber's individual aircraft letter 'L' is, for some unknown reason, painted in the colour of 3. *Staffel*, yellow.

17
Ju 88A-4 'B3+AM' of 4./KG 54, Catania, Sicily, Spring 1943
Variation on a theme. II./KG 54 arrived in the Mediterranean from the central sector of the eastern front in October 1942. It spent the first seven months on Sicily, during which time crews tried to cover all eventualities by experimenting with various camouflage schemes, including that seen here on 4. *Staffel's* 'AM'. This particular effort combined the basic desert tan (for operations over North Africa) with wavy lines of green, edged here and there in white to suggest waves. This in turn made the camouflage scheme more suitable for the crews' overwater missions. Note also the dense scribble on the undersides.

18
Ju 88A-4 'B3+DS' of 8./KG 54, Foggia, Italy, September 1943
Unequivocally attired for anti-shipping operations in a variety of individual *Wellenmuster* schemes, III./KG 54's machines, based at Foggia during the late summer/early autumn of 1943, were employed over the central Mediterranean and against the

Salerno invasion fleet, before being withdrawn to Bergamo in northern Italy.

19

Ju 88A-4 'P1+HH' of 1./KG 60, Elmas, Sardinia, January 1943

I./KG 60 had a very short-lived career. Formed in September/October 1942 for service in Finland, it was transferred to Sardinia in November in the wake of the *Torch* landings. Suffering heavy losses over Algeria and Tunisia – its *Kommandeur* was among the casualties – the *Gruppe* was disbanded on 8 February 1943 and its remaining aircraft and crews divided between II. and III./KG 30.

20

Ju 88A-4 'F1+KM' of 4./KG 76, Athens-Tatoi, Greece, November 1942

Withdrawn from the Russian front and reportedly 'tropicalised' prior to transfer to the Mediterranean, most – if not all – of KG 76's machines were still wearing standard European camouflage (with white aft fuselage band added) when they arrived in Greece in mid-November 1942. Deploying to Crete, their first missions were flown in support of the *Afrika Korps* as it retreated back across Libya post-El Alamein.

21

Ju 88A-4 '3Z+EN' of 5./KG 77, Comiso, Sicily, March 1942

II. and III./KG 77 also arrived in the Mediterranean after serving on the eastern front (albeit at the very beginning of 1942, a full ten months prior to the arrival of KG 76). They too initially retained European-style camouflage, plus the obligatory white fuselage band, but darkened the undersides of their machines when participating in the night raids on Malta during the spring of 1942. Note the red (*Staffel*) and white (*Gruppe*) spinner rings.

22

Ju 88A-5 '3Z+CT' of 9./KG 77, Libya, Summer 1942

After the easing of the Luftwaffe's air assault on Malta, the two *Gruppen* of KG 77 next supported Rommel's advance on Egypt, which had begun with his breaching the Gazala Line defences in mid-June 1942. KG 77 is known to have made use of several forward landing grounds in Libya during July and August, as witness 9. *Staffel's* 'CT' in traditional desert garb, but details are sketchy. By September III./KG 77 was based on Crete and engaged in night raids on targets in the Nile Delta region.

23

Ju 88A-17 '3Z+DR' of 7./KG 77, Orange-Caritat, southern France, April 1944

KG 77's peregrinations around the Mediterranean continued during 1943 until, by the spring of 1944 – having now been converted to a specialised torpedo-bomber *Geschwader* (KG/LT) – I. and III. *Gruppen* found themselves in the south of France flying their spectacularly scribble-patterned A-17s

against Allied convoys coming in through the Straits of Gibraltar. Note the jettisonable rocket pack mounted underwing to assist take-off.

24

Ju 88A-4 '7T+BH' of 1./KGr 606, Catania, Sicily, Spring 1942

One of two semi-autonomous *Kampfgruppen* transferred in to Sicily during the winter of 1941/42 to add weight to the early 1942 air offensive against Malta, KGr 606 had previously been based in France under the command of the *Fliegerführer Atlantik*. In September 1942 the *Gruppe* was redesignated as I./KG 77 to replace the original I./KG 77, which had become I./KG 6 the month before.

25

Ju 88A-4 'M7+DK' of 2./KGr 806, Catania, Sicily, Spring 1942

The second of the two *Kampfgruppen* to arrive at Catania to take part in the renewed air assault on Malta, KGr 806 came not from France, but from the northern sector of the Russian front, where it had been serving under the *Fliegerführer Ostsee* (Air Command Baltic). Both *Gruppen* had begun life as coastal units, hence their recent assignment to primarily anti-shipping commands. KGr 806 would also undergo redesignation in September 1942, becoming III./KG 54 to fill the slot left vacant since the original III./KG 54's disbandment back in July 1940.

26

Ju 88A-4 'B3+LX' of VFS Tours, Summer 1942

This machine bears the markings of 10./KG 54 (the *Gruppe's* three component *Staffeln*, 10., 11. and 12. being coded 'X', 'Y' and 'Z' respectively). But while KG 54's 'OTU' *Gruppe* is known to have been based at Grottaglie, on the heel of Italy, from March 1942 to May 1943, one source maintains that by the summer of 1942 this particular aircraft had been passed to the *Verbandsführerschule* (VFS, or Unit Commanders' School) at Tours, in France. It is unclear, however, whether the large training numerals on the tail and underwing date back to its days at Grottaglie or were applied at Tours.

27

Ju 88D '7A+KH' of 1.(F)/122, Fuka 1, Libya, August 1942

Although space has precluded much mention being made of the Ju 88D-equipped long-range reconnaissance *Staffeln* in the main text, these units performed a vital role in the Mediterranean – not least in locating, reporting and tracking Allied shipping movements. 1.(F)/122, the first *Staffel* to operate in the theatre, accompanied the early *Kampfgruppen* down the leg of Italy to take up residence at Catania in January 1941. Later in the year it would transfer to Greece and start rotating four aircraft at a time to Libya to act as Rommel's 'eyes' in the desert. By 1942 the entire *Staffel* was in North Africa, where it would remain – latterly based at Tunis – until February 1943.

28
Ju 88D '4U+EK' of 2.(F)/123, Kastelli, Crete, September 1942
A second reconnaissance *Staffel*, 2.(F)/123, had joined 1.(F)/121 at Catania by March 1941. It too would later be based in Greece, and on Crete, where it would be responsible for aerial reconnaissance of the eastern Mediterranean (with occasional deployments to North Africa) until the spring of 1944.

29
Ju 88A-6/U '5M+SO' of 6.(F)/122, Bergamo, northern Italy, July 1944
In all, at least nine Ju 88 long-range reconnaissance *Staffeln* are on record as having operated in the Mediterranean theatre at one time or another. Among the last of them was 6.(F)/122, formed in June 1944 by redesignating the existing

Wekusta 26 (see profile 30 below). Shortly after this date, with the withdrawal of all *Kampfgruppen* from the area following the D-Day landings, the reconnaissance units represented the only Ju 88 presence in the Mediterranean – and even these were being replaced by Ju 188s. One order of battle lists just a single operational Ju 88 (a high-speed T-3) south of the Alps by war's end!

30
Ju 88D 'Q5+B' of *Wekusta* 27, Athens-Tatoi, Greece, December 1943
Another important part in the Mediterranean air war was played by the theatre's two *Wekusta* meteorological units (We tterer kundungst affel, or Weather Observation *Staffel*). *Wekusta* 27 was formed in June 1943 from a cadre supplied by the then Sicilian-based *Wekusta* 26. Operating out of both Greece and Crete, *Wekusta* 27 monitored the weather in the eastern Mediterranean, while (from Sicily and Italy), *Wekusta* 26 was responsible for the central and western Mediterranean basins.

INDEX